LACAN

The Absolute Master

LACAN

LACAN

The Absolute Master

Mikkel Borch-Jacobsen
Translated by Douglas Brick

Stanford University Press
Stanford, California

Stanford University Press
Stanford, California
© 1991 by the Board of Trustees of the
Leland Stanford Junior University
Printed in the United States of America

CIP data appear at the end of the book

Original printing 1991
Last figure below indicates year of this printing:
03   02   01   00   99   98

ὁ πλάσας ἠφάνισεν

Contents

A Note on Citation

Because the following works by Jacques Lacan are cited so frequently in the text, all references to them are abbreviated as follows:

1953   "Some Reflections on the Ego," *International Journal of Psychoanalysis* 34 (1953).

1966   *Ecrits* (Paris: Seuil, 1966).

1968   "Proposition du 9 octobre 1967 sur le psychanalyst de l'Ecole" and "La méprise du sujet supposé savoir," *Scilicet* 1 (1968).

1970   "Radiophonie," *Scilicet* 2/3 (1970).

1973a   "L'étourdit," *Scilicet* 4 (1973).

1973b   *Le Séminaire XI: Les quatre concepts fondamentaux de la psychanalyse* (Paris: Seuil, 1973).

1975a   *De la psychose paranoïaque dans ses rapports avec la personnalité,* followed by *Premiers écrits sur la paranoïa* (Paris: Seuil, 1975).

1975b   *Le Séminaire I: Les écrits techniques de Freud* (Paris: Seuil, 1975).

1975c   *Le Séminaire XX: Encore* (Paris: Seuil, 1975).

1977a   *Ecrits: A Selection,* trans. Alan Sheridan (New York: Norton, 1977).

1977b   *The Four Fundamental Concepts of Psychoanalysis,* trans. Alan Sheridan (New York: Norton, 1977).

1978a   "Le mythe individuel du névrosé," *Ornicar?* 17/18 (1978).

1978b   *Le Séminaire II: Le moi dans la théorie de Freud et dans la technique de la psychanalyse* (Paris: Seuil, 1978).

1981   *Le Séminaire III: Les psychoses* (Paris: Seuil, 1981).

1984   *Les complexes familiaux dans la formation de l'individu* (Paris: Navarin Editeur, 1984).

1986   *Le Séminaire VII: L'éthique de la psychanalyse* (Paris: Seuil, 1986).

1988a   *The Seminar of Jacques Lacan: Book I. Freud's Papers on Technique, 1953–1954,* trans. John Forrester (New York: Norton, 1988).

1988b   *The Seminar of Jacques Lacan: Book II. The Ego in Freud's Theory and in the Technique of Psychoanalysis, 1954–1955,* trans. Sylvana Tomaselli (New York: Norton, 1988).

1990   *Television,* trans. Denis Hollier, Rosalind Krauss, and Annette Michelson (New York: Norton, 1990).

Not all publication dates in the preceding list correspond to dates of original publication, especially in the case of the works cited here as 1953 and 1984. The reader will also have noted that the works cited as 1977a, 1977b, 1988a, and 1988b are English translations of 1966, 1973b, 1975b, and 1978b, respectively. A reference to any of these translations gives the page number in question of the English version, followed by a solidus and the corresponding page number of the French original.

References to Lacan's unpublished seminars take the following form:

SIV   "La relation d'objet et les structures freudiennes," manuscript copy (1956–57).

SV   "Les formations de l'inconscient," manuscript copy (1957–58).

SVI   "Le désir et son interprétation," manuscript copy (1958–59).

SIX "L'identification," manuscript copy (1961–62).

SX   "L'angoisse," manuscript copy (1962–63).

SXVII "L'envers de la psychanalyse," manuscript copy (1969–70).

Each citation of an unpublished seminar includes the date of the lecture. For example, *SX (27 February 1963)* is a reference to a particular session of Lacan's tenth seminar, still unpublished. The unpublished material is cited courtesy of the heirs of Jacques Lacan.

  References to works other than Lacan's are indicated by consecutive superscript numbers that refer the reader to the Notes, which follow Chapter 7.

Translator's Note

Thanks to Mikkel Borch-Jacobsen's extensive participation, the reader will be spared the translator's habitual complaints about inevitable unfaithfulness to the "original," since the present volume is more a cooperative rewriting than a translation. In fact, since the "origin" of both the "original" and the "translation" was a request from Helen Tartar at Stanford University Press, it could even be said that the "translation" *precedes* the "original." Nevertheless, I would like to apologize for those instances where the English may happen to be less subtle, clear, or witty than the French. I would also like to thank the many people who helped in the production of this text, especially Terry Thomas for her sympathetic reading of successive drafts and Xavier Callahan for her editorial work, which went far beyond the normal duties of the copy editor. Thanks also are due to the members of the University of Washington's Department of Romance Languages and Literature for their support and patience.

LACAN

The Absolute Master

In Place of an Introduction

> So he had to renounce the development of his business, and that was his last attempt to eliminate his idleness. Nothing was left for him but the very emptiness of time. So he tried to see how time was passing, an enterprise as difficult as catching oneself in the act of sleeping.
> —Raymond Queneau [1]

In his seminars, Lacan liked to quote Hegel's expression that every man is the "son of his times," and this formula is eminently applicable to Lacan himself. A "son of his times," rooted in his era by every fiber of his being—who more than Jacques Marie Lacan (April 13, 1901–September 9, 1981), psychiatrist, psychoanalyst enamored of philosophy and mathematics, personal friend of Georges Bataille and Martin Heidegger, Salvador Dali and Roman Jakobson, Maurice Merleau-Ponty and Claude Lévi-Strauss, Alexandre Kojève, André Masson, Raymond Queneau, Michel Leiris, and so many others? Curious about everything, always on the lookout for anything new, Lacan took part in all the battles, all the debates of his times: those of psychoanalysis, of course, but also those of Politzer's "concrete psychology," of Surrealism (through his friendships and his contributions to the review *Le Minotaure*), of Caillois's and Bataille's *sociologie sacrée*,[2] of Hegelianism and anti-Hegelianism, of (French) Heideggerianism, and, finally, of Structuralism.

In a word, Lacan was an inspired autodidact—that is, a prodigious *assimilator*, open to every influence, quick to grasp resemblances and analogies among the most diverse fields. He was also incredibly agile at appropriating others' ideas. The autodidact, of course, owes nothing to anyone—not because he owes everything to himself, but because he owes everything to everyone. How, then, accuse him of plagiarism, since he annuls at its root the whole idea of intellectual private property? "The symbol belongs to everyone," Lacan used to say, speaking about a case of phantasmatic plagiarism analyzed by Ernst Kris: "For a psychoanalyst, an approach to the question of plagiarism in the symbolic register must center first on the idea that plagiarism does not exist. There is no such thing as symbolic private property" (1981, 93). It could not be put more clearly: "You believe you are stealing other people's ideas, but it's because you imagine that the other possesses a knowledge he does not *have*. Understand instead that ideas belong to no one, and no one can ever think by himself: it (*ça*) thinks, without you."

This thesis must be taken seriously, for it is the basis of the famous Lacanian "style," so consistently citational and allusional. ("The style is the man," Lacan recalls at the beginning of the *Ecrits*, but he adds, "Shall we accept this formula simply by extending it: 'the man to whom one speaks'? That would simply confirm the principle that we are advancing: in language, our message comes to us from the Other, and—to complete the statement—in an inverted form" [1966, 9]. In short, one always writes with the style, the pen, of the Other.) By his own criteria, Lacan—who, as we shall see, never really had a thought of his own—was still no plagiarist; no one could be, since no one could be a (proprietary, original) subject before that "discourse in whose movement his place is already inscribed at birth, if only in the form of his proper name" (1966, 495). "Jacques Lacan" (who enjoyed speaking of himself in the third person) was thus deliberately, openly, *honestly* a plagiarist. He immersed himself in the inexhaustible discourse of others, moved around, was everywhere and nowhere, finally identifying (by way of this interpolated quotation from Paul Valéry) with that voice

> which knows itself, when it sounds,
> To be no one's voice anymore
> so much as that of waves and woods.[3]

The Autodidact, son of his times, is nobody's son. Lacan, unlike Freud, was completely silent about his personal history. "Few men," notes his biographer, Elisabeth Roudinesco, "have shown such a desire to keep secret, if not intact, the part of . . . being that touched on . . . childhood or . . . family origins."⁴ Of course, we can take this as either humble anonymity or inordinate narcissism (what is more narcissistic than the phantasy of the "foundling"?). Whereas Freud, throughout his life, never stopped his self-analysis (mercilessly interrogating himself about his "family romances," his relationship with his father, his infantile megalomania, his identification with heroes), Lacan burned all his bridges, broke every filiation and every paternity (including the analytic ones), to offer the world a completely fabricated *personage*—that of the Analyst with a capital A, always Other, always Elsewhere. And this personage, naturally, masked no one: self-display (*Selbstdarstellung*) without a self (*Selbst*). Lacan, whose exhibitionism was immense (it verged on the ridiculous), exhibited nothing after all but his own histrionics— that is, his own absence of "self." This fascinating personage, who so obligingly took the stage in his seminars and in private life, was a terrific actor (or "clown," as he himself said), capable of all roles to the same extent that he was incapable of any one in particular. Was it so strange that he finally identified with the whole repertoire of the era?

Thus developed, over the years, the myth of a discourse all the more sovereign and all-encompassing for belonging to no one. Lacan the Autodidact made neighbors of Hegel, Heidegger, and Freud, read Kant "with" Sade, formulated human sexuality in terms of logico-mathematical paradoxes, assembled pell-mell Frege and the rudimentary inscriptions of the Mas d'Azil,⁵ Joyce and Borromean knots, St. Augustine and Saussure. And Lacan the Actor loaned his falsetto to Truth in person, in its anonymous rustling of words: "I, truth, speak" (1966, 409).⁶ Or again, addressing a dumbfounded television audience: "I always speak the truth. Not the whole truth, because there is no way to say it all" (1990, 3). Of course, no mouth was supposed to pronounce that oracular speech, no "I" was considered to appropriate that Truth—a spoken truth that, as Lacan often said, one can only "half-say" (*mi-dire*) (1973a, 8). The impeccably removed place from which Lacan spoke was the place (always the Other Place) from which *all* knowledge, including "absolute knowledge," was derided and its relativity proclaimed.

Yet how could his audience avoid identifying *him*, the Analyst, with that vast discourse of truth, in its prolix and multiform self-inadequacy? Who, confronted with this chameleon whose thought was as motley as his garb, did not have the marvelous and overwhelming sense of being in the presence of the *Zeitgeist* incarnate, the very spirit of our times?

Lacan had undoubtedly learned that every man is the son of his times from another inspired autodidact, Alexandre Kojève, who (apart from the psychiatrist Gaëtan Gratien de Clérambault) was the only one Lacan ever recognized as his "master": "Kojève, whom I hold to be my master for having introduced me to Hegel" (1973a, 9). For anything at all to be understood about the Lacanian adventure, it must be understood that Lacan's times (and the times of many others: Bataille, Blanchot, Sartre) were Kojèvian times[7]—that is, Hegelian-Heideggerian times. From this perspective, the best introduction to the reading of Lacan is undoubtedly Kojève's *Introduction to the Reading of Hegel*—the only trace, we must remember, that we have of what was first of all an amazing *teaching*. People flocked to Kojève's course on the *Phenomenology of Spirit*, just as they would later flock to Lacan's seminar: the same cult of oral teaching, the same bent for advancing oneself behind a mask of virtuosic commentary, the same taste for striking illustrations and paradoxical formulas, the same cynical rhetoric, the same dandyism of thought. On all these points, as on so many others, Lacan was the faithful disciple of his "master," Kojève—up to and including his derision of mastery and knowledge.

It was this last trait, indeed, that Lacan tended to emphasize when, rarely, he alluded to Kojève, and this trait in turn illuminates the rather peculiar character of the "mastery" that Lacan saw in him. Kojève, he recalls, had abandoned the teaching of philosophy to become a high international official:

He philosophized only as part of the academic discourse within which he had provisionally placed himself, fully realizing that his knowledge there was only for show and treating it accordingly. He showed this in all kinds of ways, handing his notes over to whoever could use them and posthumizing his mockery of the whole enterprise. His opening discourse, which was also the one to which he returned, sustained this contempt of his: the senior civil servant knows how to treat the jesters, as well as the others—that is, as the subjects of the sovereign that they are [1973a, 9].

Who would not recognize in this passage a rather faithful portrait of the paradoxical master that Lacan himself was, always reticent about the *"poubellication"*[8] of his seminars or his writings, and crushing his most faithful, *too* faithful, disciples with contempt?

Another passage is even more explicit, and well worth lingering over, for it will quickly help us understand what Lacan retained of Kojève. Inserted in a talk entitled "Mistake of the Subject Supposed to Know" (*"La méprise du sujet supposé savoir"*), this passage deals with the very heart of Kojève's teaching—namely, the *incarnation* of Hegel's "absolute knowledge" in the person of the Wise Man. In what subject can such knowledge be supposed, asks Lacan, if not in God, the "God of philosophers" latent "in every theory" (1968, 39), just as we still find with Einstein, who postulates a God "admittedly complicated but not dishonest" (1968, 32)? To believe that there is a subject of knowledge is to believe in God, but it is also a "mistake" that psychoanalysis permits, if not to be thwarted (it is, Lacan says, "essential"), at least to be recognized. The psychoanalyst, precisely because his patients ordinarily invest him with such omniscience, knows very well for his part that no subject contains this knowledge ("He is not God for his patient," and he "can-[not] claim to represent . . . an absolute knowledge"; 1977b, 230–232/209–210). He knows, in other words, that no subject can be sub-posed to know(ledge), unless it is the improbable "subject" of the unconscious, who (dis)appears in the *"mistake* of the subject supposed to know"—in the patient's *transference*, in other words, and, more generally, in all the symptoms, slips of the tongue, lapses, and bungled actions that inscribe themselves in such a transference to the analyst (or the teacher). Therefore, Lacan postulates, if there is a God (or a subject), he can only be unconscious (1977b, 59/58), which is also to say radically and absolutely *deceitful*.

How, then, can one possibly teach such "knowledge" (knowledge of no subject, knowledge that dupes every subject), if not precisely by deceiving one's listeners, taking them for a ride? This, for Lacan, was the supremely paradoxical and ironic lesson of Kojève, who brought Hegel's Wise Man onstage the better to scoff at absolute knowledge. Indeed, the "deceit of the unconscious" announces itself in laughter (or in the *Witz*, which is its "perfect articulation") (1968, 32)—in this, says Lacan, very different from the preposterous seriousness of Hegel's "cunning of reason":

> It is not sufficient for [the unconscious] to be cunning or even for it to seem so. To stop there is all too easy for novices, whose every inference is then burdened with that conclusion. Thank God that, for those I had to deal with, I had the Hegelian story (*histoire*) at hand—the one about the cunning of reason—to make them sense a difference where we may be able to make it understood why they are lost beforehand. Let's look at the comical aspect . . . of this reason, for which these endless detours are necessary to bring us to . . . what? To what the end of history designates as absolute knowledge. Shall we recall here the mockery of such knowledge—a derision coined by the humor of Queneau, who was educated in Hegel on the same bench as I was—namely, his "Sunday of life," or the advent of the do-nothing and the good-for-nothing, whose absolute indolence shows the knowledge suited to satisfying the animal? or only the wisdom authenticated by the sardonic laughter of Kojève, who was master of us both [1968, 33]?

The Wise Man, then, would be satisfied with knowing . . . nothing? And laughter would authenticate wisdom?

The Wise Man, in Kojève's anthropologizing version of Hegel, is the one who "realizes" absolute knowledge (omniscience) "in his own person."[9] According to Kojève, this was Hegel's "unheard-of audacity"[10]: to affirm that he, a finite man, incarnated the absolute Wisdom that, until he came on the scene, philosophy had always contented itself with *desiring*. The philosopher, he who "loves Wisdom," will never attain it, because he separates himself from it at the very moment when he poses it as the *object* of his desire. Hegel, by contrast, affirming once and for all the absolute identity of the subject and the object (of the "for-itself" and the "in-itself"), completely *fulfills* and *realizes* that desire. Knowing—with, finally, an absolute knowledge—that he himself is the object of his desire, the Hegelian Wise Man attains satisfaction, *Befriedigung*. In short, he rests. What, indeed, remains to be done, if one has attained the "goal" of knowledge—the "goal" that, Hegel said, "is the point where knowledge no longer needs to go beyond itself, where knowledge finds itself, where Concept (*Begriff*) corresponds to object and object to Concept"?[11] Not much, one suspects, and this is what Kojève, as Lacan recalls, named the "end of history." History, which is the history of desire and thus also of work, *completes itself* in the Wise Man, who finally reconciles the "week's work days" and the "Sunday of life":

The end of human Time or History—that is, the definitive annihilation of Man properly so-called or of the free and historical Individual—means quite simply the cessation of Action in the full sense of the term. . . . And also the disappearance of *Philosophy*; for since Man himself no longer changes essentially, there is no longer any reason to change the (true) principles which are at the basis of his understanding of the World and of himself. But all the rest can be preserved indefinitely; art, love, play . . . in short, everything that makes Man *happy*.[12]

Hence the title of Raymond Queneau's novel (Queneau was the editor of Kojève's course on Hegel): on Sunday, one is decidedly bored because there is nothing to do (and thus also nothing to narrate except foolish stupidities). This is what the most attentive in Kojève's listening and reading audiences—Bataille, Blanchot, and Lacan, each in his own way—would also repeat: the complete fulfillment of desire (that is, of history, of philosophy), far from satisfying desire once and for all, exacerbates it instead, beyond all limit, for then and only then does the desperate question arise of what one can possibly desire once *everything* has been accomplished. Nothing, certainly; but that is exactly what desire sets about desiring once it has been totally satisfied: *nothing*, nothing *at all*. Desire, as the desire of nothing, becomes even more insistent, and that is what Blanchot, in a friendly commentary on Bataille's "interior experience," calls the "limit experience":

What awaits this ultimate man, who is able one last time not to stop at the sufficiency he has reached, is a limit experience. It is the desire of the man who is without desire, the dissatisfaction of the one who is satisfied "in all things," pure absence wherein there is nevertheless fulfillment of being . . . it opens up in the fulfilled being a minute interstice in which everything-that-is suddenly lets itself be overwhelmed and deposed by an overabundance that escapes and exceeds. Strange surplus.[13]

Strange surplus, indeed: the "end of history" (but also, for the writers Bataille and Blanchot, the end of narrative) finally proves itself interminable, without end. That "Sunday," during which the

Man-God was supposed to rest and contemplate his work, falls irreversibly into *désoeuvrement*[14] (Blanchot), into "useless negativity" (Bataille), into pure insatiable "desire" (Lacan): no earthly paradise, no unity of Man with God, no reconciliation between finite and infinite. Blanchot's "Last Man" never ceases to die, just as the divine beatitude of Pierre Angélique, in *Madame Edwarda*, opens only into "waiting for death."[15] And, Lacan concludes, *jouissance** can be "reached [only] on the inverted ladder [*l'échelle renversée*] . . . of desire" (1977a, 324/827).

Did Kojève, too, the Wise Man, know that absolute knowledge, in the end, opens only on a dissatisfaction that is itself absolute? Could this master, who fascinated a whole generation of French intellectuals, have known what desire is about—the very definition, according to Lacan, of the "subject supposed to know" who arouses the transference (1977b, 231–232/210)? This is precisely what Lacan suggests when he cites the "sardonic laughter" that "authenticated" the wisdom of Kojève, for, as Baudelaire said, "The Wise Man does not laugh"[16]; and Bataille, in fact, had often recalled in Lacan's immediate circle that "in the [Hegelian] 'system,' poetry, laughter, and ecstasy are nothing," adding in clearly (anti-)Kojèvian terms that "poetry, laughter, and ecstasy are not the completed man, they do not give 'satisfaction.'"[17] Then how could "sardonic laughter," in Lacan's terms, "authenticate" the Wisdom of Kojève, if not by authenticating it instead as non-wisdom, non-knowledge? Beneath its cryptic exterior, Lacan's allusion is fairly clear: it is in Alexandre's laughter that Kojève's truth is to be found, in his properly *sovereign* derision of knowledge that the secret of his mastery resides.

An odd scene, to be sure: Lacan recognized Kojève as his master only insofar as the latter contemptuously proclaimed the inevitable "*mistake* of the subject supposed to know." In short, Lacan could accept as master only one who was limited, unsatisfied (or sworn to excesses of finitude—Clérambault, the other "master," killed himself in front of a mirror). This really would have made Kojève laugh: he who had taught full satisfaction, transformed here into a doctor of desire, a master of ignorance—a Lacanian analyst!

---

* Given the "orgasmic" connotation of this word in French, it took very little to carry the Hegelian-Kojèvian *jouissance* to impossible sexual satisfaction, as did Lacan (or to the no less impossible erotic "sovereignty" of Bataille)—Trans.

Could it be that Lacan—who, everyone agrees, learned very little from his analyst, Rudolph Loewenstein[18]—did his analysis (the *real* one) with Alexandre Kojève?

We shall often find this scene in Lacan: the good master (that is, the analyst; cf. 1978a, 293) is the one I recognize (*reconnaître*) beyond himself, as the "Absolute Other," without knowing (*connaître*) him (1981, 62–63), for if I were to know him (if I were to know what he knows), I would know him as myself—I would recognize *myself* in him, and then I would kill him, killing myself along with him. In other words, the "dialectic" of analysis is not the Hegelian dialectic of master and slave that Kojève (if not Alexandre) never tired of describing. For Kojève, in this respect faithful to Hegel, the famous dialectic is resolved when I recognize myself in the other, who for his part recognizes himself in me. The slave ceases to be the slave when he realizes that the Other (the Master, the God) to whom he was submitting himself is none other than himself:

> If history (in the full sense of the word) necessarily has a final term, if man who becomes must culminate in man who has become, if Desire must end in satisfaction . . . the interaction of Master and Slave must finally end in the "dialectical overcoming" of both of them. . . . It is only by being "recognized" by another [whom he recognizes], by many others, or—in the extreme—by all others, that a human being is really human, for himself as well as for others.[19]

In this sense, the "good" master is the (dialectically) suppressed master: he is the slave, *himself* become the master through liberating work and struggle, and in no way the "Absolute Other" cited by Lacan. By all the evidence, the very idea of an "Absolute Other" could not be more anti-Hegelian, and if we had to find an equivalent for it in the Hegelian text, it would fall within the domain of "death, that absolute Master" whom the slave encounters but also *avoids* from the very beginning of the dialectic of lordship and bondage. In fact, as we shall see, Lacan often returned to that swooning moment (that "sovereign" moment, as his friend Bataille would say) when the Hegelian slave had the impossible experience of his absolute freedom and did not feel "fear for this element or that, nor for this or that moment of time, [he] was afraid for [his] entire being; [he] felt the fear of death, the sovereign master."[20]

Thus, Lacan says, the analyst "makes death present" (1977a, 140/430) to his patient—very obviously an impossible task, as Lacan enjoyed repeating, for who could ever incarnate the "Master" in his sovereign escape from every mastery, every presentation, every knowledge?

For the relation of transference . . . to escape from these effects [hatred and aggressivity toward the "analyst's Ego," in which the patient's Ego (re)cognizes itself], the analyst would need to strip away from his Ego's narcissistic image all the forms of desire that had gone to make it up, in order to reduce it to the single figure that, under the masks of these forms [of desire], sustains it: that of the absolute master, death. . . . And that end would also be required for the analyst's Ego, which, we could say, should know only the prestige of a single master: death, so that life, which he must guide through so many destinies, will be his friend. . . . But this imaginary condition can be realized only in an asceticism that asserts itself in being, by way of a path where all objective knowledge is put in ever greater suspension, because the reality of the subject's own death is an unimaginable object, and the analyst, like anyone else, can know nothing about it unless he is a being promised to death [1966, 348–349].

In short, the Master is never Me (the Ego), contrary to what Kojève taught, following Hegel. Could it be said, then, that the "master" whom Lacan recognized in Kojève was other, completely Other, than the master according to Kojève? And that Lacan was consequently not Kojève, not the *same* as Kojève? That would certainly be too simple, for Kojève, too, insisted on the identification of freedom with death (or, if you will, of absolute mastery with absolute alterity). Hegel's philosophy, he wrote, is a "philosophy of death,"[21] and "there is no freedom without death . . . only a mortal being can be free. One might even say that death is the last and authentic 'manifestation' [note the quotation marks] of freedom."[22] As we shall see, this was the fundamental problem of Kojève's reading of Hegel; how, strictly speaking, can we reconcile this assertion of the mortal character (the radical finitude) of freedom with the more properly Hegelian one of the identity between the finite and the infinite (between Man and God, in Kojève's translation)? How could *man*, that "mortal being," ever reappropriate his ownmost essence, his most essential freedom, if this freedom is equivalent to a pure and simple negativity—to a "freedom-toward-death," as Kojève would say, quoting Heidegger; to a "useless negativity," as

Bataille would add? How, finally, could Desire (that same nothingness of freedom, according to Kojève) ever attain any *Befriedigung* whatsoever, if it can only be satisfied in death and, therefore, in absolute dissatisfaction? In any case, Kojève himself did not fail to emphasize this difficulty: "If man is essentially finite, he can be completely self-conscious only by becoming conscious of his death. Thus, only in knowing himself to be irremediably *mortal* can the Wise Man attain the fullness of satisfaction." [23] In *knowing* himself to be mortal—but not in *truly* dying—could Kojève's Wise Man, reputed to "fulfill" man's Desire, really be satisfied with *desiring*, with desiring his own, most impossible, death?

We can bet that Lacan for his part would have answered affirmatively, and that this very desire—the desire for death, finite desire (1977b, 31/32)—is what Lacan recognized, beyond all knowledge, in his "master," Kojève. This is a great homage, if we think about it, since it would mean recognizing his own "Desire" in Kojève's—that is, as we know, the "desire of the Other"; it is perhaps not so well known that this last formula was originally Kojève's. What human Desire desires, Kojève asserted, is Desire as such, in its pure and insatiable vacuity: "Human Desire must be directed toward another Desire. . . . Thus, in the relationship between man and woman, for example, Desire is human only if the one desires . . . the Desire of the other." [24] And so, finally, there was as much rigorous probity as fundamental dishonesty in the way Lacan appropriated Kojève's formula, which under his pen became "the formula I have given of desire as unconscious—*the desire of man is the desire of the Other*" (1977b, 115/105). After all, why in heaven's name render unto Kojève what was not Kojève's—his *desire*, which tortured him beyond himself and everything he could know about it? The desire that escaped from him was not his own, but completely Other than himself; and thus it was for another (Lacan, in this instance) to recognize it where it was—that is, nowhere: in the rift, in the breach, in the stumbling of the discourse of full satisfaction, in the unknown (otherwise translated as the unconscious: *das Unbewusste*) of absolute knowledge. Or in the Wise Man's burst of laughter.

And yet that rift, that breach, had to be inscribed somewhere in Kojève's otherwise impeccably closed and circular discourse. That breach, which Lacan would never cease to insist on reopening, has a name, and that name is "man." In this regard, it was no accident that the laughter of Kojève the man, of the Wise Man incarnated in Alexandre, is where Lacan recognized the rift of the "subject supposed to know." Indeed, Kojève proposed a "humanist" and "anthropological" interpretation of Hegel in his course, and that was how he ended up stumbling onto the problem of death and finitude, dragging his most eminent listeners into a sort of strange Hegelianism of pure negativity, which rather quickly swerved into a virulent anti-Hegelianism (and anti-humanism). Insofar as Lacan, in many ways, was the most consequential representative of this tradition of thought, it is important to pause here for a moment. This problem of "humanism" was also his, and so he remained to the end "the son of his times."

Of his *Kojèvian* times, that is, since this problem—the problem of the human, all too human, mortality of the Wise Man—is, we must emphasize, in no way a Hegelian problem, and for a very simple reason: namely, that absolute knowledge, as its name indicates, is not in any sense a knowledge or science of finite man. The *Science of Logic*, absolute knowledge's exposition, Hegel plainly defines as "the exposition of God as he is in his eternal essence before the creation of nature and a finite mind."[25] Despite certain appearances, the same is true of the work that Kojève chose to comment on, not accidentally entitled *Phenomenology of Spirit*. This phenomenology, which admittedly describes the diverse figures of human consciousness and knowledge, is nevertheless a clearly phenomenal manifestation of the Absolute—that is, of what Hegel calls, in his preface, the "life of God"[26] or the "life of the Spirit," by which he means the life of the trinitarian Spirit that "endures [death] and maintains itself in it."[27] In this sense, Hegel's *Phenomenology* is the speculative version of the Passion (as Bataille, rectifying Kojève, understood perfectly):[28] the Absolute that "rends" itself in its self-negation is strictly modeled on the kenosis of Christ (Saint Paul, Philippians 2:7; Christ "emptied himself [*ekenōsen*], taking the form of a servant"). We might as well say that this death is inseparable from the resurrection. There is in Hegel an incarnation of the Absolute (human manifestation, finite phenomenality), but this incarnation remains that of the Spirit that "maintains itself even in death" and thus "changes nothingness into being." The fact that man (the "Son of Man") dies is no problem for Hegel, since this death of the finite man is precisely the motive force behind his infinite "sublation" (*Aufhebung*),[29] the condition of the Spirit's finally absolute manifestation as trinitarian identity of Father and Son, of substance and subject, of the in-itself and the for-itself, of identity and difference: "That Substance is essentially Subject is expressed in the representation of the Absolute as *Spirit*—the most sublime Concept and the one which belongs to the modern age and its religion."[30]

It is just this Spirit, suffering its death the better to reveal itself to Itself, that Kojève proposed to translate, in a fashion as suggestive as it was aberrant, by the word "Man": "This is the meaning," he comments, "of the passage quoted from the preface to the *Phenomenology of Spirit*. Interpreted on the ontological plane, this passage signifies that it is not the (infinite) *Totality* of Being (or of the One-who-is) that reveals itself to itself, but rather that this Totality is revealed by one of its (limited) *parts*, which also reveals itself. Metaphysically speaking, the passage signifies that the Spirit— that is to say, the Being that reveals itself to itself—is not God, but Man-in-the-World."[31] It could not be put more clearly: "the suffering, the patience, and the labour of the negative"[32]—these words are spoken, not of God, but of Man, not of the Absolute, but of a "limited part" of that Absolute. Therefore, the *Phenomenology of Spirit*, Kojève repeats, is an "anthropology," a "science of man."[33]

That statement in turn could be understood in two very different ways, and this is the whole ambiguity of Kojève's strange "humanism." That Hegel's Absolute is identical to Man (with a capital M) could be understood first of all in the sense that Man reappropriates his own infinite essence, inheriting all the qualities that until then had been attributed to God. It is well known that this was the thesis of the "Hegelian left," of Feuerbach and the young Marx (whose *Manuscripts of 1844* had just been discovered), and Kojève, in fact, did not scruple to take it up again and attribute it, as generously as he did tendentiously, to Hegel himself: "In a general way, Hegelian anthropology is a laicization of Christian theology. [Hegel] repeats several times that everything Christian theology says is absolutely true on condition of its being applied, not to a transcendent God, but to real Man living in the World. The theologian is doing anthropology without realizing it."[34] The theologian, speaking of God, speaks of himself without realizing it, whereas Hegel knows he is doing it: "The Wise Man strictly ascribes to himself the *same* total content as the Religious man ascribes to his God."[35] In other words, this is the end of religious alienation and the radiant beginning of "atheistic humanism." "Existentialism," as Sartre would say, "is a humanism."

The only problem is this: How could Man (even adorned with an enormous M) claim to take the place of the Absolute if, as Kojève himself wrote, he is only a "limited part" of it? Man, like it or not, is notoriously mortal and finite; furthermore, this is what Kojève was discreetly indicating by speaking of "Man-in-the-World." Indeed, this "Man-in-the-World" is a fairly clear allusion to Heidegger's *In-der-Welt-sein* and, more generally, to the whole existential analytic put forth in *Sein und Zeit*. This analytic, which Kojève, more than anyone else, helped introduce into France (existentialism was a Kojèvism), is presented explicitly by Heidegger as one of finitude. In a word, where the metaphysical tradition had always thought of man against a background of infinite Being,[36] Heidegger proposed to reverse the current and think of Being in terms of a radical finitude (a "finitude of Being," as Kojève would say).[37] But this in no way implies that Being is reabsorbed, so to speak, in "man," as Kojève would victoriously proclaim.

Indeed, what "is" Being, according to *Sein und Zeit*? *Nothing*—nothing that man could appropriate. Being, as Heidegger defines it, is most certainly the Being of the "being that we are," but this must be understood in the sense that it is—and is *only*—the Being of an entity who does *not* have his Being in himself. That is precisely why Heidegger took great care to rebaptize the "being that we are" as *Dasein* (literally, "Being-there"), so as not to confound it with the "man" of philosophical anthropology.[38] This man would indeed continue to be thought of as what Heidegger calls *Vorhandensein* ("Being-present-at-hand"), whereas *Dasein* "ek-sists": thrown (*geworfen*) into existence, without being at the foundation of itself, it is by the same token projected (*entworfen*) beyond itself, toward its Being. Contrary to the being that subsists in the mode of *Vorhandensein*, it *has* to be, beyond all being (all "that which is"), and so is all the freer in that it is fundamentally finite. Condemned to choose among the possibilities offered to it—that is, to *negate* one possibility for the sake of another—it perpetually "goes beyond" every being, and this "transcendence" makes up its entire Being—which at the same time is no (present, subsisting, substantial, and so on) being. *Dasein*'s Being, insofar as it is "*transcendens* pure and simple," is no-being, no-thing, nothing (*Nichts*).

What this celebrated thesis means is precisely that man never rejoins or appropriates his Being. Ek-sistentialism is *not* a "humanism": the moment when human *Dasein* finally realizes its ultimate possibility is the moment of its death—that is, the impossible moment when it no longer ek-sists, or when it simply is no longer there (*Nicht-mehr-Dasein*). *Dasein*'s freedom, which makes it transcend all being, is a "freedom-toward-death" (*Freiheit zum Tode*) and, as such, cannot be appropriated. Thus, Being-there, as long as it ek-sists, is nothing but a perpetual "Being-toward-death" (*Sein-zum-Tode*).

Kojève reformulated this thesis—translating and commenting on Hegel's passage about the Spirit that "endures [death] and maintains itself in it"—by saying that "*human* Being . . . is the death which lives a *human* life,"[39] to which Lacan in turn, quoting *Oedipus at Colonus*, replied that such a life is properly *inhuman*. Yes, Oedipus "lives a life that is dead," but is the sense of this life "as human as all that?": "Am I a man," exclaims Oedipus (1988b, 232/271, 229/268), "in the hour that I cease to be?"

All of this, very briefly summarized, will have to suffice in explaining the extent to which Heidegger's *Dasein* differs not only from Hegel's Spirit but also from the Man-God of "atheistic humanism." Nevertheless, it was to precisely such an amalgam, under the name of "human reality," that Kojève invited his fascinated listeners. "Human reality" was the term proposed by Henry Corbin to translate Heidegger's *Dasein* into French. Was Kojève influenced by that translation, which in so many ways is "monstrous," to recall Derrida's term?[40] Or should we believe instead that the translation was itself an effect of Kojève's teaching, since he began using the term in 1933? (As Denis Hollier notes in his collection from the Collège de sociologie,[41] Corbin originally translated *Dasein* as "existence," and it was not until 1938 that he opted for "human reality," carrying Sartre along with him.) That matters very little here; what really matters is that, right from the second paragraph of the text which opens the *Introduction to the Reading of Hegel*, we find this philosophical monster—and in the company of that other monster, itself destined for a glorious future under Lacan's pen: "Desire."

Here is what Kojève wrote: "The analysis of 'thought,' 'reason,' 'understanding,' and so on, . . . never reveals the why or the how of the birth of the word 'I,' and consequently of self-consciousness— that is, of human reality. . . . The man who is 'absorbed' by the object that he is contemplating can be 'brought back to himself' only by a Desire. . . . The (human) I is the I of a Desire or of Desire." [42] What is going on here? This opening text, entitled "In Place of an Introduction," is really an annotated translation of Section A of the fourth chapter of the *Phenomenology of Spirit*, devoted to the (from then on) famous "dialectic of master and slave." Why, then, did Kojève choose to "introduce the reading of Hegel" by *that* particular section?

Chapter 4 of the *Phenomenology of Spirit* discusses "self-consciousness"—that is, consciousness whose object is not the object "in-itself" of theoretical consciousness (described in the first three chapters, which deal with "sense-certainty," "perception," and "understanding"), but rather the object "for-itself" of an active freedom. Self-consciousness does not contemplate the object (outside itself), it *desires* it (for itself). Thus, "self-consciousness," Hegel writes, "is desire (*Begierde*) in general," [43] in the very precise sense of knowing no alterity that it does not immediately carry back to itself. Desiring itself through the other, it negates the other (by eating it, Kojève would clarify, always careful to dot his *i*'s). This first phase of self-consciousness is thus that of "Life"—a life that develops of itself, from itself, and so is perfectly free, "independent" of any Other. But this natural life also remains profoundly un-conscious of itself: it does not *know* itself to be free, does not *know* itself to be alive. Immediately negating everything that is not itself, at bottom it has no mirror to see itself, and that is why, according to the Hegelian system, it must mediate itself—that is, it must oppose itself to itself and reflect itself in order to know *itself*. In short, it must confront death, deny itself as natural life to become conscious of itself as freedom.

This is the moment described in Section A of Chapter 4, and thus we understand why Kojève found it so interesting: this moment is that of "man," of the "human I" in its opposition to natural life. For Hegel, however, this opposition was an autoopposition of *Life* becoming conscious of itself through the experience of death, whereas Kojève for his part conceived of it as a radical opposition of *man* to the same "natural" and "immediate" life that man negates and, therefore, is not. Man, Kojève never tires of explaining, "is essentially different from animals"[44] in that he confronts death and so "goes beyond the given reality,"[45] "transcending the given that is given to [him] and that [he him]self is"[46] as a natural being. Strictly "human reality" is the reality that differs from itself, that perpetually negates itself as reality.

At the same time, this no longer has anything to do with dialectic (at least in the Hegelian sense), since here we stumble rudely upon an irreducible duality, which Kojève obligingly describes as "dualistic ontology."[47] Indeed, on one side we would have the natural, substantial, "thingish" being, always identical to itself—whether it were what Kojève called "Being pure and simple" or, to use a term that Lacan would later take up, the "Real." On the other side we would have the non-natural being that "nihilates in Being"[48] by negating, surpassing, transcending everything Real—whether it were what Kojève indiscriminately called "Man," "Subject," "Desire," or "Discourse" (for example, "Spirit is the Real revealed by Discourse. Discourse is born in Man who opposes himself to Nature. . . . From this 'rending' [*déchirement*] of the Real into Man and Nature are born Understanding and its Discourse, which reveal the Real and thus transform it into Spirit").[49] We can certainly recognize this "rending" duality (the duality of the "symbolic" and the "real," as Lacan will say later)—it is simply that of Heidegger's *Dasein* and *Vorhandensein*, here rebaptized for the occasion as "human reality" and "given reality"—just as in Kojève's "dualistic ontology" we recognize Heidegger's famous "difference" between Being and being, simply (and roughly) reinterpreted in terms of the difference between two regions of *being*.[50]

That this amalgam of Hegel and Heidegger is philosophically untenable is quite obvious. Indeed, it is hard to see how Hegel could tolerate an Absolute split in two—that is, a dialectic frozen indefinitely at the moment of finite "reflection." As for Heidegger, we know that he explicitly refuses to turn Being into a power of nihilation that human being could purely and simply appropriate (this will be the substance of his "Letter on Humanism," fundamentally as much a response to Kojève as to his philosophical heir, Jean-Paul Sartre). And yet it is just this philosophical incongruity that Kojève brought to life with all the authority of his word, under the magical names of "negativity," "historicity," "dialectic," and, to come straight to the point, "Desire."

In fact, let us return to the *Phenomenology of Spirit*, grasped through Kojève's interpretation. Hegelian desire, we have seen, desires itself in its object (it determines *itself* by negating the object, and so on). When does this desire become properly "human," "non-natural," "non-animal"? Kojève's response: when it addresses itself to a non-natural object, since desire *itself* then becomes the object abolished through its own appropriation of itself. But where are we to find such an "object," if not precisely in desire? "The only thing that goes beyond the given reality is Desire itself."[51] Note the capital letter: here there is no question of desire for this or that (which could be only an empirical *need*, as Lacan will say more than once), but rather of Desire in its essence of Desire. And what is Desire *as* Desire? It is an *empty* desire: "Desire taken as Desire— i.e., before its satisfaction—is but a revealed nothingness, an unreal emptiness. Desire, being the revelation of an emptiness, the presence of the absence of a reality, is something essentially different from the desired thing, something other than a thing, than a static and given real being that stays eternally identical to itself."[52] Will Lacan ever say anything different?

Human Desire is thus the Desire that desires itself as unsatisfied desire: pure "negativity," we would say in Hegelian terms, pure "transcendence" in Heideggerian terms. It remains to be understood in what sense Desire desires "itself": as "itself" or as "other"? That, obviously, is the whole problem of this Hegelian-Heideggerian amalgam. For Hegel, it is clear that desire desires *itself* through the other that it denies, which is precisely why Hegel, in this connection, spoke of the "doubling" of self-consciousness: self-consciousness desires itself in another that it itself is, having first to alienate itself in another desire before being able to reappropriate it for itself as its very own (and, thus, to arrive at the famous "satisfaction"). By contrast, if desire is defined, in para-Heideggerian terms, as transcendence toward nothing, it is none the less clear that it will desire "itself" only as nothingness—in other words, as pure negativity and absolute alterity: that Desire (capital D) will desire "itself" as Other (capital O), beyond itself and every "ego." Therefore, in formulas ambiguous enough to admit of all readings, we shall say that Desire is "Desire of Desire," or "Desire of the Desire of the other."[53] Human Desire, according to Kojève, is what is brought to bear on another human Desire: it desires to be desired—that is, "recognized"—as pure desire of nothing. The only strictly human Desire is "Desire of recognition," and the only "human reality" is "recognized reality" or "social reality": "If . . . human reality is a social reality, society is human only as a set of Desires mutually desiring one another as Desires."[54]

The problem, however, only becomes more acute. Aside from the difficulty of seeing where this Desire for recognition comes from (in keeping with "dualistic ontology," social-human reality arises *ex abrupto* from natural reality, with absolutely no transition and no mediation), there is also the difficulty of understanding how it could ever be "satisfied," if, as Kojève asserts, it is pure desire of nothing. For "human reality," the only way to become recognized and desired as pure Desire would be in fact to die, to radically negate itself as animal life and "given reality"—and so to go completely unrecognized. This brings us right back to the "absolute Master, death." Kojève, to resolve the difficulty, calls on the strictly Hegelian solution of the problem—namely, the struggle for recognition (for "pure prestige" says Kojève, since the consciousnesses are fighting each other for *nothing*) and the subsequent dialectic of master and slave. According to this theory, one of the two battling consciousnesses would become frightened of death (that is, of its "own" Desire) and would prefer unilateral recognition of the other as its master, thus setting off the long process of Labor and History as the Struggle for a truly final and definitive recognition. And so not until the *end* of history would Man satisfy his truly human Desire—at exactly that moment when he is no longer a Man, but a Wise Man. Let us reread Kojève's idyllic summary: "If Desire must end in satisfaction . . . the interaction of Master and Slave must finally end in the 'dialectical overcoming' of both of them. . . . It is only by being 'recognized' by another, by many others, or—in the extreme—by all others, that a human being is really human."[55]

Here, peals of laughter from Alexandre, Jacques, and Georges—for how would Desire be satisfied in the end, if it had not been satisfied at the beginning? The slave, as Bataille and Lacan have both noted, is *still alive*, having recoiled before the "absolute Master," and thus the desire that, in the end, he "satisfies" is in no way the one in question at the beginning, the pure Desire of death. In reality, this Desire of death cannot possibly be satisfied, if, as Kojève insists, it is a *human* desire: How could a man ever experience the pure negativity that he "himself" "is," if not by perpetually deferring it—by perpetually desiring it?

If strictly human Desire is the desire that desires itself as desire of nothing, then man can never take his proper place except as *desire* of himself, as *impossible* desire of himself. "Man" was the name of the impossible. Man is not in man, he is always beyond himself. And "the desire of man," Lacan would conclude, following the thread of desire straight down from Kojève, "is the desire of the Other."

> "What do you desire to know?" asked Valentin, shouting.
>
> Indeed, what could she desire to know, the poor wreck? If she wanted to hear about her past, Valentin possessed all the desired documentation.
>
> "If you are a clairvoyant," said Miss Pantruche, leaning toward him to try to glimpse his face through the veil, "if you are a clairvoyant, you should know what I desire to know."
>
> And to think that this derelict dares to be skeptical, sighed Valentin, I'll have to one-up her.
>
> "You desire to know the future," he vocalized.
>
> "That's it!" Miss Pantruche announced triumphantly.[56]

Crime and Punishment

> No experience has probed more deeply than psycho-
> analysis into that equivalence to which we are alerted
> by the pathetic call of Love: it is yourself at whom
> you are striking out, and the cold deduction of the
> Spirit: it is therefore in the fight to the death for pure
> prestige that man makes himself recognized by man.
>
> —Jacques Lacan (1966, 147)

Before becoming a psychoanalyst, Lacan was a
psychiatrist. This explains why his initial encounter with psychoanalysis took place in the field of psychosis. Whereas Freud, "doctor of nerves" ("*Nervenarzt*"), had begun by exploring neurosis,
Lacan began with madness—and not just any madness, but murderous, paranoid madness. Lacan's doctoral thesis in medicine, defended in 1932, was entitled *De la psychose paranoïaque dans ses
rapports avec la personnalité* ("On Paranoid Psychosis in its Relation to Personality"), and it centered on the case of "Aimée," a mentally disturbed woman who attempted to stab a popular actress to
death. A year later, in the journal *Le Minotaure*, he published an
article summarizing the essentials of his thesis, this time applying
them to the crime of the Papin sisters, two servants from Le Mans
who, in a particularly atrocious manner, had slit the throats of their
employer and her daughter and then dismembered the two.

The Paranoia of Self-Punishment

With Lacan, then, it all begins in hatred, violence, and murder.
More precisely, it all begins with *crime*. Lacan's thesis is that the
"aggressive drive" of the paranoiac "is itself marked with social relativity: it always has the intentionality of a crime" and thus also a

"human signification" (1975a, 392). The criminal knows the law that he transgresses (he admits it at the very moment he denies it), and, according to Lacan, this applies equally to the paranoid criminal. Far from being a ferocious beast or an automaton driven by his instincts, he detaches himself from the human community for motives that are themselves human and social.

In other words, the paranoiac is a *person* (in the moral and legal sense). Similarly, paranoia must be understood "in its relation to *personality*." As a matter of fact, under Lacan's pen these terms remain rather vague, but in all likelihood they echo the "concrete psychology" of George Politzer; witness the "Dogmatic Conclusions" of the young thesis writer: "The key to the nosologic, prognostic, and therapeutic problem of paranoid psychosis must be sought in a *concrete* psychological analysis that applies itself to the entire *personality development* of the subject, that is, to the events of his *history*, to the progress of his *consciousness*, to his reactions in *social* surroundings" (1975a, 346). This, as we know, was the general program of Politzer's critique of the foundations of psychology,[1] and this, on the whole, is what Lacan tries to apply here to the more particular problem of paranoia: let us stop viewing the paranoiac "in the third person"; instead, we must penetrate his personal "drama," his concrete relations with others, his conflictual relations with society. Thus the Marxist look of this thesis, which explains the favorable reception accorded Lacan's work by *L'Humanité* and *La Critique Sociale*:[2] "We have admitted as explicative of the facts of psychosis the dynamic notion of *social tensions*, whose state of equilibrium or disequilibrium normally defines the personality in the individual" (1975a, 392).

But what exactly are these "social tensions" cited by Lacan? To attempt a response to this question, we must first ask what paranoia is. In its classic definition, briefly summarized by Lacan in his article on the Papin sisters, paranoia is characterized by "(a) an intellectual delirium, whose themes range from ideas of grandeur to ideas of persecution; (b) aggressive reactions, very often murderous; (c) a chronic evolution" (1975a, 391). The paranoiac, who often believes himself invested with a religious or political mission of redemption, has the impression of being spied on, invaded, obsessed by one or more malefactors whom, for that very reason, he feels authorized to hate and, sometimes, to kill. Now, where does this unmotivated hatred come from, which often erupts suddenly, on the most trivial pretexts (for the Papin sisters, it was a simple electrical blackout)? In his thesis, Lacan starts by dismissing the classic explanations. Delirium is neither the development of a supposed "morbid constitution" (another name for "bad temper") nor an attempt to rationalize perceptual disorders (Clérambault's famous "elementary phenomena"). If the explanation for delirious hatred must be sought somewhere, it should be sought, Lacan believes, in psychoanalysis, which he was discovering at the time in Freud's texts and on the couch of Rudolph Loewenstein.

Indeed, it is well known that Freud,[3] in his classic study of President Schreber, proposed to link the various forms of paranoid delirium (persecution, jealousy, erotomania, megalomania) to one and the same thing: the disavowal of homosexuality. In reality, according to this study, the paranoiac *loves* his persecutor homosexually, and this love turns to hatred only because of its vehement rejection (*Verwerfung*). The homosexual tendency, Lacan writes, summing up Freud's position, "expresses itself only in a distraught self-negation, which establishes the conviction of being persecuted and designates the beloved as the persecutor" (1975a, 395–396). Freud himself illustrated this with the different ways of "denying" the basic proposition of that delirium: *I (a man) love him.* The delirium of persecution reverses the verb (*I do not love him*, projected into *He hates me*); that of jealousy permutes the subject (*She loves him*); erotomania contests the complement (*I love her*, projected into *She loves me*); and, finally, megalomania rejects the whole proposition (*I do not love anyone, I love only myself*).

Without entering at this point into the complexities of the Freudian thesis, we should at least note that Freud, engaged at the time in a theoretical rivalry with Jung, strongly emphasized the homo*sexual* character of that paranoid "love." Lacan (who in 1930 had done an internship at Jung's famous Burghölzli clinic) was much more interested in its *homo*sexual character. This nuance is fundamental, and it must be emphasized from the very start. The paranoiac, according to Lacan, "loves" a *counterpart* (*semblable*): the delirious person's "chosen object" "is as similar as possible to the subject" (1975a, 396). In other words, the "object" is nothing but the "subject" himself: far from desiring an object of erotic love, as Freud would have it, the paranoiac loves *himself* (hates *himself*) in a lifelike double. Thus Lacan notes that the persecuting figures in Aimée's delirium—and especially the unfortunate actress who was finally struck down—all represented what Aimée herself wanted to be:

From that point, one sees the meaning, more representative than personal, of the persecutor chosen by the patient. The persecutor is the type of the celebrated woman, adored by the public, having "arrived," living in luxury. And if the patient in her writings [Aimée wrote two novels] vigorously finds fault with such lives and the artifice and corruption she imputes to them, the ambivalence of her attitude must be emphasized, for she too, as we shall see, would like to be a novelist, lead a grand life, have an influence on the world [1975a, 164].

"What [one] would like to be [oneself]": this was Freud's[4] definition of the narcissistic "ego-ideal" [*Ichideal*], and Lacan takes up the term. "In her victim," he says, "Aimée strikes out at her exteriorized ideal" (1975a, 253), by which Lacan means first of all a *social* "ideal" (in agreement, moreover, with Freud, who saw in the narcissistic "ego-ideal" the root of the "conscience"). This amounts to saying that in Lacan's eyes the paranoiac's ideal figure is much more social than erotic—much more "homosocial," one could say, than "homosexual." Hence his insistence, for example, on the social or religious content of delirium (1975a, 269), or on the "social repercussions of the paranoiac's acts and, often, of the delirium itself" (1975a, 403). Madness, for Lacan, is essentially a social affair: "Delirium . . . is a delirium of the hallway, the street, the forum" (1975a, 212).

And how, in fact, could it be otherwise, if delirium always pivots on what one would (ideally) like *to be*, and not on what one would like *to have* (in the name of sexual pleasure)? What I myself am not (namely, *a subject*: free, autonomous, independent, and so on) is always another (another *subject*: rich, famous, admired, recognized) who is taking my place—that place or social position where I would like to be. The problem, of course, is that I will then compete savagely with that other for that "being," for that "place," because if the other is in my place, it goes without saying that I shall never cease my efforts to dislodge him, in order finally to be myself. What begins in admiration ends in murder.

Now it is easier to see what Lacan means by "social tension." As we may have suspected, it has nothing to do with "class struggle." It is the much more fundamental and paradoxical "tension" of *rivalry* as simultaneously a social relation with the other and a passionate denial of that relation. Thus the somehow "hypersocial" character of what is at first sight an asocial delirium, paranoia: the paranoiac, a passionate idealist, really does nothing but exhibit in broad daylight the aggressivity inherent in social relations with others, relations that Freud called "sublimated" and "inhibited as to sexual aim." Thus, too, the paradoxically "hypermoral" character of the paranoid crime: obviously, by striking out at the rival he wants to be, the delirious person strikes out at and punishes himself. This is how Lacan explains delirium's not infrequent remission after what he calls the "fertile moment" of the crime, as if the crime's only goal had been expiation. Freud had already spoken of those "criminals from a sense of guilt" who break the law only in order to be punished for misdeeds of which they are unconscious,[5] and this is fundamentally the same mechanism Lacan finds in the paranoia of Aimée and the Papin sisters: they are criminals because of an obscure desire to glorify the law that they flout. Therefore, Lacan says, their paranoia is a "*paranoia of self-punishment*," a clinical entity he was the first to isolate and whose curable nature he emphasizes:

What, for Aimée, is the representative value of her persecutors? Women of letters, actresses, women of the world, they represent the image that Aimée has formed of women who to whatever degree enjoy freedom and social power. But here is where the imaginary identity between the themes of grandeur and the themes of persecution emerges: that type of woman is exactly what she herself dreams of becoming. The same image that represents her ideal is also the object of her hatred. Therefore, in her victim, Aimée strikes out at her exteriorized ideal, just as the *criminal of passion* strikes out at the single object of her hatred and love. . . . Nevertheless, through the same action that renders her guilty before the law, Aimée has struck out at herself, and when she understands this, she feels the satisfaction of desire fulfilled: the delirium, now useless, vanishes. The nature of the cure, it seems to me, demonstrates the nature of the disease [1975a, 253].

Mistress and Slave

The deeply Hegelian character of this "paranoia of self-punishment" is obvious. Besides, Lacan makes no mystery of it. The "fertile moment" of the delirium, he says, has a *dialectical* value: the cure that follows the criminal act "represents nothing less than the liberation of a conception of oneself and the world," which "suffices to ensure for it, at least in principle, the value of a dialectical progress" (1975a, 317). In Hegelian terms, the paranoid criminal passes from the opposition of the "in-itself" and the "for-itself" to their dialectical resolution. Realizing that he has struck out at *himself* in the *other*, whom he thought he hated, he reconciles himself with himself, since now he knows himself to exist in that other.

Mental alienation, when we think about it, turns out to be nothing but alienation in the Hegelian sense. Christine Papin's "desperate experience of the crime," Lacan writes, "tears her from her other self" (1975a, 397). Need we recall that this, according to Hegel, is the very "experience" of consciousness, its "path of doubt and despair"? Hegelian self-consciousness also places itself outside itself, negates and opposes itself to itself the better to know itself. In fact, it is enough to read Lacan's thesis to see that his description of paranoia is organized entirely around what, in homage to Christine and Léa Papin, could be called a "dialectic of mistress and slave." Here, everything revolves around a struggle (to the death, for "pure prestige") for freedom, the persecutor occupying the place of the master and the sick person that of the slave.

Why, indeed, does Aimée not instigate the "struggle" with her sister, in whom Lacan recognizes the prototype of her later persecutors? Because Aimée, just like Hegel's slave, is *herself* alienated in that "dominatrix" whom she "envies":

Aimée's personality does not allow her to react directly in a combative way. . . . Indeed, the sister draws her main strength against Aimée not from the praise and authority conferred by their circle but from Aimée's own consciousness. Aimée recognizes the virtues, qualities, and efforts of her sister for what they are. She is dominated by her sister, who, from a certain point of view, represents the very image of the being Aimée is powerless to attain [1975a, 233].

Therefore, she must repress the aggression she harbors toward her, or, if you will, must negate herself as pure freedom—a typically Hegelian process of self-negation, which Lacan then compares to Freud's negation (*Verneinung*) by recognizing in it "the avowal of what is so vigorously denied" (1975a, 233). Divided against herself,

Aimée the paranoiac, as "a consciousness repressed within [her]self
. . . will [as a result] withdraw into [her]self," just like Hegel's slave,
until the fertile moment of the crime, when, by a reversal, she "will
be transformed into a truly independent consciousness"[6]—that is,
into *autodetermination*, since, by punishing herself through her
action, she will finally recognize in the "oppression" of others her
ownmost law.

Fourteen years later, in his "Remarks on Psychic Causality,"
Lacan repeats the same thesis even more clearly. This time, support
is sought in Hegel's sequence on the "law of the heart" and the
"frenzy of self-conceit" (illustrated by the "case of Alceste" in Mo-
lière's *Le Misanthrope*), but the schema remains exactly the same:

The madman [note that now it is the "madman" in general, and no longer
simply the self-punishing paranoiac] wants to impose the law of his heart
on what appears to him as the disorder of the world, a "mad" enterprise
. . . in that . . . the subject does not recognize in the world's disorder the
very manifestation of his present being, and insofar as what he feels to be
the law of his heart is only the image, both inverted and virtual, of that
same being. . . . His being is thus enclosed in a circle, unless he breaks it
with some act of violence in which, directing his blows against what seems
to him disorder, he strikes out at himself by way of social repercussion.
Such is the general formula for madness that we find in Hegel; do not think
that I am saying anything new. . . . I say, "general formula for madness," in
the sense that it can be applied to any one of those phases by which, in each
destiny, the dialectical development of the human being is more or less
completed [1966, 171–172].

This is a "formula" that gives one pause, for here the "*general*
formula for madness" is identified with nothing less than the *general* "dialectical development of the human being." Does this mean,
then, that the dialectic as such is mad—and that the human being,
by the same token, is profoundly paranoid? If the "fertile moment"
of the dialectic of madness—of the dialectic *and* of madness—is a
crime, can it ever engender anything other than a violence that is
itself general?

"Psychoanalysis of the Ego"

In 1932, the references to Hegel were far from being so numerous and explicit. Lacan, who of course was already steeped in the

era's Hegelian atmosphere (Jean Wahl, Alexandre Koyré, André Breton), had not yet heard Kojève (whose course on the *Phenomenology of Spirit* would not begin until 1933). Thus, Lacan's Hegelianism remained relatively veiled, covered as it was by the much more apparent references to Freudian theory. But let us make no mistake: what would later become a triumphant "return to Freud" was for the moment only a simple detour via Freud. Lacan put it nicely himself: "The help we appear to have taken from the data of psychoanalysis should be viewed as a corroboration imposed by the facts" (1975a, 318). In reality, Lacan was searching through Freud only for what would serve to confirm "facts" that he had already interpreted in para-Hegelian terms. As Philippe Julien has noted, the young Lacan "[took] from Freud what [would] serve him"[7]: the theory of narcissism and identification, to the detriment of the theory of sexuality; the "psychoanalysis of the ego," to the detriment of the "psychology of the unconscious" (1975a, 280)—to which we need add only that the selection was made from an entirely Hegelian point of view.

What, in fact, does Lacan retain of Freud? Roughly speaking, everything concerned with the "analysis of the ego." As we know, Freud, starting from a decided opposition between the (conscious, social, censuring) ego and the sexual libido, found himself progressively constrained to make room, somewhere between the "ego instincts" and the "sexual instincts," for a singular "ego-libido." Far from being only the representative of reality's demands and society's prohibitions, the ego becomes equally an "object" of love: it loves itself, sometimes to the point of madness and death. This strange "self-love" is what Freud, from 1910 on, called "narcissism," adding in 1914 that *all* libido could very well be an "ego-libido" alternatively "yielded up to" and "withdrawn from" objects. Thus, the love object would actually be a narcissistic object, as it is, for example, in homosexuality (where the ego loves a counterpart) or in passionate love (where the man loves himself in a narcissistic woman).

We can already see what interest this theory of "narcissistic object-choice" could have held for Lacan. After all, if I love myself in the object, what distinguishes the narcissistic libido from the Hegelian *Begierde*, from the "desire" of self-consciousness that looks for itself in its other, or from that "disporting of Love with itself" spoken of in the preface to the *Phenomenology of Spirit*?[8] In short, all Lacan had to do was pick up the obscure and "confused" doctrine of narcissism (1975a, 321) in order to carry it into the light of the Hegelian concept, and he sketches out just such a program in the theoretical section of his thesis, proudly entitled "Critical Exposition . . . of the Method of a Science of Personality and of Its Import in the Study of the Psychoses": "In fact, in the economy of the psychoanalytic doctrine, narcissism is presented as a *terra incognita*, whose borders could be mapped by the investigative means born from the study of the neuroses, but whose interior remained mythical and unknown. For our part, we claim to have furthered the study of this domain, following a doctrine whose *premises* we have defined" (1975a, 322–323). These "premises" being largely borrowed from dialectic, we see that Lacan declares his colors rather clearly: what begins here is a Hegelian reinterpretation of Freud that only later, in the 1950's, would become a "Freudian" rereading of Hegel.

But that is not all. We must also understand that the exploration of narcissism was accompanied, in Freud, by a question bearing on the social tie. Indeed, since the ego, according to the first Freudian theory, is supposed to represent society's interests and values, doesn't the discovery of narcissism permit the *libidinal* ground of sociality and morality to be unveiled? After all, doesn't this "love of self" furnish the key to the *internalization* of the prohibitions decreed by society, as well as the key to the social relation with the *counterpart*? It is this hypothesis—highly risky, as we shall see—that Freud, during the years from 1910 to 1920, tried in many ways to elaborate, finally concluding with the famous "second topography" introduced in *The Ego and the Id*. In the 1911 article on the case of President Schreber, he imagines that the genesis of the "social instincts" lies in narcissistic homosexuality: beginning by loving itself, the little asocial-narcissistic ego reaches sociality by loving itself in a counterpart. Thus, all sociality would be of a profoundly homosexual nature (and this "homosexuality," Freud adds, is what the paranoiac rejects with such vehemence). In *Totem and Taboo*, written the following year, the hypothesis is advanced with even more temerity and grandiosity: human sociality and morality are rooted in the murder of a "primal father," whose sons kill and devour him in order to take his place while still loving and obeying him "retrospectively," as the result of that narcissistic-identificatory incorporation. This same internalization of a narcissistic "ego-ideal," which one "wants oneself to be," is what Freud then places (in "On Narcissism: An Introduction") at the root of the individual "conscience" and what, from the 1920's on, he finally calls "identification." The social tie, he states in 1921 (*Group Psychology and the Analysis of the Ego*), rests on an identification among "egos" on the basis of a common love for an "object put in the place of the ego-ideal." As for that "ego-ideal" itself, according to *The Ego and the Id*, it is born of a normative identification with the parent of the same sex: the infant surmounts the Oedipal rivalry in which it is engaged with one of the parents by introjecting that same parental personage in the form of a special psychic agency, henceforth called the "superego."

Here then, briefly, is what we have: the strictly social (not "directly sexual") relation with another is a relation with "an other-self," whether a homosexual counterpart or a model of identification, a narcissistic reflection or an interiorized "object." Here again, we see how much grist Freud's text brings to Lacan's Hegelian mill, since Freud allows him to envision the social relation with the other as a relation with oneself. Thus Lacan carefully emphasizes, even more than Freud does himself, the simultaneously social *and* narcissistic (which is also to say, sexually "neuter") character of the famous paranoid "homosexuality." The latter, Lacan tells us, reflects "the first, and usually instinctively inclined, integration of what we call *social tensions*," an integration formed "according to the law of least resistance, by an affective fixation very close to the solipsistic ego, a fixation that deserves to be called narcissistic, and in which the chosen object is as similar as possible to the subject: such is the reason for its homosexual character" (1975a, 396).

This doctrine is visibly inspired by the hypotheses Freud advanced in his article on the case of President Schreber, and Lacan blends it quite elegantly with the Freudian theory of the superego, to explain the self-punitive (or, if you will, the "masochistic-moral") character of paranoia. "This *Superego*," Lacan recalls, is what "Freud conceives of . . . as the *reincorporation* . . . into the

Ego of a part of the external world. This *reincorporation* is carried out on objects whose *personal*—from the same social genetic point of view we ourselves use in defining the term 'personal'—value is maximized. Indeed, it is carried out on those objects that summarize in themselves all the constraints exercised by society over the subject, be they parents or parental substitutes. It is as such, at least, that they are reintegrated at that moment into the individual structure, in accordance with a *secondary identification* of the Ego, whose fundamental genetic difference from the *primary identification* of 'the Oedipus'[9] Freud was careful to emphasize" (1975a, 325). In other words, little "Oedipus," after hatefully identifying with the fraternal or parental *rival*, on the level of the "primary" identification, peaceably identifies with the social or parental *prohibition* on the level of the "secondary" identification. Here is a dialectical reversal bound to please Lacan: instead of vainly hurling itself against the other's law, the ego makes that law its own and thus becomes *auto*determining, in the mode of *auto*nomy, since "this [secondary] identification supplements the repressive constraints by reproducing their agency in the subject himself" (1975a, 325).

As for the paranoiacs, they remain in the "emotional ambivalence" proper to the narcissistic and rivalrous stage of Oedipal identification, until the resolving and fatal moment of self-punishment:

The "affliction of being two," from which these patients suffer, only slightly frees them from the affliction of Narcissus. This is a mortal passion, and one that ends by killing itself. Aimée strikes out at the brilliant being whom she hates, precisely because this being represents the ideal she has of herself. This need for self-punishment, this enormous feeling of guilt, can also be read in the actions of the Papin sisters, if only in Christine's genuflection at the denouement [1975a, 397].

Moral and even hypermoral, these sick people are madly so, given the lack of a dialectical solution to the narcissistic conflict of the "ego" and the "other," of the "Ego" and the "Superego." Hence the "Dogmatic Conclusion" of the thesis, which retranslates this aborted dialectic into the terms of genetic fixation: "*The paranoia of self-punishment* and *the paranoia of righteousness* . . . are determined . . . by *arrested development of the personality* at the genetic stage of the *Superego*" (1975a, 349).

The Dialectic of Oedipus

The dogmatic nature of this conclusion should not, however, conceal the enormous problem it raises, for what is said here about the paranoiac's mad morality and sociality inevitably reflects on morality and sociality themselves, as soon as Lacan, along with Freud, acknowledges that the mechanism for "resolving" the Oedipal conflict (identification) is exactly the same as the one that instigates it (again, identification). Indeed, what guarantees that the so-called secondary identification with the Oedipal law does not reproduce the so-called primary identification with the Oedipal rival? Or, in the vocabulary of the young Lacan, what guarantees that the so-called normal personality is not fundamentally paranoid? What allows us to decide whether the "dialectic" of Oedipus, rather than giving birth to a moral and social *subject*, does not lead instead into alienation, madness, and crime?

Note that this was already the whole problem of the Freudian theory of sociality, and it is no accident that it was elaborated in the vicinity of paranoid hatred, murder of the "primal father," and Oedipal rivalry. How, in fact, can sociality be peaceful if it is rooted in a narcissistic and/or identificatory relation with the other? That other, being an other-me (an alter ego, as Lacan will say), will never truly be another, or he will be other only when *dead* (the members of the primal horde respecting the "primal father" only after having devoured him—thus, respecting him in a profoundly guilty way). By the same token, the superego never ceases to reproach the ego with the latter's having interiorized-killed it by identifying with it (the superego, says Freud in *The Ego and the Id*, is essentially guilt-producing and "sadistic"—"obscene and savage," Lacan later adds). In reality, the other-me is never anything but a rival, all the more detested for being admired, all the more violently negated for being amorously incorporated. Therefore, it should not surprise us that Freud so often took his theory of sociality and morality back to the drawing board. This theory could not have avoided being miscarried, since Freud, by making the relation with others a relation with oneself, necessarily made it a relation of non-relation—of violence, hatred, and guilt. This, of course, should not necessarily be interpreted as *failure*. Setting out to solve the problem of the "source of morality"[10] and the social tie, perhaps Freud did nothing but demonstrate en route the pointlessness of the problem as such. If the essence of the social tie is identification (the "emotional tie" of identification, as it is called in *Group Psychology*), then that ultimately means that this "essence" itself has nothing social about it: there is no good relation to the moral law, society is based on a crime (*Totem and Taboo*), and humanity's guilt is inextinguishable (*Civilization and Its Discontents*).

Nevertheless, Freud most often presented the problem *as its own solution*, by repeatedly resorting to a sort of enigmatic transmutation of narcissistic-identificatory hostility into social love and moral respect. Already in *Totem and Taboo*, he supposed that the murderers of the "primal father" obeyed him "retrospectively" for the same reason that they had killed him: because they "loved and admired" this "feared and envied model."[11] Identification (since that is really what we are dealing with in the devouring of the *Urvater*) thus leads to the most savage violence and at the same time puts an end to it, as Freud says continually in his later works. "Social feeling," he explains in *Group Psychology and the Analysis of the Ego*, "is based upon the reversal (*Umwendung*) of what was first a hostile feeling into a positively toned tie in the nature of an identification."[12] The same can be said for the moral superego that, according to *The Ego and the Id*, emerges by means of a "reversal" or a "turning" of the rivalrous identification of the Oedipus into a normative identification: the superego's

relation to the ego is not exhausted by the precept "You *ought to be* like this (like your father)." It also comprises the prohibition "You *may not be* like this (like your father)—that is, you may not do all that he does; some things are his prerogative." This double aspect [*Doppelangesicht*; literally, "double face"] of the ego ideal [*alias* the superego] derives from the fact that the ego ideal had the task of repressing the Oedipus complex; indeed, it is to that reversal (*Umschwung*) that it owes its existence. Clearly, the repression of the Oedipus complex was no easy task. The child's parents, and especially his father, were perceived as the obstacle to a realization of his Oedipus wishes; so his infantile ego fortified itself for the carrying out of the repression by erecting this same obstacle within itself. It borrowed strength to do this, so to speak, from the father, and this loan was an extraordinarily momentous act.[13]

And the same can be said, finally, for the "conversion" of fraternal rivalry into a "feeling of social identification," according to the 1922 article "Some Neurotic Mechanisms in Jealousy, Paranoia and Homosexuality":

Observation has directed my attention to several cases in which during early childhood impulses of jealousy, derived from the mother-complex and of very great intensity, arose [in a boy] against rivals, usually older brothers. . . . These impulses yielded to repression and underwent a transformation (*Gefühlsumwandlung*), so that the rivals of the earlier period became the first homosexual love-objects. Such an outcome of the attachment to the mother . . . is [in] complete contrast to the development of persecutory paranoia, in which the person who has before been loved becomes the hated persecutor, whereas here the hated rivals are transformed into love-objects. It represents, too, an exaggeration of the process which, according to my view, leads to the birth of social instincts in the individual. In both processes there is first the presence of jealous and hostile impulses which cannot achieve satisfaction; and both the affectionate and the social feelings of identification arise as reactive formations against the repressed aggressive impulses.[14]

Umwendung, Umschwung, Umwandlung: each case, as we see, concerns a reversal of negative to positive—in short, a process that bears a strong resemblance to a dialectical *Aufhebung* and thus to "magic," as Hegel himself remarked.[15] Once again, it is difficult to see how a hateful identification with the rival could be transformed, by a single stroke of the magic wand, into a good and affectionate social identification. It is even more profoundly difficult to see how that relation of identification with the other would cease to be a relation to another *oneself*—that is, to a *negated* other (dialectic, as everyone knows, leaves piles of corpses behind).

Note that Lacan himself, in his thesis, chooses to refer to just this perfectly mythical process of "reversal" with respect to Freud's theory of the "genesis of the social instincts" (1975a, 260). The "point of psychoanalytic doctrine" that seems "immediately to integrate itself" into his own "doctrine is precisely the conception given to the functions of *self-punishment* or, according to the terminology, of the *Super-Ego*" (1975a, 323), and the Freudian texts that he uses more generally for support are the very ones we have just quoted: *Totem and Taboo, Group Psychology and the Analysis of the Ego* (1975a, 260), and *The Ego and the Id* (1975a, 323 ff.). Moreover, and this is clearly no accident, Lacan himself translated, and published in the *Revue Française de Psychanalyse*, the 1922 article on jealousy, paranoia, and homosexuality, which he calls "admirable":

Freud, in an admirable article . . . shows . . . that when, in the now recognized first stages of infantile sexuality, the enforced reduction of primal hostility between brothers occurs, an abnormal inversion of that hostility into desire may be produced, and this mechanism engenders a special type of homosexual in whom social activities and instincts predominate. In fact, this mechanism is constant: this amorous fixation is the primordial condition for the first integration of what we call *social tensions* into the instinctual tendencies" [1975a, 396].

In short, the "*abnormal* inversion" of hostility into homosexual-narcissistic love, where the paranoiac remains, is at the same time the fundamental process of social *normalization*.

What does this mean, if not that Lacan, trusting too much in dialectic, still believes it possible to maintain the classical schema of the Oedipus, by the same token inheriting the *problem* bequeathed by Freud? The "problem" of the Oedipus, we can now understand, is nothing other than that of dialectic as a supposed "*solution*" to the narcissistic-identifying conflict (the "fight to the death for pure prestige"), and this explains the strangely interdependent destiny of these two questions in Lacan. Indeed, for Lacan, keeping the Freudian model of the Oedipus is equivalent to keeping dialectic; and, inversely, whenever the "dialectic" of Oedipus is called into question, dialectic in general must also be challenged. Under these conditions, it is not surprising that this problem took some twenty years to dawn on Lacan: behind Freud, nothing less than the crushing shade of Hegel had to be exorcized.

Totem or Taboo

That the Freudian "solution" to the Oedipal conflict was already a problem for Lacan can clearly be seen in the article he published six years later in Monzie's *Encyclopédie Française*, on the theme of the family.

Once more centering the problem of access to sociality on the mechanism of identification (and, more particularly, on identification with the *father*, as we shall see), Lacan certainly continued to see the Oedipus complex and its "dialectical interplay" (1984, 94) as a normative and pacifying process: "Indeed, starting from an ambivalent identification with its counterpart, through jealous participation and sympathetic competition, the ego differentiates itself, in joint progress, from the other and from the object" (1984, 94; see also 1984, 46). Now, how does this "progress" work? Once again, through a "process of identification" that "resolves the Oedipal complex" (1984, 103). In this resolving identification, it is easy to recognize the "secondary" identification that, according to Freud, is responsible for the surpassing of Oedipal rivalry and the formation of the "ego-ideal"/"superego," with its "double aspect." In fact, Lacan himself also speaks of the "double role played by the father, insofar as he represents authority and is the center of sexual revelation" (1984, 103); and yet again:

By this double process, the parent of the same sex appears to the child as both the agent of sexual interdiction and the example of its transgression. The tension established is thus resolved, on the one hand, by repression of the sexual tendency, which then remains latent . . . until puberty; and, on the other hand, by the sublimation of the parental image, which will perpetuate in consciousness a representative ideal, the guarantee of the future coincidence of psychic and physiological attitudes at the moment of puberty" [1984, 50–51].

Therefore, in accordance with Freudian theory, the father is both the one whom the little boy must imitate (with respect to the task of assuming masculine sexuality or, as Lacan would also say, "psychic" sexuality; 1984, 52) and the one whom he must not imitate (with respect to possession of the mother).

The significant fact remains that Lacan *decomposes* the "ambiguity" of the parental "imago" (1984, 103) by proposing to "revise the Freudian schema of the Oedipus" (1984, 49) and distinguish between two aspects (or two "faces," if you will) of the father. On one side is the unconscious "superego," prohibiting identification ("Do not be like me") and thereby repressing "the biologically inadequate object that desire's first maturation proposes to desire" (1984, 94). On the other side is the conscious "ego-ideal," which says, "Be like me," and which through "imaginary identification . . . will orient the choice toward the biologically adequate object of pubescent maturation" (1984, 94). Now, why does Lacan feel the need to introduce this distinction between the superego and the ego-ideal (to be found nowhere in Freud, as Lacan himself notes; 1984, 93), if not because he sees that identification with the Oedipal "obstacle" resolves nothing? Indeed, if I myself am the rival, there is fundamentally no reason why I should stop competing with "myself," nor is there any reason why this fantastic dialectical "progress," by which "the ego differentiates itself from the other and from the object," should come about. In other words, the Oedipal dialectic will remain undecidable: nothing can guarantee that the "reversal" proper to Oedipal identification will go from negative to positive. Thus Lacan tries to cut the Gordian knot of the Oedipus (of dialectic) by separating the two "faces" of identification: on one side, the somber "specular double" of the superego (1984, 61), whose archaic and ambivalent character Lacan stresses—archaic and ambivalent because it is profoundly narcissistic (and thus profoundly sadomasochistic and castrating) (1984, 60–61); on the other side, the good "example" of the ego-ideal (1984, 64), which "substitutes for the double" and represents its properly sublimating "completion and metamorphosis" (1984, 107). In short, the other who I must be (the ego-ideal) is not the *same* as the one who I must not be (the superego); or the other with whom I identify must be *other* than the "other-me."

Lacan's rectification shows that he is already very conscious of the problem posed by the Oedipus, but it also shows that he persists meanwhile in looking to it for the solution. Lacan, remarkably, continues to believe that the Oedipus is the "solution" to the Oedipal conflict (or, if you will, that there is a "good" Oedipal identification as opposed to a "bad" one). The Oedipus, he reiterates, has a function of normalization, of "psychic correction of sexual prematurity" (1984, 94), of "regulation of individual sexuality" (1984, 95). As for the psychoses and neuroses, they arise, respectively, from "an anomaly of the familial situation" (1984, 86), and from an "anomie" (cf. Durkheim's *Le Suicide*) of the modern family (1984, 96)— in short, from a *failure* of the Oedipus: paranoid fixation on the homosexual counterpart, neurotic disequilibrium in the relation between ego-ideal and superego.

The problem, however, is that this "failure" may very well be structural. Indeed, how to keep the "ideal" identification, deemed sexually normative, from being made with the "superegoic" and homosexual rival? In this respect, it takes no genius to see what is hidden beneath Lacan's brilliant terminological innovations. It is quite simply the Freudian identity of the "ego-ideal" and the "superego": With whom should one identify in order to achieve sexual normality, if not with precisely the same "biologically inadequate [homosexual] object" with whom one *must not* identify? Consequently, on what grounds can Lacan claim to distinguish the "ego-ideal" from the "superego," since these two "faces" belong to one and the same person?

On this point, it is worth emphasizing Lacan's train of thought, for his argument takes the form of an appeal to "primitive societies," in some ways anticipating what will later become, through the structural anthropology of Lévi-Strauss, the famous "symbolic order." Lacan, as we have just seen, perceives very clearly the fragility of the Oedipus, as he has reconstructed it after Freud: normative, the Oedipus is also, like it or not, "neurotive" and "psychotive." And so Lacan settles the matter by attributing that fragility, not to the Oedipus as such, but to what he calls the "degraded form of the Oedipus" (1984, 96) proper to modern societies. It is only in *our* societies, Lacan says, that the (sublimating) ego-ideal and the (repressive) superego converge on a single person. Lacan, leaning on Durkheim and Malinowski, reminds us that the family has not always had a "conjugal" form (1984, 12–17), and especially that repressive authority has not always been the prerogative of the biological father: "The imago of the father concentrates in itself the function of repression with that of sublimation; but this is the result of a social determination, that of the paternalistic family. In matriarchal cultures, the authority of the family is not represented by the father but, ordinarily, by the maternal uncle" (1984, 66). In other words, only in conjugal-patriarchal societies is the holder of repressive authority confounded with the "familiar figure" and "the singularly transgressive example" (1984, 70–71) of the *real* father.

The result, according to Lacan, is an "antinomy" (1984, 67), the source simultaneously of cultural progress and neurosis. On the one hand, the paternal imago "invested with repression . . . projects repression's original force into the very sublimations that must overcome it" (1984, 67); hence, for example, the potentialities for "creative subversion" (1984, 70) of authority proper to conjugal-patriarchal societies, or the fruitful "dialectical crises" that "exalt to the highest degree the tension of the libido and the consequences of sublimation" (1984, 70–71). Inversely, "by causing the family to evolve toward the conjugal family," these societies turn the normative process of identification over to "individual variations" (1984, 95–96) and, by the same token, to neurosis, since the "personality of the father . . . absent, humiliated, divided, or superfluous" (1984, 73), may prove unequal to the double function assigned to it. This explains the proliferation of neurosis in our strictly modern societies, marked, Lacan says, by a "deficiency" (1984, 73) and a "social decline of the paternal imago" (1984, 72):

On that "anomie," which favored the discovery of the [Oedipus] complex, depends the degraded form in which analysts know it, a form that we define according to incomplete repression of desire for the mother, along with reactivation of anxiety and inquiry, both inherent in the relationship of birth, and according to a narcissistic degeneracy in the idealization of the father, causing in the Oedipal identification a revival of the aggressive ambivalence immanent in the primal relationship to the counterpart [1984, 96].

By contrast, Lacan says, things are quite different in "primitive societies," which "ensure a less fragile ease to the sexual development of the individual" (1984, 20). Why is this so? First of all, as we have seen, these societies strictly separate the real father from the *function* of sexual repression; but to this first argument Lacan adds a second, this one bearing on the separation of the real father from the function of sexual *sublimation*. The train of argument is apparently reversed, but the important thing (as could be expected) is that the two "functions," in this second argument as in the first, are not united in the same person. Indeed, in primitive societies the accession to the sexual ego-ideal is carried out not through identification with the real father (the *taboo* father, who prohibits identification), but through initiatory identification with a *totem* (that is, in Lacan's later vocabulary, with a pure "symbol" or "name" of the father: this or that symbolic animal or plant). Lacan is alluding, of course, to the theory of totemism set forth by Freud in *Totem and Taboo*. But whereas Freud proposed to interpret the totem on the basis of the "Oedipus complex"—that is, on the basis of the *modern* form of the Oedipus, characterized by an ambivalent and "devouring" identification with the real father—Lacan reverses the order of things. Instead, he says, let us understand "bastardized" identification, which belongs to modern neurosis, on the basis of the *primitive* form of the Oedipus: "Primitive societies, which involve a more positive regulation of individual sexuality, manifest the meaning of that irrational integration [the 'integration of sexuality'] in the initiatory function of the totem, inasmuch as the individual identifies his vital essence with it and ritually assimilates it; the meaning of the totem, which Freud reduces to that of the Oedipus, seems to us instead to be the equivalent of one of the Oedipal functions: that of the ego-ideal" (1984, 18–19).

In other words, do not confuse the Oedipus and the Oedipus complex, the normative function of the ego-ideal and its neurotic/superegoic/modern degradation, good totemic identification and bad ambivalent identification with the taboo. Identification with an ego-ideal is certainly necessary, as Freud said, to the assumption of sexuality and the cessation of "Oedipal" hostilities, but this normative identification does not, by right (totemic right), have any bearing on the paternal rival—that is, the one who prohibits the identification. If Freud confuses these two identifications, it is because he is part of the modern, conjugal-familial Oedipus, where the normative and rival models are one and the same person. Lacan is quite clear about it, linking the Freudian discovery to the "social decline" of traditional patriarchy and, in a larger sense, to the desacralization ("detotemization," if you will) of modern societies:

Whatever its future may be, this decline constitutes a psychological crisis. Perhaps the advent of psychoanalysis itself should be attributed to this crisis. Perhaps the grand accident of genius is not itself enough to explain why it was in Vienna—at the time, the center of a State that was the melting pot of the most diverse forms of family, from the most archaic to the most evolved . . .—that a son of the Jewish patriarchy imagined the Oedipus complex [1984, 72–73].

Therefore, the Oedipus, in the Freudian sense, is nothing but the neurotic Oedipus, the Oedipus of the modern *crisis* of identification (the "mimetic crisis," as Girard would say), and this is what Lacan repeats in 1948, in his account of aggressivity in psychoanalysis: "We have often said that the initial emphasis, in [psychoanalytic] doctrine, on the Oedipal conflict's aggressive wrenching within the subject is due to the fact that the complex's effects were first noticed in its *failed* resolutions" (1966, 119).

We see, then, that Lacan in 1938, and even more in 1948, was very conscious of the problem Freud had bequeathed under the name of "Oedipus," and that he was already attempting to solve it—but, we could say, only at the price of keeping it whole, since he continued to believe *that there was a solution, beyond its "failures."* Whereas Freud—in this respect, very modern indeed—went stubbornly on butting up against the paradox of an identification that was normative *and* neurotic, socializing *and* desocializing, Lacan no less stubbornly sought to resolve it: by cutting through Freud's ambiguity between the ego-ideal and the superego; by separating the good, normalizing identification from the bad, rivalrous identification; and by making the latter a "failure" of the former, making the Oedipus complex a "failure" of the Oedipus, and, finally, making modern societies on the whole a gigantic "failure" of good old traditional societies, where one still knew *who* one was.

Eventually there would come a time when the solution would cause the problem to be forgotten. The so-called imaginary identification with the alter ego would be deemed incompatible with the so-called symbolic identification with the Other, and the bad, undecidable "dialectic" of Oedipus would be rejected for a completely different "dialectic," that of the "desire of the desire of the Other." But that time was still to come.

The Statue Man

Beneath the rays, I feel my statue shudder.

—Paul Valéry[1]

Is it possible to meet oneself? Strange question; and yet it happened to Freud one day, as he relates in his article "The 'Uncanny'":

I was sitting alone in my *wagon-lit* compartment when a more than usually violent jolt of the train swung back the door of the adjoining washing-cabinet, and an elderly gentleman in a dressing-gown and a travelling cap came in. I assumed that in leaving the washing-cabinet, which lay between the two compartments, he had taken the wrong direction and come into my compartment by mistake. Jumping up with the intention of putting him right, I at once realized to my dismay that the intruder was nothing but my own reflection in the looking-glass on the open door. I can still recollect that I thoroughly disliked his appearance.[2]

Freud and His Doubles

What happened in this improbable encounter? It could be said that Freud made an ordinary mistake in perception. He failed to recognize his image, to the point of confusing it with reality (as Lacan would add, to the point of *méconnaissance*). The mistake was quickly corrected: Freud hardly had time to jump up, before reality reasserted its rights and pushed the disagreeable intruder back into the mirror, which he should never have left. This episode was only a brief failure of "reality testing" (*Realitätsprüfung*), in no way a hallucination. That, Freud explains, is why he had no feeling of "uncanniness," unlike someone less sure of the difference between thought and reality (an "obsessional neurotic," for example). But he himself, he assures us, had not the least superstitious fear of that kind, only a bit of irritation. Nevertheless, he notes admirably, "Is it not possible . . . that our dislike . . . was a vestigial trace of the archaic reaction which feels the 'double' to be something uncanny?" [3]

Indeed, there is nothing more "dislikable"—and, in the extreme, nothing more agonizing—than someone who resembles oneself. As Lacan repeats with respect to the analytic situation, "Imagine what would happen inside a patient who saw in his analyst an exact replica of himself. Everyone feels that the excess of aggressive tension would pose such an obstacle to the appearance of the transference that its useful effect could be brought about only with extreme slowness. . . . If, to take an extreme case, this were experienced in the form of strangeness proper to apprehensions of the *double*, this situation would unleash an uncontrollable anxiety" (1977a, 15–16/109; translation modified).

But why does this happen? Why is the image of what, by all accounts, is most "familiar" and *heimlich* to us—our ego—so "uncanny," so *unheimlich*? We know what Freud answers in this article: it is because that image takes us back to a "surmounted" stage of psychic development, when the distinction between ego and image did not yet exist.[4] At that time, there was no space to interfere between the ego and the world, nor was there any delay between a wish and its representation. The division between "interior" and "exterior" did not exist; the thought was equivalent to the act, the wish to its fulfillment. Everything was in everything, the "ego" in the "other" and the "other" in the "ego":

Our analysis of instances of the uncanny has led us back to the old, animistic conception of the universe. This was characterized by the idea that the world was peopled with the spirits of human beings; by the subject's narcissistic overvaluation of his own mental processes; by the belief in the omnipotence of thoughts and the technique of magic based on that belief; by the attribution to various outside persons and things of carefully graded magical powers, or "*mana*"; as well as by all the other creations with the help of which man, in the unrestricted narcissism of that stage of development, strove to fend off the manifest prohibitions of reality.[5]

Therefore, it is this "narcissistic" or "animistic" phase that returns so strangely in the image or figure of the Double. In the presence of this figure, I am once more in an absolutely familiar relation with the not-me, with the other—but in the form of a no less absolute uncanniness, since this other me is now seen on the *outside*, as the result of my repressing the narcissistic apprehension of the world. This, according to Freud, is the source of the Double's *un-heimlich* character: the ego *sees* itself outside itself, in an image all the more estranging because it is narcissistic, all the more alienating because it is perfectly similar. What had been one's own living identity (or identification) becomes, once represented, an expropriated, deadly resemblance—a frozen mirror, a cold statue:

The theme of the "double" has been very thoroughly treated by Otto Rank. . . . He has gone into the connections that the "double" has with reflections in mirrors, with shadows, with guardian spirits, with the belief in the soul and with the fear of death; but he also lets in a flood of light on the surprising evolution of the idea. For the "double" was originally an insurance against the destruction of the ego, an "energetic denial of the power of death," as Rank says; and probably the "immortal" soul was the first "double" of the body. This invention of doubling as a preservation against extinction has its counterpart in the language of dreams, which is fond of representing castration by a doubling or a multiplication of a genital symbol. The same desire led the Ancient Egyptians to develop the art of making images of the dead in lasting materials. Such ideas, however, have sprung from the soil of unbounded self-love, from the primary narcissism which dominates the mind of the child and of primitive man. But when this stage has been surmounted, the "double" reverses its aspect. From having been an assurance of immortality, it becomes the uncanny harbinger of death.[6]

Narcissus in Ecstasy

The principal ingredients of Lacan's "mirror stage" are easily recognizable in the preceding passage by Freud: the mirror, the image, the double, narcissism, castration (imaginary fragmentation), and death. Even the statue is there (the making of images in "lasting materials") and the future $(-\phi)$ of the Lacanian algebra (the change in "algebraic sign"). Is this to say that Lacan simply reprised the logic sketched out in "The 'Uncanny'" and applied it to the phenomenon of recognition in the mirror? Far from it, as we shall see. Freud had based his interpretation on the hypothesis of the ego's "primary narcissism," by which he meant a state preceding the representational split introduced by the specular image; Lacan, by contrast, proposes to conceive of the ego in the image *of the image*: far from preceding the image, the ego is outside itself from the start, transported into its image. Thus, the double comes first. Already, in his thesis, Lacan had put us on notice: the Freudian theory of primary narcissism was still "confused," "obscure"; now, here it is, clarified, thanks to that marvelous instrument the mirror.

Everyone is familiar with the famous "mirror stage," which Lacan first presented in a speech to the Sixteenth International Psychoanalytic Congress, held in 1936 at Marienbad (the article reproduced under that speech's title in *Ecrits* was written in 1949). Place a baby who is still uncoordinated, *infans*, in front of a mirror, and you will notice not only that it already recognizes its image but also that it takes great pleasure in it:

This event can take place, as we have known since Baldwin, from the age of six months, and its repetition has often made me reflect upon the startling spectacle of the infant in front of the mirror. Unable as yet to walk, or even to stand up, and held tightly as he is by some support, human or artificial, . . . he nevertheless overcomes, in a flutter of jubilant activity, the obstructions of his support and, fixing his attitude in a slightly leaning-forward position, in order to hold it in his gaze, brings back an instantaneous aspect of the image [1977a, 1–2/93–94].

It will not be particularly useful to spend too much time on this "spectacular" observation, available to any parent who is even slightly attentive. Lacan later declared that he "invented" "Jacques Lacan's classical mirror stage" (1966, 67, 184; 1988a, 146/169), but that is saying a great deal if we stick to the observation itself. In fact, it had already been given a detailed presentation in 1931–32 by the psychologist Henri Wallon, who relied on previous work by Darwin, Guillaume, Preyer, and Charlotte Bühler.[7] Moreover, Wallon had already drawn much the same conclusions as Lacan. Just as Lacan would make the mirror stage "a particular case of the function of the imago, which is to establish a relation between the organism and its reality—or, as they say, of the *Innenwelt* to the *Umwelt*" (1977a, 4/97), so Wallon saw in it only "a more or less episodic process" among those that serve the child's finally grasping itself "as a body among bodies, as a being among beings."[8] Noting that the baby starts by looking in the mirror each time its name is called, Wallon attributed this fact to the child's more general need to apprehend its "proprioceptive ego" through an "exteroceptive image." The body proper, Wallon emphasized, is first of all an *image* of the body—that is, a *visual* image: "What other exteroceptive image could he have of himself but the one given him by the body's eyes, that is, one that is necessarily exterior to him who perceives it?"[9] First of all, the child must see itself *other* than it feels; this would be the condition *sine qua non* of the child's emergence from "immediate experience":

Between the immediate experience of things and their representation, a dissociation necessarily intervenes that detaches the qualities and the existence proper to the object from the impressions and the actions in which it is initially implicated, by attributing to the object, among other essential traits, those of exteriority. Representation is possible only at that price. The representation of the body proper insofar as it exists, necessarily satisfies that condition and can be formed only through self-exteriorization. . . . The whole work [of the child] therefore consists in the child's giving himself images of himself analogous to those he can form outside himself, and which, moreover, he can form in no other way. . . . For it is in the nature of images to belong to space.[10]

This is what Lacan constantly says about the ego: it is an "image," an "object" (1988b, 44/60, 49/66) among other objects in space, and thus pertains to an "optic" and a "topic of the imaginary" (title of the second section of work cited here as 1988a). From this perspective, Lacan's description of the mirror stage is far from being truly original, no matter what may have been said in various quarters.[11] In truth, its originality lies elsewhere; as always with Lacan, its originality is in the nature of a generalizing combination. In short, Lacan mixed Wallon's examination of the mirror with Freud's narcissism and Hegel's dialectic, at the same time raising the psychologist Wallon's modest proposals to the level of a grandiose "ontological structure of the human world" (1977a, 2/94).

In this respect, the term "mirror stage" should not lead us astray. It is not merely a question of one more stage or phase among the many already discovered by developmental psychologists and psychoanalysts. Rather, this concerns a global reinterpretation of the human ego's development, a reinterpretation based on the particular case (1977a, 4/96) of the mirror stage, understood as a "stasis of being" (1966, 172). Thus, whereas Freud and his followers imagined a series of phases in libidinal development, from autoerotism and/or narcissism to the genital stage, Lacan from the beginning conceived the evolution of relations between the "ego" and its "objects" on the basis of the narcissistic phase alone, itself deciphered in light of the child's experience before the mirror.

It must be further specified that this is hardly a question of a *stage*, if by that we mean a datable moment or period in the ego's evolution. If there is a "stage" here, it is one that is both unstable and instantaneous, that of an ek-stasis that pro-jects the ego before itself. (The Heideggerian vocabulary imposes itself here, for it seems to be what Lacan is alluding to when he writes, for example, that the "development [of the ego] is experienced as a temporal dialectic that decisively projects the formation of the individual into history. The mirror stage is a drama whose internal thrust is precipitated from insufficiency to anticipation" [1977a, 4/97]. Still elsewhere, Lacan connects the subject's "constant pursuit" of an "illusory unity" to the Heideggerian "thrown Being"—that is, as he formulates it in the vocabulary of the era, "to that agony of dereliction that is Man's particular and tragic destiny" [1953, 16].)

The ego erects itself (raises itself permanently and stably upright) only before "itself," by *anticipating* itself on the basis of an irreducible falling behind itself. As Freud had already said in "On Narcissism: An Introduction," a unity comparable to the ego does not exist "from the beginning," [12] and Lacan adds that this is because the human ego (by contrast with the animals) is fundamentally premature. It is born too soon, before being an "ego": there is, Lacan recalls, relying on data from embryology and especially on the work of Bolk, [13] a true "*specific prematurity of birth* in man" (1977a, 4/96; see also 1984, 31). If the ego projects itself before itself—by falling—it is because, among other reasons, it does not hold itself upright. Therefore, it can erect itself as a stable ego only

through "precipitation," imaginary anticipation: the infant, delivered as he is into a sort of primordial "dehiscence" (1977a, 4/96),
anticipates his bodily unity and mastery in an image, whether his
own specular image or that of some counterpart (*semblable*) whose
stature or commanding presence happens to fascinate him. In this
sense, the unity of the ego is fundamentally *imaginary*—that is, both
fundamentally illusory (with respect to the chaotic reality of the
body) and fundamentally visual. Indeed, only through vision can
the ego raise itself before itself as a self-enclosed "beautiful totality." The erection of the ego is always the erection of a statue that I
see, over there—triumphant, unshakable, fixed for eternity:

> The tendency by which the subject restores his lost unity has its place from
> the start in the center of consciousness. It is the energetic source of his men-
> tal progress, a progress whose structure is determined by *the predominance
> of the visual functions* [my emphasis]. If the search for his affective unity
> promotes within the subject the forms by which he represents his identity
> with himself, its most intuitive form is provided, at this stage, by the
> specular image. What the subject greets there is his inherent mental unity.
> What he recognizes is the ideal of the imago of the double. What he ac-
> claims is the triumph of the salutary tendency [1984, 44].

Hence the "jubilation," the "interminable ecstasy" (1953, 14)
that seizes the child at the sight of this image, and which, according
to Lacan, is nothing but the first manifestation of the child's narcissism, for narcissism is ecstatic. If the ego loves itself, as Freud
would have it, this is first of all because it is precisely *not* "itself." It
will always love itself as an object, in that adorable *other* who
presents it with the mirage of its own omnipotence. The ego is an
object, which also means that man, because of his specific prematurity, has no natural, instinctive relation to any sexual "object"
whatsoever. That "object" will always be a false object, a decoy, a
trap in which the ego pursues its own image—"an odd puppet . . . a
baroque doll . . . a trophy made of limbs, in which must be recognized the narcissistic object whose genesis we have cited: [a genesis]
conditioned by the precedence, in man, of the body's imaginary
forms over the mastery of the body itself, by the defense value that
the subject gives these forms against the distress of the vital tearing
caused by prematurity" (1984, 60). Human sexuality, as Lacan
never tires of saying, is fundamentally "baitable" because it deals

with images, simulacra: "The libidinal drive is centered on the imaginary function" (1975b, 141; see also 1981, 107–108).

In short, far from having different types of libidinal relations *to* the object, the ego *is* an object (an image) from the very start; and, symmetrically, every love object *is* the ego (an image). Libidinal development, as Lacan says quite unambiguously in all the texts from this period, is therefore a dialectical development: the initial "alienation" of the ego in the specular image (1977a, 2/95, 4/97; 1966, 181) inaugurates the "dialectic of identification with the other" (1977a, 2/94), which, through successive "dialectical syntheses," will end at the time of the Oedipus in the "asymptotic" "resolution" of the "discordance" of the *I* "with [its] own reality" (1977a, 2/94, 6/98).

This could not be stated more clearly. Freudian narcissism is linked to Wallon's *specular* image (as the myth of Narcissus certainly permits; 1984, 44), and that image in turn is linked to the *speculative* dialectic of Hegel. From this perspective, it is clear enough that Wallon's remarks about the specular image could only encourage Lacan's Hegelian bent by furnishing it with a sort of experimental guarantee. Indeed, that there is no "possible representation" except at the price of an initial "exteriorization" and of a "dissociation" from "immediate experience"—isn't this what Hegel says of the Absolute and its "reflection in otherness within itself"?[14] In short, it was very easy for Lacan to translate from one to the other, from the "specular image" of Wallon to the "reflection" of Hegel. After all, isn't the very word "reflection" used above all with the mirror, that fascinating surface which reverses light or returns (*re-flectere*) it to its point of departure? And doesn't a deep-rooted etymology continue to link "speculation"—another of Hegel's key words—to *speculum*, to the mirror?

Reflection and Speculation

One might object that Hegel's *speculative* philosophy is explicitly proposed as a critique of the "philosophy of *reflection*," and that the two should not be confounded under the pretext of etymology. Indeed, Hegel tells us (notably in the writings of his youth, but also later on), the "philosophy of reflection" is content to pose the Absolute in purely formal terms and to project it "beyond" the conceptual oppositions (subject/object, form/content, and so on) that it cannot transcend. Therefore, it never arrives at truly speculative thought, which knows itself to be the thought of the Absolute reflecting *itself* in order to appear to itself, all formal opposition being understood as *auto*opposition, *auto*formation, and *auto*-determination. For example, "The speculative stage or stage of positive reason apprehends the unity of terms in their opposition—the affirmative which is involved in their disintegration and transition." [15] As for reflection, it is (nothing but) a "moment" of the Absolute—its strictly formal, abstract moment—which should not be separated from its content, from its "result": "Reason is, therefore, misunderstood when reflection is excluded from the True, and is not grasped as a positive moment of the Absolute. It is reflection that makes the True a result, but it is equally reflection that overcomes the antithesis between the process of its becoming and the result." [16] We see, then, that Hegel's "reflection" could very well be described as a mirror (since the Absolute does reflect *itself* there)—but only on the express condition that the mirror is understood as suppressing itself "speculatively" (since the Absolute *is* its own mirror).

Now, to return to the mirror stage: Isn't Lacan holding instead to a merely formal reflection when he writes, for example, "This jubilant assumption of his specular image by the child at the *infans* stage, still sunk in his motor incapacity, . . . would seem to exhibit in an exemplary situation the symbolic matrix in which the *I* is precipitated in a primordial form. . . . This form situates the agency of the *ego*, before its social determination, in a fictional direction, which will always remain irreducible for the individual" (1977a, 2/94). Nothing is less "speculative," in the Hegelian sense, than the "precipitation" that "forever" stops, fixes, and blocks the ego in the form in which it fictitiously anticipates itself. In fact, as we shall see, it is precisely this same "formalism" of the ego (1977a, 20/114) that later furnishes Lacan with the pretext for breaking with Hegel. And once he has come to his senses, so to speak, Lacan emphasizes the motif of reflection, to the detriment of the resolving motif of speculation. He then says that specular alienation is "irreducible, with no way out," and that it "must last until the end" (1988b, 72/92).

Consequently, there is no speculative reunion of the ego with itself, and no reconciliation with the image. The mirror remains outside, and the ego with it: immobile, frozen, "statuefied."

Is this to say that the motif of reflection would have sufficed *in itself* to make Lacan break so profoundly with the Hegelian problematic? Not at all, and we should emphasize this point right away, the better to measure, later on, the stakes of the "critique" of Hegel that Lacan launched in the early 1950's, for, along with the mirror, Hegel and the whole "ontological structure of the human world" described in the article on the mirror stage remain firmly intact. In a word, that structure is the structure of vision, and in Hegel it is absolutely fundamental, foundational, extending far beyond the distinction between "reflection" and "speculation." In this regard, we should note that speculative thought, even for Hegel himself, is nothing other than absolute reflection, carried to the absolute. As Jean Hyppolite reminds us in *Logique et existence*, speculative thought is an "absolute reflection of Being itself": "It transcends merely human reflection on experience and its constitution; it seizes content itself as reflection; it is Being that knows itself through man, and not man who reflects on Being." [17] Therefore, not only is reflection absolutely necessary to the speculative process, it is wholly maintained in and as Being, beyond its suppression as finite reflection.

Now, if this is the case, it is because Being can appear to itself (present itself, manifest itself, phenomenalize itself) only by posing before itself, by dividing itself, the better to know itself—in other words, the better to *see itself*. If, for Hegel, Being must absolutely reflect itself, it is first of all because for him the only Being is luminous, visible, and thus *exterior* to the eye that perceives it. Therefore, Being can *be* only by ex-posing itself, exactly as the eye can see itself only by exorbiting itself in a mirror. In this respect, it is no accident that Hegel always criticized the philosophies of identity and immediacy on grounds of unconsciousness and night ("that night," says the preface to the *Phenomenology* "in which . . all the cows are black"), nor is it any accident that Hegel always relegated any "inner" feeling to the ineffable obscurity of non-knowledge. For him, the only consciousness is luminous, consciousness of what "pro-poses" itself to view, and this is also why any self-consciousness must first pass through the reflecting mediation of a *speculum*. His youthful essay "The Spirit of Christianity and Its Fate" states the matter quite clearly, and here it is Light itself that expresses itself as Being: "Only a consciousness that is equivalent to life is φῶς [light], and in it, consciousness and life differ only in that the latter is being, while the former is being as reflected upon."[18] Being must think itself and reflect itself in order to be, for the only Being is luminous.

Story of the Eye

This luminous ontology ("photology," as Rodolphe Gasché aptly names it) is not at all unique to Hegel, and we should briefly review it here before returning to its strictly Lacanian version. As Heidegger (whose thoughtful summary of the history of metaphysics we shall be following here) has suggested, Being has certainly been thought of in terms of vision ever since the beginning of Western philosophy:

The Greeks . . . conceived knowledge as a kind of seeing and viewing, a state of affairs suggested by the expression "theoretical," an expression that is still common today. In it, the words *thea*, "view," and *horan*, "seeing" (compare with *theater* and *spectacle*), speak. . . . But that can have its sufficient reason only in an interpretation of Being which was decisive for the Greeks. Because Being means presence and permanence, "seeing" is especially apt to serve as an explanation for the grasping of what is present and what is permanent.[19]

That which *is* contains itself stably and permanently in the clearing of light. What is spoken of as Being is initially the presence within the heart of the "non-occulted," and this luminous unveiling[20] still shines, according to Heidegger, in the Platonic Idea: "According to Plato's doctrine, Being is *idea*, visuality, presence as outward appearance"[21]—with the slight difference, Heidegger adds, that along with the Platonic Idea an ambiguity is introduced, which will progressively swing the brilliance of Being toward human vision (and the truth, as *a-lētheia* and non-veiling, toward truth as *homoiōsis*, *adaequatio*, and correct vision). Indeed, in Plato's *Republic* one must already turn one's vision "toward more real things [that which has more being]," in order to see "more truly"[22]: "The ambiguity of Being as Idea (pure presence and making-possible) also announces itself in the fact that, through the interpretation of Being (*physis*) as *idea*, the reference to 'seeing' evokes human knowing. As visual, Being is presence, but at the same time is what man brings before his eyes." [23] So begins the progressive transformation, or "rescendence," [24] of the *idea* into perception and representation that, according to Heidegger, characterizes the Cartesian *cogito* and, more generally, the modern metaphysics of subject(iv)ity that culminates in Hegel.

Indeed, we know that in the certitude of the *ego cogito, ego sum* Descartes finds the *fundamentum inconcussum veritatis*, which is also to say the foundation pure and simple (*to hupokeimenon* in Greek, *subjectum* in Latin). This new foundation of the totality of being—thus, this new *subject*—is certainly the ego, but only insofar as it thinks, cogitates: the ego that knows itself (as being) to be at the extremity of hyperbolic doubt knows itself only insofar as it thinks ("for as long as I think," says Descartes), the whole question, then, being to know what it is that we call "thinking." Now, for that German who goes here by the name Heidegger, it goes without saying: *cogitatio* (also named *perceptio* or *idea* by Descartes) is a *Vorstellung*—that is, a "representation" and, even more literally, a "posing-before." It follows that, once again, the certitude of the *cogito* derives from its visibility: *cogitatio* means *Vor-stellung*— that is, "the bringing-before-itself and what-is-brought-before-itself and made 'visible' in the widest sense." [25] In this sense, the ego knows itself as the foundation of all things because it "sees" itself in everything: "Every *ego cogito* is a *cogito me cogitare*; every 'I represent [I pose before myself] something' simultaneously represents a 'myself' [poses me before myself], me, the one representing (for myself, in my representing). Every human representing is—in a manner of speaking, and one that is easily misunderstood—a 'self'-representing [a 'self'-posing before oneself]." [26]

The Cartesian "subject," therefore, is primarily an eye (as Lacan very consciously repeats in his first seminar: "The eye is here . . . symbolic of the subject. The whole of science [Cartesian-Galilean science, let us add] is based on reducing the subject to an eye, and that is why it is projected in front of you, that is to say, objectivated" (1988a, 80/95). But, above all, this eye that is the subject sees itself in everything it self-ob-jects by way of the *Vor-stellung*.

Thus it takes possession of everything it sees, through inspection and the scrutinizing gaze. What starts as a solitary meditation on the *ego cogito* ends as a general enframing (*Ge-stell*) of being by science and technology.

As we can see, Heidegger's interpretation rests entirely on the assimilation of the "I think" to an "I/represent/myself," which in turn is assimilated to a theoretical "I/see/myself." In truth, it is quite possible that this reduction of the "I think" to the *Vorstellung* violates the singular experience of the Cartesian *cogito*, as has been suggested more than once,[27] and that the evidence of the *ego sum* actually has nothing to do with the evidence of a representation. As Descartes says of the *res cogitans*, it is "a thing that thinks. What is that? A thing that doubts, understands, affirms, denies, is willing, is unwilling, and imagines also and *feels*."[28] Now, feeling is not a (self-)representation. Therefore, it is quite possible that the experience of the *cogito* is finally that perfectly unexposable and unrepresentable experience of an affect. But this objection—which, obviously, is a major one for the interpretation of the *cogito*—in no way diminishes the relative validity of Heidegger's reading. However forced it may be, Heidegger's reading remains incontestably pertinent to the destiny of the "metaphysics of subject(iv)ity" proceeding from Descartes, and, for our present purposes, it has the advantage of taking into account the Hegelian and Lacanian versions of this same metaphysics.

Indeed, if, as Heidegger claims, the evidence of the *cogito* is that of a "posing-oneself-*before*-oneself," it is easy to understand how Hegel comes to make the division and exteriorization of self the very condition for the manifestation of absolute subjectivity. The *cogito*, interpreted in terms of representation, supposes from the very start a certain *spacing*, however thin and tenuous, of the "before-oneself," and so we could say that Hegel only took to its ultimate limit the banal paradox that one never sees oneself except at a distance. On the level of representation, it is self-evident that the ego never grasps itself except as (an) other (ego)—and that is self-evidence itself, the self-evidence of the *videre*: the self-evidence of the ego is the "transcendence of the ego" (Sartre).[29] As Lacan says later, in essential agreement with the Heideggerian interpretation and with the presuppositions of the modern problematic of the subject, the evidence of the *cogito* is a visual evidence, all the stronger for not being immediate, unlike that of sensation:

"*I saw myself seeing myself*," the young Parque says someplace. . . . What evidence can we really attach to this formula? How is it that it remains, in fact, correlative with that fundamental mode to which we referred in the Cartesian *cogito*, by which the subject apprehends himself as thought? . . . How is it, then, that the *I see myself seeing myself* remains its envelope and base, and, perhaps more than one thinks, grounds its certainty? For *I warm myself by warming myself* is a reference to the body as body—I feel the sensation of warmth that, from some point inside me, is diffused and locates me as body. Whereas in the *I see myself seeing myself* there is no such sensation of being absorbed by vision. Furthermore, the phenomenologists have succeeded in articulating with precision . . . that it is quite clear that I see *outside*, that perception is not in me, that it is on the object it apprehends. And yet I apprehend the world in a perception that seems to concern the immanence of the *I see myself seeing myself*. The privilege of the subject seems to be established here from that bipolar reflexive relation by which, as soon as I perceive, my representations belong to me [1977b, 80−81/76].

This brief detour by way of the onto-photo-logy of the Moderns will have made it plain that the Lacanian interpretation of the ego—as visual form and specular image—stops far short of calling the fundamental Hegelian problematic into question, nor does it do so even virtually in the article on the mirror stage. Even less does it "oppose," as Lacan rashly declares at the beginning of the same article, "any philosophy directly issuing from the *cogito*" (1977a, 1/93). The reverse is true: the theory of the mirror stage prolongs and, in its own way, even completes the modern problematic of the subject by exhibiting one of its major presuppositions in broad daylight. That the *ego* is outside itself from the very first, always already represented and ex-posed in front of itself, is what the subject's thought has never ceased to proclaim, at the very moment when it insisted on the transparency of that mirror. Consequently, insisting on the irreducible capture of the ego by its own specular image may reverse but in no way overthrows this schema (this "optical schema"). Like it or not, an eye is still there to see itself, an ego is still there to pose before itself as . . . self (ego). In any case, no type of relation with the world or the other—except the specular, spectacular, scopic one, as it defines the subject of representation through and through—is ever taken into account. The Lacanian ego is the ego as it theorizes itself, never as it feels "itself" or experiences "itself."

Paranoid Knowledge

Lacan says this quite clearly himself, when he obligingly defines the ego as an "object" ("The ego really is an object"; 1988b, 49/66), or when he adds that this object is the very object of knowledge (1981, 49–50). To designate this knowledge with the "term, designed to be striking, *paranoid knowledge*" (1966, 180) obviously changes nothing. This "paranoid knowledge," which Lacan very suggestively and perspicaciously describes, is only another name for the Moderns' representational knowledge, where everything is an object (of perception, inspection, appropriation) for a subject.

Lacan sketched out a first definition of "paranoid knowledge" in his thesis, insisting on the identificatory character of the paranoid relation to the world:

The genesis of the *self-punishing* function clearly reveals the concrete structure, imitative in its nature, of one of the vital foundations of knowledge. On the other hand, the social determinism of that genesis takes on a highly generalized meaning from the fact of all knowledge's primordial anthropomorphism, recognized as much in the child as in the "primitive" [an allusion to the "animism" in *Totem and Taboo*, but also to Lévy-Brühl's "primitive mentality," which Lacan so savagely ridicules later on; cf. 1966, 306, 859]. Let us say—to stay consistent with our terminology—that the question arises of knowing whether all knowledge is not originally *knowledge of a person* before being *knowledge of an object*, and whether even the notion of an object is not, for humanity, a secondary acquisition [1975a, 326].

As can be seen, knowledge, already described as fundamentally paranoid (because it is identificatory and "imitative"), is nevertheless thought of here as non-objective (because the ego is "itself" what it knows). Thus, in 1932, Lacan was very close to conceiving the archiknowledge of the world and of the other in terms of an "emotional communication," just as he would do again briefly in 1936, in the article "Beyond the Reality Principle." "The 'nature' of man," the passage reads, "is his relation to man," which is precisely not the relation of scientific "knowledge" to a nature stripped of all anthropomorphism:

His relations with his counterpart proceed by much more direct routes: here, we are designating neither language nor the elementary social institutions, which, whatever their genesis, have structures marked by artificiality; we are thinking of that emotional communication, essential to social grouping [an allusion this time to the Freudian theory of social identification as an "emotional tie," *Gefühlsbindung*], which makes itself known directly enough in that it is his counterpart whom man exploits, his counterpart in whom he recognizes himself, and his counterpart to whom he is attached by the indelible psychic tie that perpetuates the vital, really specific, misery of his first years. These relations, as *relations of connaturality*, can be opposed to those that constitute knowledge in the strict sense [1966, 87].

In short, before knowing (*connaître*) another and the world as objects, the human ego, according to the Claudelian pun (1984, 29), is born with them (*co-naît*)—immediately, prior to any language and representation, according to a "sym-pathy" in which any resolvable separation between the "ego" and the "other," the "subject" and the "object," is totally scrambled. This is a truly decisive hypothesis, one that could have led Lacan a long way toward a non-theoretical (affective) problematic of the "ego" and identification.

Once the mirror stage is introduced, however, the primacy of the theoretical installs itself definitively and solidly in Lacan's thought. The ego is certainly always deemed to know *itself* in the world and in another, but now it is by virtue of being an object in a world of objects where it alienates itself through an "objectifying identification" (1977a, 17/111). If things proceed in this way, it is not only because the world of paranoid knowledge is structured by "transitivistic" rivalry for the object of the other, as Lacan has proposed more than once. Thus, emphasizing in his seminar on the psychoses the "paranoiac affinities of all object-knowledge as such," he explains that "all human knowledge has its source in the dialectic of jealousy. . . . This is the basis on which the human world is differentiated from the animal world. The human object is distinguished by its neutrality and its indefinite proliferation. . . . What makes the human world a world covered with objects is based on this fact: that the object of human interest is the object of the other's desire" (1981, 49–50; 1953, 12). But, as Lacan immediately adds, this is possible only because the ego itself is already an object—which is to say, that other in which the ego sees itself through its rivalry with itself (1977a, 22–23/117): "How is this possible? Because the human ego is the other, and in the beginning the subject is closer to the form of the other than to the springing up of his own bent" (1981, 50). In other words, the ego that apprehends itself in the world does so only through a strictly theoretical knowledge, since all "feeling of Self" is immediately captured, captivated, by the "image of the other" (1966, 181). Out, then, with the feeling of "self," since now it is *seen* in the other, instead of being *felt* in him, as him; and theorized or reflected affect, as everyone knows, is no longer lived affect.

Thus is the world described by Lacan so strangely petrified and static, a sort of immense museum peopled with immobile "statues," "images" of stone, and hieratic "forms." The world Lacan describes as strictly "human" is simultaneously the most inhuman of possible worlds, the most *unheimlich*, in any case: it is the world of Freud's doubles, a shadowy world where every image of the ego is already an "uncanny harbinger" of its death. In accordance with the fundamental structure of the objectifying *Vor-stellung*, the ego here takes its "pose" for eternity in what Lacan (evidently playing quite consciously on the root *sta*) calls an "*instantané*" (snapshot), an "*instance*" (agency), a "*relief de stature*" (contrasting size) (1977a, 2/95), a "static," a "statue" (1977a, 2/95, 43/251), a "stasis of being" (1966, 172), or a

stagnation . . . similar in [its] strangeness to the faces of actors when a film is suddenly stopped in mid-action. Now, this formal stagnation is akin to the most general structure of human knowledge: that which constitutes the ego and its objects with attributes of permanence, identity, and substantiality, in short, with entities or "things" that are very different from the *Gestalten* that experience enables us to isolate in the shifting field, stretched in accordance with the lines of animal desire [1977a, 17/111; see also 1953, 12].

The world of knowledge (the "human" world, the "paranoid" world) is therefore that of the *stability* of substance and of what holds itself straight, raised, erected in the light, just as, imaginarily, the infant in the mirror did: "The stability of the standing posture, the prestige of stature, the impressiveness of statues [are what] set the style for the identification in which the ego finds its starting-point and leave their imprint in it forever" (1953, 15). Is this why Being, as Heidegger recalls, has been thought of since the Greeks as being-stable-and-upright?[30] Perhaps; but it is also what Lacan wholly *subscribes* to at the very moment when he makes a show of proposing an explanation for it, under the name of "paranoid knowledge." In reality, the only Being, for Lacan, is static Being—coming to a standstill before a "theoretical" and stabilizing gaze—and this is equally true for the Being of the ego, as soon as the ego itself *is* that world at which it gazes. The "ego-world" is a statue: as hard as stone, as cold as ice, it is *standing in front of* the ego that is petrified there—that is, in the ego-world, it both gazes at and petrifies itself.

In that world, visual through and through, entirely given over to the "vertigo of the domination of space" (1977a, 28/123), everything becomes a "statue in which man projects himself" and produces himself in front of himself, to the point of transforming himself into that "automaton in which, in an ambiguous relation, the world of his own making tends to find completion" (1977a, 2–3/95). A mechanical, persecuting world, much like the one that Nathanael, Hoffmann's hero, sees through the Sandman's diabolical glasses: there, man puts himself "in the service of the machine" (1977a, 27/122), his ego molds itself into the "protective shell" of his automobile (1953, 17), his movements decompose into "kaleidoscopic" images (1977a, 27/122), his living arm transforms itself into an "instrument" of technical aggression (1977a, 16–17/111). Finally, his whole body is cut up into "those organs represented in exoscopy, growing wings and taking up arms for intestine persecutions, which the visionary Hieronymus Bosch has fixed, for all time, in painting, in their ascent from the fifteenth century to the imaginary zenith of modern man" (1977a, 4–5/97; translation modified). Then the eye of paranoid knowledge, in its tireless self-curiosity, rises up against itself, in a monstrous persecutive erection, and it must be castrated with a vengeance, as in the case of Christine and Léa Papin: "Like the castrating bacchantes, they tear out eyes. Sacrilegious curiosity, which has caused man anguish since the beginning of time, is what drives them when they desire their victims, when they search in their gaping wounds for what Christine—later, before the judge—would call, in her innocence, 'the mystery of life'" (1975a, 358).

In this somber painting, we recognize the description of the technological world where, according to Heidegger, the modern metaphysics of the subject reaches its limit. We recognize the *description*, but not the *problematization*—for, in the end, Lacan never questions (as Heidegger does, for example) the non-technical essence of technology that brings about the situation wherein "man everywhere and always encounters only himself," even though "precisely nowhere does man today any longer encounter himself."[31] Lacan, by contrast, describes the technological world "from within," following the subject's thought and resting content with stating the *alienation* of that subject in the objects of its fabricating. Hence Lacan's diagnosis, admittedly quite lucid, but which really only "translates" into psychiatric terms the fundamental structure of the subject of representation: the "paranoia" of the modern world, the "persecutive" structure of technology.

The era, we must admit, certainly seemed to confirm that apocalyptic suspicion. The problem, however, is to know whether such a diagnosis could, in being made, bring relief from this evil, so judiciously noted. That is doubtful, since Lacan, as if fascinated by his "object," simultaneously describes both the paranoid world as *the* human world and paranoid knowledge as the very basis of *all* knowledge. In reality, the theory of "paranoid knowledge," which Lacan proposed in those dark years of total war, is rigorously congruent with paranoid knowledge itself in maintaining the major presupposition of the reduction of knowledge to the *theoretical* relation and to the *optic* of representation. How, then, could this theory shatter the mirror and escape its fatal fascination, once it had made the mirror, in accordance with the most steadfast ontophoto-logy of the Moderns, the "ontological structure of the human world"?

Plato with the Moderns

But that is not all. We could go so far as to say that the theory of the mirror stage and of paranoid knowledge not only does not call the essentials of the modern problematic of the subject into question but even reintroduces (and rather oddly) a previous motif, a strictly Platonic one. Indeed, we recall that Heidegger, referring to the Cartesian *cogito*, spoke of a "rescendence" of the Platonic Idea into a subjective representation:[32] from being transcendent and "meta-physical" in Plato, the Idea was progressively transformed into the *perceptum* of a *perceptio*, into the "perceived" of a human "perceiving." Now Lacan, for his part, and under the various names of "image," "form," and "ideal identification" (1966, 172), proceeds toward an astonishing "reascendence" of the *perceptio* into *idea*. Indeed, for Lacan, the specular image, although admittedly an image of the ego, is simultaneously what *gives form to* the ego. The image is exterior (the Sartrean theme of the "transcendence of the ego") and "superior" (the prestige of standing erect, of the human "statue" to which the infant *raises* its eyes), and, moreover, formative: the ego (or the eye, if you will) forms itself in the image of the image, which by the same token reacquires the stature (and the "standing") of a true Idea.

This is what Lacan continually spells out, starting with the 1936 article "Beyond the Reality Principle." He finds support for his argument in both Freud and *Gestalttheorie*. First of all, he says, the image must not be understood as a simple, "enfeebled" (and, as such, "imaginary" and "illusory"), re-presentation of reality (1966, 77–78). It is instead the very reality of the ego: such, according to Lacan, was Freud's inspired discovery, relentlessly asserting the "psychic reality" of phantasms, dreams, and symptoms (1966, 79). If this is so, however, it is not only because the subject *is* what it represents to itself, and thus also what it imagines (here we must place Lacan's momentary recourse to phenomenology and intentionality; cf. 1966, 76, 78); it is also because the image has a "function of *in*formation" (1966, 77). It forms, in-forms, the ego—the proof being those imagoes, discovered by psychoanalysis, that determine the subject's behavior and personality, well beyond what the subject can know about them: "the image of the father or the mother, of the all-powerful adult, tender or terrible, beneficent or punishing, the image of the brother, rival child, self-reflection or companion" (1966, 84).

These imagoes, far from being simply phantasmatic, are actually "real"—first of all because they are figures from the ego's personal history, which have presented themselves to it in the element of exteriority (the Latin word *imago*, as Lacan does not fail to remind us, means statue; cf. 1977a, 2/94), but above all because these images organize and schematize the ego's reality, well beyond any relation of simple imitation or reproduction: captivated by such an imago, the ego is thus also captured by "a certain number of typical psychic relations, wherein a particular social structure is expressed"—that is, by a "complex" (1966, 89). Therefore, the imago has the superior (so to speak) "reality" of a true ideal form, and that is why Lacan continually assimilates it to a *Gestalt*, in the sense of the "theory of form." What captivates and thus "forms" the ego is not the sight of this or that image but rather of *the* image, in its character of essential scheme or "type" (1988a, 121–122/140–141); hence, too, the instantaneity of that capture, since the image-diagram does not present itself *partes extra partes*, but globally (1966, 179).

To summarize, the image in the mirror, far from being a simple reflection, forms the ego. Even more precisely, the gaze (that is, as we now know, the subject) forms *itself* in the image of what it sees, of what it perceives in the way of a "vision of essences." Now, what does this mean, if not that the gaze is established here by what it sees (rather than the reverse)? Besides, as Lacan himself says in "Remarks on Psychic Causality," the "causality of madness" is psychic causality in general, and it is that "support which the symbolism of thought finds in visual perception, and which, with Husserl, I shall call a relation of *Fundierung*, of foundation" (1966, 162). In this psychic "cause," this "foundation" of the ego, how can we fail to recognize a modern, "subjective" version of the Platonic Idea (rather than the Aristotelian *morphē* to which Lacan refers; 1953, 13)? The *perceptum*, while remaining the object of a subjective *perceptio*, has once more become, in the form of a "visual *Gestalt*" (1977a, 18/113), the ideal foundation of the gaze directed toward it.

It is not simply that the Lacanian image, like the Platonic Idea, is a matter of essential vision. Above all, it is a question of that vision's forming the gaze. This is what Heidegger shows in his famous commentary on Plato's myth of the cave (a commentary that Lacan must have known very well, to judge from the astonishing resemblances between the vocabulary of the article on the mirror stage and that of Heidegger's article). It is no accident, Heidegger says, that the myth of the cave is presented in the *Republic* as a myth that concerns education (*formation*),[33] *paideia,* for what occurs in it is a transformation of truth, conceived as *alētheia* and pure unveiling, into *homoiōsis,* into correctness of the resembling gaze. Truth, for Plato, becomes a question of "education" (*formation*) because now it is a question of directing one's gaze to what "has more being"— that is, toward the Idea as "Cause" of what is: "Everything depends on the ὀρθότης, the correctness of the gaze. . . . In this directing of self, perception matches itself to what should be sighted. . . . In consequence of this matching of perception as ἰδεῖν to the ἰδέα, there arises a ὁμοίωσις, an agreement between cognition and the thing itself."[34] In this sense, the Idea "forms" the gaze that is directed toward and founded on it. Heidegger, referring to the motif of the *paideia,* comments thus: "The German *Bildung* [*formation*, education], although not an exact equivalent, most closely approximates παιδεία. . . . '*Bildung*' means two things: first, a forming (*Bilden*), in the sense of an explicating imprinting. At the same time, however, this 'forming' 'forms' (imprints) by the anticipatory fitting to a determining view, which is thus called the model (*Vorbild*). '*Bildung*' is guidance and, especially, imprinting by an image (*Bild*)."[35]

It is hardly necessary to emphasize this point, but the Lacanian "image" (which, indeed, is often referred to as an *Urbild*; cf. 1977a, 21/116; 1966, 180; 1988b, 248/289) has all the traits of the Idea as *Bildung,* with the slight difference that, in the guise of the mirror, this "image" remains an "idea" (or "ideal") *of the ego.* Then is the theory of the "imaginary" simply a twentieth-century Platonism? This suspicion may seem strange, but it is only reinforced when we read from Lacan's pen that the "psychic causality proper to the image" is of the same order as "ideal identification" (1966, 172). Indeed, the imago, Lacan says, is "the proper object for psychology," and "it is established by a form of causality that is psychic causality itself: *identification,* which is an irreducible phenomenon" (1966, 188). Or again, the imago is "formative of identification" (1966, 106), and this identification is "the transformation that takes place in the subject when he assumes an image" (1977a, 2/94). In brief, the ego forms through identification, by *conforming* to the image in which it sees *itself.*

It is easy to recognize here the major concept of Freud's second topography: the ego, Freud was already saying in *The Ego and the Id*, is formed through successive identifications, whether with "abandoned objects" (which account for its "character") or with the "father in [the ego's] own personal prehistory" (which accounts for the "ego-ideal" or "superego").[36] In fact, it is always to identification, in the Freudian sense, that Lacan refers when he cites the "brilliant use that Freud was able to make of the image" (1966, 88). But how can we not also see that he constantly interprets it in a Platonic sense, by making it a homoiōtic con-formation of the gaze to what it gazes at, or a visual "orthopedics"? This is the term used in the article on the mirror stage, and it obviously leads us back to the Platonic *orthotēs* and *paideia*: "The mirror stage is a drama . . . which manufactures for the subject, caught up in the lure of spatial identification, the succession of phantasies that extends from a fragmented body-image to a form of its totality that I shall call orthopaedic" (1977a, 4/97). Thus, in the same way that the deformed foot ends up adopting the form of the so-called orthopedic shoe, the subject learns to hold itself straight, upright, by spatially identifying with the specular image: as Lacan was still saying in 1951, the "dialectic" of psychoanalysis, as "ortho-dramatization of the subjectivity of the subject" (1966, 226), assigns itself the task of the subject's optical erection.

An Affective Identification?

Here, in concluding this chapter, is the place for us to pose a few elementary questions. Is it so obvious, after all, that identification is always specular, always identification with a *Vor-bild* (an "image-before")? Is mimesis (since this is really what we are talking about) necessarily spatial, as Lacan says, finding support for his argument in the work of Caillois (1977a, 3/96)? There is certainly nothing more persistent than this Platonic interpretation of mimesis,[37] and it is also true that it dominates Freud's theory of identification to some extent. It is enough to recall, in this connection, that in Chapter 7 of *Group Psychology and the Analysis of the Ego* Freud describes the identification with the father (from the "prehistory of the Oedipus complex") in terms of "ideal" and *vorbildliche Identi-*

fizierung: "Identification endeavors to mold [to form] a person's own ego (*das eigene Ich zu gestalten*) after the fashion of the one that has been taken as a model (*Vorbild*)."[38] But this description, which makes ceramic dogs of the ego and its "image," in no way prevents Freud from simultaneously describing identification in terms of *Gefühlsbindung*, "*emotional* [affective] tie" with another: "Identification," he says, "is the original form of emotional tie with an object."[39] This is certainly a difficult proposition, but one that nevertheless means that identification is not initially a question of optical representation (not an "ideal," "objectivizing," "spatial" identification). Not only is identification "possible before any sexual object-choice has been made," as Freud also writes,[40] but it must also, by all rights, precede every ob-jection, and every view in general, because it gives birth to the "ego." How, then, could this ego see anything at all—and particularly any "model" or "image"— since it is nothing *before* the identification?

Identification, if we take Freud seriously, escapes from the mirror stage at the very moment when it makes this "stage" possible. It presupposes some ante-specular apprehension of the other (and of the) ego, on the order of the "affective communication" that Lacan cites briefly in "Beyond the Reality Principle" before he finally takes exception to any idea of a possible *Einfühlung* that would precede the mirror stage (1977a, 19/113).[41] If there is a specular identification (and who would deny it?), it cannot really be produced elsewhere than on the (abyssal, non-"subjectal") ground of a preliminary *affection*, by the "other" that "I" *am* "myself" prior to any perception, any representation, any "posing-before." If there is a Freudian *cogito*, it is profoundly blind and therefore also unconscious, since it is "self-conscious" before any light in which self-seeing, self-posing, or self-apprehension, and so on, could take place. For example, it is the *cogito*, of the "I am the breast" from Freud's posthumous notes: "Children like expressing an object-relation by an identification: 'I am the object.' Having is the later of the two; after loss of the object it relapses into 'being.' Example: the breast. 'The breast is a part of me, I am the breast.' Only later: 'I have it'—that is, 'I am not it.'"[42]

Lacan, oddly enough, knew about this, as his 1938 article on the family complexes testifies (1984). This point deserves emphasis, for here we see a sort of vestige in him of a (properly speaking) *aborted* theory of identification, which later on he will do every-thing in his power to cast back into the outermost shadows of the ineffable. Identification, he concedes in that article, is not specular at first but "affective" (1984, 41). Admittedly, he refers to this Freudian concept only with reticence, already proposing to inte-grate it into "a theory of that identification whose developmental moment we designate by the term 'mirror stage'" (1984, 41). But with even a bit of attention to the text, we see that this matter is still not completely settled for him. At this point, moreover, Lacan has no trouble conceding that the mirror stage (which he now prefers to call the "intrusion complex") is developmentally second: the very first imago is not the imago of the "fraternal" counterpart but rather the maternal imago (characteristic of what he now calls the "weaning complex").

This archimago, in Lacan's description of it, is remarkable pre-cisely in its *not being an image*: "The content of this image is given by the sensations proper to earliest childhood, but it has *form* [my emphasis] only insofar as the sensations are mentally organized. Now, since this stage is anterior to the advent of the object's form, it seems that these contents cannot be represented in consciousness" (1984, 28). A bit farther on, emphasizing (like Freud) the funda-mentally ambivalent character of the primal (non-)relation with the maternal breast, Lacan adds:

The proprioceptive sensations of sucking and grasping obviously form the basis of this experience's ambivalence, which arises from the [following] situation: the being who is absorbing is completely absorbed. . . . We are not speaking here, with Freud, of autoerotism, since the ego is not formed, nor of narcissism, *since there is no ego image* [my emphasis]. . . . A "canni-balism," but a fusional, ineffable cannibalism, both active and passive . . .— we recognize in these terms the relation with reality on which the maternal imago rests [1984, 29–30].

It would be difficult to state this more clearly. The maternal imago is not an image or an object or a form or a representation— and that is precisely why, on this subject, Lacan constantly speaks of "sensations," of "lived experience" (*vécu*), or of "affective . . . knowledge" (*co-naissance*) (1984, 29). As Freud said, "the original form of . . tie with an object" is an "emotional" one, and its nature is profoundly one of identification, since it precedes the very distinction between "subject" and "object," between "ego" and "other." The important thing here is not merely that Lacan explicitly recognizes the existence, previous to the mirror stage, of a pre-specular relation to the imago. More important, he plants—something he will never do again—the subsequent dialectic of specular identifications in that initial affective ambivalence, seeing in this ambivalence the "undialecticizable matrix" of that dialectic.

Indeed, he suggests that the specular dialectic only prolongs and, so to speak, makes *ex*plicit (by placing it outside) the arch-ambivalence that makes up this strange "rapport without rapport" with the maternal imago. We must read *in extenso* that extraordinary genesis of dialectics, which traces the coming to light of the "ego" and the "other" (of representative ob-position), starting in the night of affective identification:

Traumatic or not, weaning leaves in the human psyche the permanent trace of the biological relation that it interrupts. Indeed, that vital crisis is replicated in a crisis of the psyche, undoubtedly the first whose resolution will have a dialectical structure. For the first time, it would seem, a vital tension is resolved in a mental intention. By means of that intention, weaning is accepted or refused; admittedly, the intention is very elementary, since it cannot even be attributed to an ego still in a rudimentary state; acceptance and rejection cannot be conceived as choices, since, in the absence of an ego that affirms or denies, they are not contradictory; but, as coexistent and contrary poles, they determine an essentially ambivalent attitude, although one of them does prevail. At the time of the crises that ensure further development, this primordial ambivalence is resolved in psychic differentiations whose dialectic is of an increasingly high level and whose irreversibility is also increasing. The original prevalence changes direction several times and is thereby subject to very diverse outcomes; nevertheless, it will recover itself in them, both in the time and in the tone that it imposes on the new crises and on the new categories with which each of these crises will endow the experience [1984, 27–28].

In other words, the dialectic never suppresses the ambivalence that sub-tends it, no more than it balances or resolves its fundamental "tone": indissolubly active and passive, the relation of the ego to its specular alter egos will always be *rather* active (sadistic, voyeuristic, despotic) or *rather* passive (masochistic, exhibitionistic, servile). But there is more to it than that. A bit farther on, Lacan adds that the specular imagoes, in which that primordial ambivalence comes to be reflected and refracted dialectically, form the ego only because they have first been "*informed*" by the maternal imago. This expression is all the more curious (and thus significant) because at that moment Lacan is speaking of the "*contents*" of the maternal imago, emphasizing the absolute unrepresentability that results from their anteriority to the "form of the object": "Nevertheless, they reproduce themselves in the mental structures that, as we have said, model the subsequent psychic experiences. They will be reevoked by association to the occurrence of these later experiences, but they will be inseparable from the objective contents that they will have *informed* (1984, 28; Lacan's emphasis).

Would the "content" thus in-form the "form" that "models" it? Lacan's quasi-systematic blurring of the opposition between form and content says it clearly enough: the specular imagoes, far from giving form to a sort of indeterminate and passive "matter" (far from mediating a pure and simple immediacy), actually only reproduce and develop, in the ob-positive space of the visible, a more primordial ambi-valence of the "ego" and the "other." Now, this ambivalence has nothing to do with the relation of an eye to a "model." On the contrary, this "model" that is the specular imago (or the "form of the object") forms the ego only by modeling itself on a prior identification—one that is absolutely blind (non-imaginary)—with the maternal imago. Behind—or, better yet, *in*—the visible image of the counterpart, or the "brother," there would remain the invisible, unimaginable maternal imago from which the image would receive its formative power.

This can only mean that "formative" identification, well before it is a question of vision and ideal modeling, is first and essentially a matter of *affection* of the "ego" by the "other," preceding any representational scission and, more generally, any opposition, whether between activity and passivity, spontaneity and receptivity, or form and content. This is unmistakably what Lacan ends up saying, in an astonishing passage that, strictly speaking, should have ruined the whole *theory* of the imaginary in advance. Indeed, he writes that the image forms the ego not because it is seen, *over there*, but rather because it "intrudes," *here*, in and as the ego; and this intrusion is that of an affect, experienced im-mediately, body and soul, as an "emotional or motive suggestion":

The perception of the activity of others is not actually enough to break the affective isolation of the subject. As long as the image of the counterpart plays only its primary role, limited to the function of expressivity, it unleashes similar emotions and postures in the subject, at least to the extent that the current structure of the subject's systems permits this. But while the subject is under the influence of that emotional or motive suggestion, *the subject does not distinguish itself from the image* [my emphasis]. Furthermore, in the discordance characteristic of that phase, the image only adds the temporary intrusion of a foreign bent. Let us call this a narcissistic intrusion; nevertheless, the unity that it introduces into the [various] tendencies will contribute to the formation of the ego. Before the ego asserts its identity, however, it confounds itself with the image that forms it but that first of all alienates it [1984, 45].

In other words, the pathetic intrusion precedes and makes possible the ecstasy of alienation: I *am* the other, through a corporeal-affective mimesis, and it is only on condition of this initial and blind "suggestion" that I will then be able to see myself in the other, in the image that inexplicably steals my feeling of "my-self." And Lacan adds:

Let us say that, from this origin, the ego retains the ambiguous structure of the spectacle that—manifest in . . . despotism, seduction, and display . . .—will give form to sadomasochistic and scoptophilic . . . drives that are essentially destructive of others. Let us also note that this primordial intrusion allows us to understand every projection of the constituted ego, whether that projection shows itself as mythomaniacal in the child whose personal identification is still wavering, as transitivistic in the paranoiac whose ego is regressing to an archaic stage, or as comprehensive when it is integrated into a normal ego [1984, 45–46].

Thus, the spectacle of the imaginary was only the projection, on the world's stage, of the mime that the "ego" initially is. Why did Lacan forget that so quickly? Was it because this spec(tac)ular staging was the only way of objectifying a mimesis that otherwise would have been untheorizable, ineffable, and unrepresentable? No doubt; but who says that the stakes for the actor are knowledge, self-knowledge via (the gaze of) the other that freezes him into a statue, an idol? Isn't his joy (or his anguish) above all to *play* his role, to move *inside* the pathetic scene that he incarnates? And why, after all, should true life always be elsewhere, in front of me, in that double who augurs my death? That other: as Freud said of the mother's breast, I am it, I feel it, I give it life—and it is "me" (*moi*, ego), "my" life, never *the* ego. "Only later" will I run up against that hard, frozen "object" that I am and am not, that I am not all the while I am ravished in it. So, yes, I will be able to meet myself, run into myself in mirrors, struggle with my doubles, love myself in them while hating myself, project myself into them while losing myself.

But then I will no longer be what "I am," in the invisible and untheorizable affect of my identification. I will be, as Lacan rightly says, "alienated"—but alienated because I will seek myself in objects, whereas I am no "ego" and no "object."

Through the Looking-Glass

> . . . .
> . . . .
> . . . .
> . . . .
> . . . . the mirrors
> lining the walls, and even the ceiling, multiplied the
> animal image of a coupling: at the slightest movement,
> our broken hearts opened themselves to the void,
> where the infinity of our reflections overwhelmed us.
>
> —Georges Bataille [1]

For Lacan during those somber wartime years, while the theory of the mirror stage was being elaborated, what was the analytic cure? It was a *dialogue*—that is, an exchange of words between two people (1977a, 12/106): the first, lying down, speaks to the other, who sits behind (and is therefore invisible) and answers parsimoniously. The whole question, however, is to know *who* speaks, and *to whom*. This is the question of the dia-lectic of the cure.

You Are This

To begin with, we should note that from 1936 on Lacan designates the first person (the one who speaks) by the name "subject." The analyst, he writes in "Beyond the Reality Principle," is placed "in the situation of *interlocutor*," and "the subject solicits him to take that role" (1966, 83). Does this mean that the "subject," named almost in passing, is different from the "ego" that we have been dealing with until now? Far from it, at first anyway; and we shall see that it took Lacan all of fifteen years to distinguish between these two persons (the *I* and the *ego*, as he baptizes them in the first seminars; cf. 1988a, 166/188, and 1988b, 44/59). Nevertheless, this fine terminological distinction is not immaterial. The ego is the "one" who *sees* himself in the other (and who remains mute in admiration, or in rage). The subject, although the same "one," is the subject insofar as he *speaks* to the other and seeks to express himself to the other's intention.

This definition of the subject is introduced very early, and it always remains fundamentally valid for Lacan, beyond the conceptual modifications yet to come: the only subject is a speaking one; and, inversely, all speech supposes a subject. Why is this so? Because the very fact of speaking, according to Lacan's first formulations, implies a *vouloir-dire*, or an "intention" to signify (1966, 83). It is what makes the difference between, on the one hand, the tracks that alert an experienced hunter to the passage of game and, on the other, the trail marker with which the same hunter signals his own passage to another hunter who follows him. Whereas the tracks imply no *vouloir-dire* on the part of the unfortunate game, the trail marker, even if undecipherable, will always manifest an intention to signify. Indeed, suppose that the first hunter uses a convention or code unknown to the second. At the very least, the second hunter will know that someone—call him "X"—has tried to make his presence known. In other words, the trail marker will represent "X": it will signify not an object but a subject. And for Lacan, that is precisely the essence of language: "Language, before signifying something, signifies for someone" (1966, 82). It follows that all speech, even if "insignificant," has a *meaning*—which is nothing other than the subject insofar as he expresses *himself*. Language, which signifies or represents this or that, presupposes speech (*parole*), in which a subject signifies himself and engages in auto-representation by *ex*-pressing himself to another's intention. Thus, in essence, language (statement, *énoncé*) is autoenunciation.

What about the analytic dialogue, then, since that is what we are attempting to define here? It is a good bet that, at the beginning, it will strongly resemble the "dialogue of deaf-mutes" that we have just been imagining between our two hunters. At first glance, this may seem to be an obstacle to communication, but it only shows more clearly communication's essence of dialogue: "What he [the patient] says may indeed make no sense; what he says *to him* [the analyst] receives a meaning" (1966, 82–83). Analytic speech, precisely because confused, illogical things are said within it, represents the essence of speech for Lacan—its dialectical essence:

It can be said that psychoanalytic action is developed in and through verbal communication, that is, in a dialectical grasp of meaning. It presupposes, therefore, a subject who manifests himself as such to the intention of another. . . . Only a subject can understand a meaning; conversely, every phenomenon of meaning implies a subject. In analysis a subject offers himself as being capable of being understood, and indeed *is* capable of being understood [1977a, 9/102].

At bottom, an ear (even a deaf ear, even a "mis-understanding" one) is enough, and it is this ear, as Lacan repeats in the opening of his seminar, that Freud knew how to open, in contrast to the scientistic prejudices of his day: "From the scientistic point of view, Freud appeared . . . to revert to the most archaic thinking—reading something in dreams. . . . But when one interprets a dream, one is always up to one's neck in meaning. What is at issue is the subjectivity of the subject, in his desires, his relation to his environment, to others, to life itself" (1988a, 1/7).

Dreams, symptoms, slips of the tongue, bungled actions—which furnish the essentials of abracadabricating analytic speech—therefore have meaning because a subject expresses *himself* in them and thus constitutes *himself* in and by the mediation of the interlocution. But who is this *himself*? And how does he express *himself*? As Lacan recalls in "Beyond the Reality Principle," the "experience of language" proper to analysis is singular. On the one hand, the subject is asked to say everything, even if it is meaningless (the so-called rule of free association). On the other hand, the "interlocutor," the analyst, remains silent most of the time, or at any rate does not respond directly to the discourse addressed to him (the rule of neutrality and abstinence). The astonishing thing is that this situation, far from interrupting the flow of words, excites it—except that the subject, as if dragged down into the silence that the analyst sets against him, begins speaking to "some other, imaginary but more real" (1966, 84). In other words, he starts to speak—in an ever more imploring or demanding, ashamed or aggressive, way—to an *image*, the very one from which he suffers, and which he was already expressing through all his symptoms. As Lacan writes—in a particularly wily (or confused?) sentence, where everything seems calculated to make the attribution of the possessive adjectives uncertain—the analyst discovers in the patient's discourse

that very *image* which, by means of his game, he has aroused from the subject [note this formulation: it concerns a self-image], whose trace he recognized imprinted in his [the patient's] person, that image which he certainly knew to have a human essence, since it provokes passion and exerts oppression, but which, as he himself does for the subject, hid its features from his [the patient's] gaze. He discovers those features in a family portrait [which is also, in terms of the preceding, a self-portrait]: the image of the father or the mother, of the all-powerful adult, tender or terrible, beneficent or punishing, the image of the brother, rival child, self-reflection or companion [1966, 84].

In this description, we recognize the very peculiar phenomenon that Freud called "transference." The patient in analysis, Freud said, "transfers" to the analyst the feelings that he experiences unconsciously for this or that character from his personal history. More precisely, he *acts*[2] and *repeats* these emotions in the current relation with the physician, rather than *remembering* the distant events that aroused them—the objective of the cure thus being to "dissolve" the transference by making it conscious.[3]

Note, however, the important nuances that Lacan brings to this picture. First of all, what Freud had described in terms of affect (love, hatred, anxiety, guilt) is entirely retranscribed in terms of "signifying intention" and "social expression" (1966, 83). This feature remains constant in Lacan's later descriptions of the transference, to the point of hardening into outright dogma; affect, as experienced "beyond language," is hardly important (1977a, 40/248, 57/267); what matters is affect only as "transmitted by language" (1966, 83)—that is, only as exteriorized in intersubjective dialogue. The profoundly Hegelian nature of this thesis deserves passing notice. Hegel had said long ago that inner feeling remains ineffable (it cannot know itself) so long as it refuses to bring itself "into the light of day" in the form of discourse: he who "makes his appeal to feeling, to an oracle within his breast, . . . tramples underfoot the roots of humanity. For it is the nature of humanity to press onward to agreement with others; human nature only really exists in an achieved community of minds. The anti-human, the merely animal, consists in staying within the sphere of feeling, and being able to communicate only at that level."[4] Lacan repeats this in relation to the "community of minds" that is transference: "Transference does not depend on any mysterious property of affectivity, and even when it betrays itself under the appearance of emotion, this emotion takes on meaning only in terms of the dialectical moment in which it is produced" (1966, 225). There is no question, then, of the cure's outcome depending on this or that catharsis of affects, nor even on that "working through" of transferential affects in which Freud saw an equivalent of abreaction.[5] In the analytic cure, affect has citizenship rights only as it is formulated in a communal discourse, where it makes itself recognized and so shows itself in the full light of exteriority (of the *agora*).

Next—and this second aspect is especially dominant in Lacan's early texts, contrary to what will happen when transference comes to be conceived exclusively in terms of speech (1988a, 107–109/ 125–127)—the transference of affect becomes a transference of image, "imaginary transference." Thus, in "Aggressivity in Psychoanalysis," regarding the "negative transference": "This phenomenon represents in the patient the imaginary transference onto our person of one of the more or less archaic imagoes that, by an effect of symbolic subduction, degrades, diverts, or inhibits the cycle which, by an accident of repression, has excluded from the ego this or that bodily function or corporal segment and which, by an action of identification, has given its form to this or that agency of the personality" (1977a, 14/107; translation modified). Thus the "intense emotional relationship" (*intensive Gefühlsbeziehung*) that Freud spoke of[6] becomes for Lacan a relation of identification. It is true that this movement was already implicit (if not explicit) in Freud himself, since transference, defined as repetition of the earliest emotional relations with others, had for this very reason to be a repetition of identification, understood as "the most primordial form of emotional tie to an object." The fact remains, however, that Freud spoke in this regard of an "*emotional* tie," whereas for Lacan, as we have seen, identification is conceived in specular terms, as a relation to an image. By the same token, what Freud described as an affective and essentially blind "repetition" becomes under Lacan's pen a process of exteriorization—that is, of "theoretical" knowledge: transference is the *projection* onto the analyst of the "image of the subject" that until then was "imprinted in his person" and that the subject "repeated in his conduct," knowing nothing of this all the while (1966, 84).

In short, transference is the projection of that "intrusive" "suggestive," "emotionalizing" image also spoken of in the article on family complexes (1984). It is the ex-pression, through speech, of the im-printed (and therefore invisible, unimaginable) image ("hidden from his gaze") that the "subject" initially was. This, by the same token, allows us all the better to identify the characters who are present in the psychoanalytic dialogue. Indeed, it should now be fairly obvious that the "subject" who speaks is the "ego." As for the one to whom he speaks, this is also the "ego" (or, what amounts to the same thing, its image). If the subject *speaks himself*[7] to the other's (the analyst's) intention, it is first of all in the sense of speaking *with* his ego: he speaks *to* his ego and *by means of* his ego (1981, 23, 196). Therefore, this dialogue is, all things considered, a monologue, the more so (despite appearances) as the subject, in the strangest and liveliest way, experiences the analyst's presence. This agonizing moment, which Lacan later describes as the pivot of the transference (1966, 373; 1988a, 42/53 ff.), is the one in which "the speech of the subject tips toward the presence of the listener" (1966, 373), but only in order to "hook on to the other" and coagulate into that "alienated form of being that one calls the *ego*" (1988a, 49/60, 52/63). The subject then calls the analyst to witness, tries to interest him, and seeks to obtain from him the confirmation of his affliction (that is, of his ego). In short, he puts him in the position of alter ego, the very definition of resistance, according to Lacan's later formulations: "The subject . . . begins the analysis by speaking of himself without speaking to you, or by speaking to you without speaking of himself. When he can speak to you of himself, the analysis will be finished" (1966, 373).

Now, how is this mirage of the transference, which transforms the analyst into the image of the subject, produced? We can already guess the answer: the analyst, by removing himself from the patient's gaze and providing "dialogue with a participant . . . as devoid as possible of individual characteristics" (1977a, 13/106), holds a *mirror* up to the subject. If the subject can now see, on the outside, the image of himself that until then, "as [the analyst] him-self does for the subject, hid its features from his gaze" (1966, 84), it is, Lacan says, to the extent that "our attitude offers the subject the pure mirror of an unruffled surface" (1977a, 15/109). Lacan will repeat this, but at a moment when the schema of analysis will have been profoundly transformed with respect to the present topic: the analyst should not be "a living mirror, but an empty mirror" (1988b, 246/288)—that is, a mirror pure and simple (for where but in *Snow White and the Seven Dwarfs* have we ever seen an ani-mated mirror?).

The analyst's action, hardly active, is thus limited to reflecting for the subject the image that he, unaware, has been reproducing (miming) up to that point, until the moment when he can finally see himself (*se voir*) in it—and thus once again know himself (*se sa-voir*) in it. Here, as brief as it is triumphant, is the description of this process that Lacan gives in "Beyond the Reality Principle":

From then on . . . the analyst acts in such a way that the subject becomes conscious of the unity of the *image* that is refracted in him with such differ-ent effects, according to whether he plays it, incarnates it [in a mimetic style], or knows it. We shall not describe here how the analyst proceeds with his intervention. . . . Let us simply say that insofar as the subject pur-sues the experience and process in which the image is reconstituted, his conduct will cease to mime the suggestion of the image [the "emotional suggestion" of the article on family complexes]; his memories will recap-ture their real density, and the analyst will see the end of his power, which will have become unnecessary because of an end to the symptoms and the completion of the personality [1966, 85].

One almost feels like applauding—and why not, since every-thing shows that we are at the theater. Lacan himself says so quite clearly several pages later, referring to those "images" of the Oedipal complex "with which, one after another, the subject identifies in order to play out, as the only actor, the drama of their conflicts. That play, which the genius of the species has placed under the sign of laughter and tears, is a *commedia dell'arte* in that each individual improvises and makes it mediocre or highly expressive. . . . It is also a *commedia dell'arte* in that it is played out according to a typi-cal scenario and traditional roles" (1966, 90). The subject, as we see, is a mime, and one possessed by his role to the point of not even perceiving that he is playing ("repeating"[8] and "acting," as Freud said: the patient, we read in "The Question of Lay Analysis," is "obliged to stage a revival of an old piece," "he is reproducing it tangibly, as though it were actually happening, instead of remembering it").[9] Hence the comical character of this marionette for the outside observer, the theoretical spectator, since he sees what the marionette does not see (repetition, identification).

As for the progression of the analysis, with its peripeties and sensational "happy ending," it conforms to Aristotle's good old rule of "recognition." It is the progression from blind (non-specular and thus hypnotic or, as Lacan notes, "suggestive") identification to true and authentic self-identification: at the end of that tragicomedy in which, through méconnaissance, he has "played" and "mimed" all the roles imposed upon him by the imago, the subject finally *recognizes himself* in his image and thus passes, as Aristotle said, "from ignorance to knowledge."[10] Like Oedipus, who furiously acts out his fate until the moment when he becomes conscious of his true identity, the subject is cured of his symptoms when he becomes conscious of himself in the mirror that the analyst holds up to him.

Could the obscure passion animating the transference be the passion to see (*voir*), the desire to know (*savoir*)? Could the non-knowledge of transference have a *view* toward knowledge? Lacan, following Freud's example,[11] often compares the progression of the analysis to the tragedy of Oedipus (1988b, 214/250, 229/267 ff.; SXVII, 18 March 1970; 1981, 70), and this is obviously no accident. Of the desire to know, understood as the desire to know oneself, Oedipus is the lofty hero, the one who, Hegel says in his *Lessons on the Philosophy of History*, becomes self-conscious by solving the riddle of the Sphinx and ultimately hurling that enigmatic, stonelike "statue (*Bild*) of Egypt" into the "Oriental" night of non-knowledge.[12] Therefore, to say that every patient in analysis is an "Oedipus" means that every analysis essentially unfolds on the level of self-knowledge (and not, for example, on that of affective communication, passion, or "acting"). For the young Lacan, the progress of the analysis is clearly a progress in self-consciousness, and its (dialectical) mainspring is the analyst as simple reflecting mirror. The analyst speaks very little, and if he does speak, it is only from the mirror, from which emerges the "You are this" in which analysis culminates: "The point to which analysis leads, the end point of the dialectic of existential recognition, is—*You are this*" (1988a, 3/9). Again, according to the conclusion of the article on the mirror stage, "In the recourse of subject to subject that we preserve, psychoanalysis may accompany the patient to the ecstatic limit of the '*You are this,*' in which is revealed to him the cipher of his mortal destiny, but it is not in our mere power as practitioners to bring him to that point where the real journey begins" (1977a, 7/100).

It is true that the preceding lines, by their very clear allusion to the *tragic* fate of Oedipus, also give us a glimpse of a "beyond" the mirror, a "beyond" that would no longer be a simple dialectical dissolution of the specular mirage. Oedipus, as we know, expiates his passion for knowledge:[13] "His eyes fall from him like scales," as Lacan says later (SXVII, 18 March 1970), and he must go unreconciled toward that sacred grove where he will disappear from men's view after having uttered terrible maledictions (1988b, 229/268 ff.; 1986, 292, 330–331). The "ecstasy" in question here is thus no longer the ek-stasis of the ego into its specular image. It is already—akin to Heidegger—an ek-stasis into nothing and a journey toward death. The time was soon to come when, for Lacan, it would no longer be a question of recognizing oneself in the mirror; on the contrary, the issue would be *not* to recognize oneself in the mirror, to shatter it and move on, bloodied, into the void of its absence.

You Are Me, the Ego

The problem raised by Lacan's description, in the 1940's, of the analytic cure is the following: How can the subject be kept from seeing *himself* in the mirror that the analyst holds up to him? Even more precisely, how can he be kept from seeing himself in the mirror as an *ego*? Who could be authenticated by the analyst's "You are this," if not the unsinkable "ego" from which one claims to deliver the "subject"? Therefore, what difference is there between "You are this" and "You are me/ego," between the de-alienating mirror of the analyst and the captivating mirror of the specular image?

We have already seen that Lacan describes the mirror as both the source of all the subject's afflictions and the mainspring of his cure. On the one hand, the mirror captures, freezes, and alienates the subject by expatriating him in an image that dominates, subjugates, and "suggests" him. On the other hand, and simultaneously, it permits him to see himself—that is, to separate himself from his image by seeing himself in front of himself. Thus, it should not surprise us that Lacan, in all the texts of this period, remains particularly reserved about the technique of the cure and especially its "end." In reality, there is no way to break out of the mirror's enchanted circle, since it is the very circle of the *subject in general*, as Lacan understands it during this period. The "ego" is certainly an alienation of the "subject," but that "subject" in turn receives only a specular definition; in reality, he is the "ego" in its character of being incapable of knowing itself (de-alienating itself) *except* in the mode of self-vision (which is the mode of alienation, of being-out-of-oneself).

This circle has a name, and we already know it: "dialectic." First of all, if Lacan does not see the contradiction in which he is trapped, it is not because he is insensitive to it; on the contrary, it is precisely because he thinks dialectically, stubbornly searching for the solution (or the "resolution") of that contradiction in contradiction and ob-position as such. We have seen this again and again: to resolve the conflict between the subject and his specular alter ego, Lacan always calls upon a dialectical mechanism, whether the "dialectical progress" implied in the paranoiac's self-punishing crime, the "inversion" of brotherly hostility into homosexual love, or the "dialectic of identifications" (1977a, 1/94, 18/112) through which imaginary rivalry is finally resolved into a normalizing identification with the Oedipal ego-ideal. "The imago's function," we read in "Remarks on Psychic Causation," "is to bring about the resolving identification of a psychic phase—in other words, a metamorphosis of the individual's relations with his counterpart" (1966, 118). In this way, then, imaginary identification is simultaneously alienation and de-alienation, the source of conflict and the means of its resolution. Identification with one's counterpart is perhaps the mainspring of madness (of mental illness, in the broadest sense of the term), but madness in turn is only a trick of reason, a simple "phase" in the "dialectical development of the human being" (1966, 172).

This is another way of saying that true madness is refusal of madness—the imaginary alienation, as Lacan says over and over, that is the "being of man" (1966, 154), or that leads "to the heart of the dialectic of being" (1966, 171). Therefore, one must accept alienation and recognize oneself in the other, in order to live in peace with him. As Lévi-Strauss so aptly puts it, summing up in his own fashion "the conclusion that emerges from Dr. J. Lacan's profound study, 'Aggressivity in Psychoanalysis,'" "Strictly speaking, the person whom we call sane is the one who is capable of alienating himself, since he consents to an existence in a world definable only by the self-other relationship." [14] And, during this whole period, it is precisely this profoundly dialectical schema that Lacan applies to the unfolding of the cure: the object of the cure is not to suppress the egoic image from which the patient suffers, but rather to authenticate it as the subject's true image, so that he can recognize (rather than "miscognize") himself in it.

Let us confirm this by examining what is in many ways a pivotal text: "Intervention sur le transfert," from 1951. Here, the insistence on the imaginary relationship is already becoming more cautious, but the schema of recognition in the mirror, as we shall see, is still solidly dominant. Recalling yet again that the "psychoanalytical experience . . . unfolds entirely in the relation of subject to subject" (and not in an objectivizing relation, a typical error of psychology), Lacan proposes to define the transference "in purely dialectical terms" (1966, 216–218). The example chosen to illustrate this not really unexpected thesis is the analysis of Dora, which Lacan then describes quite brilliantly in terms of "dialectical reversals" or "scansions of structures where truth is transmuted for the subject, touching not only on his comprehension of things but also on his very position as subject, of which his 'objects' are a function" (1966, 218).

Indeed, what does Freud do in this famous (and, as we know, aborted) analysis? According to Lacan, he contents himself with showing Dora (the "subject") where her "ego" is. Dora, the hysteric, complains bitterly of being the object of a sordid bargain: her father, who for several years has carried on a liaison with a certain Mrs. K., has turned Dora over to the attentions of the husband,

Mr. K., as a sort of exchange. According to Lacan, Freud counters by saying, "If this situation has been going on for such a long time, it must be because of your complicity." In other words, "*You are the reality that you denounce*" (the typical schema of the Hegelian "beautiful soul," as Lacan does not fail to recall; 1966, 219). Thus, this is a first reversal, from which follows a second question—for, under these conditions, what is the significance of Dora's sudden jealousy with respect to her father? Could it be, as it may first appear, a jealousy motivated by the desire to possess that (masculine, Oedipal) *object*—the father? Freud's second response is just as much a reversal as the first: "Your jealousy with respect to your father hides a much deeper jealousy toward Mrs. K. She is the object of your desire"—that is, "*You are* a man (your father; Mr. K.) with whom you identify in the form of an aggressive rivalry."

This discovery should have led Freud to a final reversal, which should have caused him to recognize in Mrs. K. the very "image" of Dora (1966, 221): "That woman whom you desire as an object, by identifying yourself with the man (Mr. K.), is yourself." In short, "*You are* the 'ravishing whiteness of the body of Mrs. K.' *You are* the pseudo-object that incarnates 'the mystery of your own femininity'" (1966, 220). As Lacan emphasizes, however, it is precisely this ultimate step that Freud did not take, reluctant at the time—1905—to recognize the "homosexual tie uniting Dora to Mrs. K." (1966, 223). Instead, he tried to persuade Dora that her true object was Mr. K., thus taking Mr. K's place in the transference, and by the same token provoking the same aggressive identification (the same "negative transference"). If Mrs. K. "is nothing" to Mr. K., as the latter ends up telling Dora, in order to make her yield to his advances, then what is he himself to Dora? The man is nothing but an identificatory prop for her own desiring of herself as a woman. And so Dora slaps Mr. K.—and runs away from Freud.

Desire of Recognition, Recognition of Desire

We see that Freud, according to Lacan, demonstrates a dialectical immaturity: he asks what the *object* of Dora's desire is, without seeing that she actually desires *herself* in her so-called objects. Thus he cannot recognize this desire—and neither can Dora. The cure fails because Dora has aggressively identified with the analyst, without his being able to return her reflection in the form of a "You are Mr. K.," "You are Mrs. K."

Would things have gone any differently if Freud had succeeded in showing Dora her own image in the "ravishing whiteness" of Mrs. K.'s body? This is what Lacan still seemed to believe in 1951, but by 1955, in his seminar on the psychoses, he had completely changed his tune: "To authenticate . . . in the subject everything of the imaginary order is literally to turn analysis into the anteroom of madness, and we can only marvel that this does not lead to a deeper alienation" (1981, 23). Thus, in Lacan's eyes, to return the subject's own image to him is no longer to de-alienate him; rather, it is exactly the opposite: it is (as Lacan had already said in his famous "Discourse of Rome" of 1953) to trap him once again in "an objectification—no less imaginary than before—of his static state or of his 'statue,' in a renewed status of his alienation" (1977a, 43/251), for the "ego" in which he recognizes himself, "even if it were his [spit and] image, can never become one with the assumption of his desire" (1977a, 45/254). On the contrary, it only frustrates him more, locking him into an endless aggressivity:

This ego . . . is the essence of frustration—not the frustration of a desire of the subject, but the frustration of an object in which his desire is alienated, and the more it is elaborated, the deeper the subject's alienation from his *jouissance*. It is frustration at one remove, then, and of such a kind that, even if the subject were to reintroduce its form into his discourse to the point of reconstituting the passivating image through which he makes himself an object by displaying himself in front of the mirror, he could not be satisfied with it, since even if he achieved his most perfect likeness in that image, it would still be the *jouissance* of the other that he would cause to be recognized in it. . . . The aggressivity that the subject experiences at this point has nothing to do with the animal aggressivity of frustrated desire. The latter explanation, which seems to satisfy most people, actually masks another that is less agreeable for each of us: the aggressivity of the slave who responds to the frustration of his labor with a desire for death [1977a, 42/250; translation considerably modified].

In other words, the analytic mirror no longer works—and neither does dialectic. Or, if it does work, it is with no goal, as if it has gone mad, with neither resolution nor reconciliation possible. Therefore, something happened in the pivotal years of the 1950's that led Lacan to reconsider his earlier positions: the "imaginary transference" is not *all* of transference, and dialectic is not *all* of the "ontological structure of the human world." Something else transcends that dialectic of the ego and/or the other, which Lacan variously calls the "Other-Thing" of desire, the "Other Place" of the unconscious, or the symbolic "Other" (capital O) in its radical difference from the imaginary "other" (small o). Thus begins, under the auspices of speech and language, the vast movement of the "return to Freud," which will finally make the subject a "subject of the signifier," and his desire a desire of nothing.

To what should we attribute this wrenching revision (for it really is one, even if Lacan never deigned to make it explicit)? The question is all the more difficult in that references to dialectic, far from disappearing, remain just as positive, becoming even more emphatic. Apparently the "return to Freud" is still accomplished by way of Hegel: "In order to rediscover the effect of Freud's speech," we read in the "Discourse of Rome," "it is not to its terms that we shall have recourse, but to the principles that govern it. These principles are simply the dialectic of the consciousness-of-self, as realized from Socrates to Hegel" (1977a, 79–80/292). It is true that Lacan immediately adds (this time returning to Hegel by way of Freud), "But Freud's discovery was to demonstrate that this verifying process authentically attains the subject only by decentering him from the consciousness-of-self, in the axis of which the Hegelian reconstruction of the phenomenology of mind maintained it" (1977a, 79–80/292; see also 1977a, 293/794 ff., where we learn with interest that Lacan's references to Hegel were "entirely didactic"). Thus, we must understand that the "dialectic" governing the analytic dialogue is now *other* than the one to which he had earlier had such abundant recourse. But what dialectic is it, then? What is this strange dialectic, no longer completely Hegelian but, Freudian as it is, still a dialectic?

The answer can undoubtedly be found in several terms whose insistent appearance under Lacan's pen we have already noted: "desire," "assumption of desire," "recognition," "satisfaction," "*jouissance*." The dialectic to which Lacan now refers is a "dialectic of recognition" (1966, 353)—that is, a "dialectic of desire," understood as "desire of the desire of the other" (1977a, 58/268) and "desire to have one's desire recognized" (1966, 343). Now, these terms, which are obviously not Freudian, are also not, appearances to the contrary, strictly Hegelian. They are actually linked to the anthropologizing and para-Heideggerian *interpretation* of Hegel that Kojève proposed in his course on the *Phenomenology of Spirit*.[15] And so haven't we also found the solution to our problem? Isn't Lacan's "other" dialectic simply Kojève's dialectic—that is, the dialectic of master and slave, interpreted from over Heidegger's shoulder in terms of a "philosophy of death" and finitude?

To confirm this suspicion, let us begin by briefly recalling the dialectic of master and slave according to Hegel and/or Kojève.[16] This dialectic, as Lacan correctly says, is a dialectic of "self-consciousness"; it is also, as he no less faithfully repeats, a dialectic of "desire." Indeed, Hegel writes that "self-consciousness is desire (*Begierde*) in general,"[17] in the precise sense of a desire desiring itself in "objects" (in "others") that it immediately negates as such. Thus, according to the Hegelian system, self-consciousness must begin with the painful discovery of objects' "independence," since it cannot really satisfy its desire except through their mediation: "It is in fact something other than self-consciousness that is the essence of Desire; and through this experience self-consciousness has itself realized this truth."[18] As we know, this happens to desire as soon as it becomes desire of recognition—that is, as soon as it *reflects* itself in another consciousness (in another desire). To know itself, self-consciousness wants to see itself "outside" (indeed, desire of recognition is fundamentally a desire of self-manifestation), and by the same token it enters into the fatal "duplication"[19] that makes it ever more dependent on that other self-consciousness (that other desire) by which it wants to be recognized (as a pure "independent" desire).

This is what Kojève, as we recall, translated by saying that desire—strictly "human" desire—is a "desire of desire" or a "desire of the desire of the other." Since "non-animal" desire is what negates and freely transcends every "given," it cannot reflect itself (that is, "manifest" itself) except in another negativity, another freedom—another desire. Desire (from now on adorned with a capital D) is the desire to be desired by and as pure Desire:

Human Desire must be directed toward another Desire. . . . Thus, in the relationship between man and woman, for example, Desire is human only if the one desires, not the body [the animal, natural, "given" body], but the Desire of the other; if he wants "to possess" or "to assimilate" the Desire taken as Desire—that is to say, if he wants to be "desired" or "loved," or, rather, "recognized" in his human value, in his reality as a human individual. Likewise, Desire directed toward a natural object is human only to the extent that it is "mediated" by the Desire of another directed toward the same object: it is human to desire what others desire, because they desire it. Thus, an object perfectly useless from the biological point of view (such as a medal, or the enemy's flag) can be desired because it is the object of other desires. Such a Desire can only be a human Desire, and human reality, as distinguished from animal reality, is created only by action that satisfies such Desires: human history is the history of desired Desires.[20]

That is to say—let us begin here—that human history is a violent, conflictual, murderous history, for this Desire, which Kojève oddly styles "social,"[21] is the most "asocial" or, in any case, the most violent one there is. Indeed, let us suppose that "desire of desire" is interpreted as a desire *to be desired* by the other. This desire (if we restrict ourselves to the strictly Hegelian version) being a desire of oneself, it is evident that my Desire can be satisfied only at the price of the other's Desire. Since there is room for only one self-consciousness, we will have to fight it out to decide which one of us will be able to extort the coveted recognition from the other—who will be the master and who the slave, who the beloved and who the lover. The dialectic of the desire of desire opens unfailingly onto a dialectic of domination and servitude, and that is what Lacan also says more than once with respect to the imaginary relation. That man's desire is for the desire of the other means above all that man is a rival (and not a wolf; 1966, 147) for man:

Desire is first grasped in the other, and in the most confused form. The relativity of human desire in relation to the desire of the other is what we recognize in every reaction of rivalry, of competition, and even in the entire development of civilization, including this sympathetic and fundamental exploitation of man by man whose end is by no means yet in sight, for the reason that it is absolutely structural to, and constitutes, as Hegel acknowledged once and for all, the very structure of the idea of labour [1988a, 147/169; see also 1977a, 26/121].

The same will certainly be true if we define "desire of desire" in terms of desire for the *object* of the other's desire (a strictly Kojèvian illustration of the desire of recognition, to be found nowhere in Hegel). Here again, as Lacan emphasizes (and as, later on, Girard[22] will also stress), rivalry will be ferocious, inevitable. Indeed, since the object of my desire is the same as that of my neighbor's, it will necessarily become an object of rivalry: "The human object is originally mediated through rivalry, through the exacerbation of the relation to the rival, through the relationship of prestige and presence [bearing, *prestance*]. . . . Here we have a destructive and fatal relation among human beings" (1988a, 176–177/199–200, translation modified; see also 1977a, 19/113). Consequently, no matter how we characterize "desire of desire"—whether as desire-of-being-desired or as desire-of-the-object-of-the-desire-of-the-other—the fact remains that it will be congealed in violence and hatred, aggressivity and jealousy, *at least so long as it is interpreted as desire of oneself (desire to be an ego).* As that charming little girl cited by Lacan put it, "Me break Francis head"; and Lacan continues, "She spoke that with assurance and peace of mind. Nonetheless, I . . . don't predict a criminal future for her. She simply displayed the most fundamental structure of the human being on the imaginary plane—to destroy the person who is the site of alienation" (1988a, 172/194).

It is true that, up to this point, nothing really new has flowed from Lacan's pen. This is exactly the way Lacan had always described the "paranoid," "narcissistic," or "identificatory" relation with others, and its reformulation in Kojèvian vocabulary obviously does not change the picture much (we can scarcely even say that the picture has grown darker and more disenchanted). Thus it is really not the description of the imaginary relation that has changed, but rather its interpretation: at the outset of the 1950's, Lacan no longer saw any escape from it—at least not a dialectical one. On the contrary, dialectic *as a whole* (still identified, as Kojève would have it, only with the dialectic of master and slave) was now characterized as imaginary "impasse" (1988a, 223/248) and irreducible alienation. Why is this? It is essentially because Lacan no longer believed that the subject's desire of recognition could be "satisfied" through a recognition of *self* in the other: that alter ego would "never become one with the assumption of [the subject's] desire," and the "You are this" in which the "dialectic of existential recognition" culminates could not, should not any longer, come from a mirror.

This may very well amaze us, since this is precisely the official "Hegelian" solution that Kojève assigns to the dialectic of master and slave, understood as the dialectic of desire, for history (as the "history of desired Desires") is the history of a constant alienation of desire in the desire of the other: the slave recognizes the master, without being recognized by him; and the master, for his part, is recognized only by a slave, "that is to say, someone . . . he does not recognize as a man" (1988a, 223/248); hence the reciprocal dissatisfaction and the historical drudgery of Desire. But all of that is supposed to stop when the slave (alias the proletarian) manages to make himself recognized by the master and at the same time recognizes himself in the master, thereby abolishing their opposition in the universal and homogeneous State (alias the classless society). "You are me" and "I am you": each one recognizes himself in each one, and the desire of desire, finally satisfied, peacefully breathes its last on the bosom of an " 'I' that is [a] 'We' and [a] 'We' that is [an] 'I.' "[23]

It is to precisely all of this (the whole political and totalitarian conception of the "realization" of desire) that Lacan very explicitly takes exception. Indeed, suppose that Kojève's dreamed-of "universal and homogeneous State" were actually to come to pass. Rivalry between egos would be no less venomous and savage, Lacan says: the "scientists" would envy those who amused themselves in nightclubs, and the latter—"the good fellows, the nice guys, the libidinal types" (1988b, 72/92)—would in turn envy the scientists' knowledge. What this little "existentialist" apologue claims to teach us is that desire can never be satisfied with reciprocity of any kind between egos. If desire must be "satisfied"—*that is, recognized* (and Lacan never doubts this for a second)—it will not be through any recognition in a mirror.

Why not? Simply because the desire that is to be recognized is not—is not any longer, for Lacan—a desire to be oneself. The "self" (the "subject") of desire is not identical to himself. He is now "something other" than himself. He is nothing, or dead.

The Absolute Master

This, indeed, was Kojève's essential lesson (at least the one retained at the time by his most attentive listeners and readers), beyond his official "Hegelian" teaching. Bataille has offered the best summary of this unofficial lesson (shared with Lacan, Sartre, Blanchot, and a few others): "Man always becomes *other*. Man is the animal who continually differs from himself."[24]

To say "man" is also to say "Desire," understood as a perpetual desire for "something other." It must not be overlooked that the "Desire" which Kojève supposed would be wholly "satisfied" and "recognized" at the *end* of history is not at all the same one he was talking about *in the beginning*. The latter, we recall, was initially defined as pure negativity: "revealed nothingness," Kojève said, the "revelation of an emptiness."[25] "Transcending" every "given," "exceeding" every "real and static being," this Desire was described as a desire of nothing (or, again, of death), and that, according to Kojève, was precisely why it had to bear upon another Desire. Where is "nothing" to be found, if not in the "unreal void" of Desire?

For there to be Self-Consciousness, Desire must . . . be directed toward a non-natural object, toward something that goes beyond the given reality. Now, the only thing that goes beyond the given reality is Desire itself. . . . Desire, being the revelation of an emptiness, the presence of the absence of a reality, is something essentially different from the desired thing, something other than a thing, than a static and given real being that stays eternally identical to itself."[26]

Here, we touch the heart of what Lacan retains of Kojève in his "own" doctrine of desire, for now we see the very peculiar sense in which Desire is "Desire of the Desire of the other": desiring the Desire of the other, it certainly desires "itself"—*but precisely insofar as it is never "itself," never "identical to itself."* What Kojève ("Hegelianism *oblige*") here calls "Self-Consciousness" is actually anything but consciousness of a *self*. It is much more a question (akin to the "ipseity" of Heidegger's *Dasein*) of an *ek-stasis* and, in this instance, of a radical ek-stasis, since Desire cannot even pose itself in front of itself in order to (re)cognize itself in another itself (another "self-consciousness"). If Desire "recognizes itself" in another Desire, this happens only to the extent that the latter "reveals" to Desire its own non-identity to itself—or, if you will, it happens because the other's Desire does not "reveal" anything to Desire; it reveals Desire's own nothingness. Therefore, this mirror does not reflect anything—and is thus no longer a mirror, but rather a hole, a void, a dizzying, vertiginously distressing escape from all "self-consciousness."

That is why, in the eyes of the "hyper-Kojèvian" Lacan, the so-called desire of recognition can no longer satisfy itself by recognizing *itself* in another desire, for this is desire not of itself but of "something other"—or, better yet, of "being other." From this point on, how could it ever reveal itself, manifest or phenomenalize itself, by posing itself before itself, since it is always "beyond" itself, always ek-stasized in the pure nothingness that "is" "itself"? The only way for desiring man to reveal himself to himself—and thus be "satisfied," since desire of recognition is a question of self-manifestation—would be to plunge into nothingness, to die.

This, moreover, is exactly what Kojève, following Hegel, proposed. Man, he said, manifests his liberty (that is, his Desire) in the fight to the death for pure prestige: "Man's humanity 'comes to light' only in [his] risking his life to satisfy his human Desire—that is, his Desire directed toward another Desire."[27] The problem is that this manifestation is impossible, being the very manifestation of nothingness. Since man (finite man) can "satisfy" his Desire only when he is dead, he will never satisfy it—at least not in the sense of any sort of self-manifestation. As Lacan and Bataille hasten to emphasize, "with" and "against" Kojève (with Heidegger and against Hegel, if you will), death is nowhere phenomenalized in the *Phenomenology of Spirit*, for the good reason that it is avoided, postponed.

Indeed, as we know, at the moment of manifesting its pure negativity (its pure desire), one of the two self-consciousnesses who had been engaged in the fight to the death became frightened of it"self" (it "gave up on its desire," according to Lacan's later formula; 1986, 368 ff.). It felt, says Hegel, anguish over the integrity of its essence, for "it felt the fear of death, the sovereign master (*des absoluten Herrn*)."[28] Thus it preferred to put something—or rather someone: the master, in which it objectivizes its Desire *as if it could be "satisfied," as if that nothingness could be "revealed"*—in front of the perfectly unrevealable void that is it"self." For the one who becomes the slave, then, the master manifests what Lacan, using a term borrowed from Kojève, calls his (the slave's) own impossible *"jouissance"*:[29] "Ah," says the slave to himself, "how happy the master is in enjoying being master!" (1988b, 72/92)

Thus the figure (the *Gestalt*) of the master comes to take the place of the unfaceable, unfigurable Desire of the slave, and that figure is so fundamentally terrible only because the slave *objectivizes* in it his own death, his own nothingness (or, if you will, because in it he *imagines* himself dead). "Knowledge of death," Bataille writes in this regard, "cannot do without a subterfuge—the spectacle," for "death does not actually reveal anything. . . . In order for man finally to reveal himself, he would have to die, but he would have to do it living, by *seeing* [my emphasis] himself cease to be"—which he cannot do, Bataille continues, except through the expedient of the image, the spectacle, in which "it is a question . . . of *identifying* [my emphasis] with some character who dies and of believing that we ourselves die while we are still alive. Besides, imagination pure and simple is enough."[30]

"Image," "spectacle," "gaze," "identification": we recognize here the master-words of the imaginary relation according to Lacan. Thus there is no reason to be surprised if we find in Lacan exactly the same idea as in Bataille (with whom he had very probably discussed it), and in relation to the same motifs. The specular image, Lacan now says, presents to man his own unpresentable death, in the sense of his seeing himself in it as he will never see himself: "This image of the master, which is what he sees in the form of a specular image, becomes confused in him with the image of death. Man can be in the presence of the absolute master. He is in his presence from the beginning, whether he has been taught this or not, insofar as he is subjected to this image" (1988a, 149/172). And "only to man does this image reveal its deadly significance. . . . But that image is given to him only as the image of the other, that is, it is stolen from him" (1966, 346)—stolen indeed, since his *own* death can never reveal *"itself"*: "Death is never experienced as such, is it—it is never real. Man is only ever afraid of an imaginary fear"

(1988a, 223/249). And again, at the end of the 1953 lecture on the individual myth of the neurotic:

One can say that the theory of narcissism . . . explains certain facts that remain enigmatic in Hegel. After all, for the dialectic of the fight to the death, the fight for pure prestige, even to begin, it is still necessary for death to remain unrealized, because otherwise the whole dialectic would have stopped for lack of combatants; death must be imagined. And indeed, imaginary and imagined death is what is at stake in the narcissistic relation. Imaginary and imagined death, insofar as it is introduced into the Oedipal drama, is equally the issue in the formation of the neurotic—and perhaps also, to a certain extent, in something that far surpasses the formation of the neurotic: namely, the existential attitude characteristic of modern man [1978a, 306–307].

The neurotic (modern man), rather than confront the deadly void of his desire (or castration, as Lacan will say later on), prefers to vie with the imaginary alter ego who, he believes, frustrates him in his *jouissance*. In this sense, Oedipal rivalry is a pure neurotic *alibi*:

In that rivalry with the father . . . lies the narrow footbridge thanks to which the subject does not feel directly invaded, directly swallowed up by the yawning chasm that opens itself to him as pure and simple confrontation with the anguish of death . . . indeed, we know that the death of the father, whenever it occurs, is felt by the subject as the disappearance . . . of that shield of intervention, or substitution, that the father [forms between the subject and] the absolute Master—that is, death [SVI, 7 January 1959].[31]

And so the "dialectic of the Oedipal drama," with its classically triangular structure, was nothing but a *defense* intended to occult the undialecticizable "fourth element" that is death (1978a, 306): better to ceaselessly resurrect the image of the rival than be confronted by the abyss of desire, better guiltily to identify with the one who forbids *jouissance* than be handed over to the void of its absence.

In this way, for example, the hysteric "identifies himself with the spectacle" of his desire, by placing "his ego in the third party by whose mediation [he] enjoys (*jouit*)" (1977a, 87–88/303–304) (an allusion to the Freudian concept of hysterical identification). The obsessional, by contrast, "shows" himself to "the spectator, invisible from the stage, to whom he is united by the mediation of death" (1977a, 87–88/303–304). Rather than confront his desire to be the "absolute Master, death," he prefers to await the death of the master while offering him the expiating spectacle of his labor (an allusion to the ambivalent ritualism of the obsessional according to Freud): "He *is* in the anticipated moment of the master's death, from which moment he will begin to live, but in the meantime he identifies himself with the master as dead, and as a result of this he is himself already dead" (1977a, 100/314; see also 1966, 452–453; 1977a, 309/811).

Already dead, yet still alive (living-dead): the obsessional is "dead" only by means of an identification with the master, just as the hysteric "realizes" his desire only by identification with the third, enjoying, party. Therefore, as we see, the manifestation of death (the "realization" of desire) requires a whole theater. More precisely, it requires the whole distance of theatrical representation—that is, the protective spacing that permits one to fulfill desire *in effigy*, without suffering its consequences. Only a specular identification—indeed, only a specular mimesis—allows one to *see* oneself dead. As Freud also wrote, "It is indeed impossible to imagine our own death; and whenever we attempt to do so we can perceive that we are in fact still present as spectators."[32] Thus, he continues, "in the realm of fiction . . . we die with the hero with whom we have identified ourselves; yet we survive him and are ready to die again just as safely with another hero."[33]

In any case, we note that this in no way prevents Freud from admitting that we do *die* by identifying with the hero who realizes our desire.[34] The whole Freudian theory of phantasmatic "wish-fulfillment" (*Wunscherfüllung*) remains fundamentally incomprehensible if we do not admit, "under" the structure of spec(tac)ular representation, a non-representative and non-specular identification (a non-visual *mimesis*, if you will). If phantasy has a "psychic reality," as Freud constantly reiterates, it is because in it I *am* the identificatory character who "fulfills" the wish—immediately, without the mediation of any representation, any theater, or any mirror.[35] It is, however, just at this crucial point (crucial, since on it depends our whole conception of desire, of representation, and of their relationships) that Lacan implicitly separates himself from Freud: identification, in his eyes, can neither "fulfill" the wish nor "satisfy" desire. Indeed, for Lacan—insofar as his only concept of identification is specular, spectacular, and imaginary—it goes without saying that to identify with the dead one (with the one who enjoys [*jouit*]) amounts to identifying with a simple *image* of death, and thus to postponing enjoyment (*jouissance*) *itself.*

By the same token, *jouissance,* understood to be what the image both occults and presents, is transferred beyond the specular image. *Jouissance,* which is nothing—nothing that could ever be presented—*is none the less thought of as what is "hidden," "veiled," "disguised" by the image that represents it.* The imaginary, which for Freud is the very "place" of desire's fulfillment (its "other scene," understood as a "beyond all scenes"), becomes for Lacan the place of its un-fulfillment (or, if you will, of its "fictional" fulfillment). With respect to the deadly truth of desire, no specular image can any longer be anything but a decay: the more I identify with such and such an image of my desire, the more I avoid my "self" as pure desire of death, as pure abysmal ek-stasis in the "nothing" of the other's desire. Under these conditions, how could such an image ever "become one" with the "assumption" of my desire? On the contrary, that image would actually be its *méconnaissance,* its denial and refusal. The truth of desire—the truth of the subject—from now on is "*beyond*" the mirror, *behind* the reflections that claim to present it.

4

How Can We Speak the Truth?

> For God's sake!—quick!—quick!—put me to sleep—
> or, quick!—waken me!—quick!—*I say to you that I
> am dead*!
>   —Edgar Allan Poe [1]

The imaginary, we have just been saying, is a "denial" of death, a *méconnaissance* of desire, a "defense" against the anxiety of the absolute Master. Must we conclude, then, that desire is *repressed* in the specular relation (in the "imaginary transference")? Indeed, according to good Freudian doctrine, it could be argued that desire—or, rather, the wish (*Wunsch*) [2]—is fulfilled "in the imaginary," in phantasy (*Phantasie*), only on condition that repression and censorship forbid its fulfillment in reality. "*A dream*," Freud declares, "*is a (disguised) fulfillment of a (suppressed or repressed) wish*," [3] and the same goes for all phantasmatic productions, not to mention the symptoms and transferences that prolong them. To reconcile Freud and Lacan, then, could we say that the analyst's action consists in disengaging desire from the various imaginary formations in which it is *deceptively* "fulfilled" because of repression?

What *is* the goal of an analysis (and, more generally, of an analytic interpretation)? To become conscious of the repressed wish, says Freud; to recognize the desire of the subject, says Lacan ("That the subject should come to recognize and to name his desire, that is the efficacious action of analysis"; 1988b, 228–229/267). Isn't

this the same thing? Once the Freudian *Wunsch* has been reinterpreted in terms of Kojèvian "Desire," doesn't Lacan, in sum, propose to conceive of analysis as an unveiling of desire from its imaginary coverings—in short, as a progression through the realm of
truth, as a "passage from ignorance to knowledge"?

Yes; but how can we continue to speak of the repression, disguising, veiling of desire, if this repression represses *nothing*, veils
nothing? And how can we unveil "nothing"? How can we speak
(name, recognize) the truth of desire?

"Herr, What Is there to Be Said?"

Let us take a famous example of repression: the forgetting of
the name Signorelli, an incident that Freud analyzed in the opening
chapter of *Psychopathology of Everyday Life*. Freud is on a train
that is taking him from Ragusa to Herzegovina, and he is talking
with a fellow traveler. At one point in the conversation, he has just
mentioned the impressive frescoes in Orvieto cathedral, representing the Apocalypse (Death, Judgment, Hell, and Heaven) and
painted by . . . by whom? Botticelli? Boltraffio? No, that's not it.
Freud can see the *images* of the Apocalypse quite clearly before
him—and even the image of the painter himself.[4] Nevertheless, no
matter how hard he tries, he can no longer remember the painter's
name: Signorelli. Why not?

It was, Freud tells us, as if this name had been swallowed up by
the repression of other thoughts that the immediately preceding
conversation had evoked. This conversation concerned the customs
of the Turks living in *Bosnia* and *Herzegovina*, especially their fa-
talistic attitude toward death: "*Herr* [Sir], what is there to be said?"
was their customary reply to the doctor who gave them the bad
news. At that moment, Freud had also thought of their diametri-
cally opposed attitude toward the loss of sexual potency: "*Herr*,
you must know that if *that* comes to an end, then life is of no
value." But Freud had said nothing about this to his companion,
out of a sense of propriety. Sex? Death? At any rate, Freud preferred
not to think about it any more, shaken as he was at the time by the
news, which he had learned at *Trafoi*, about the suicide of one of
his patients, who suffered from "an incurable sexual disorder." He,

too, *Herr Doktor* Freud, had failed in the face of death. Well, what was there for him to say?

Right away, he said what there was to say, without saying it, by forgetting (repressing) the name Signorelli into the Hell of the expressible, where it was henceforth to burn along with *Herr* (*Signor*), in *Herz*egovina. All that remains now are halves of words (rather like the chosen ones in the fresco of Judgment, whose half-bodies emerge from the earth where they had been lying): *Bottic*e*lli,* *Bol*traffio . . . which gives us the following "fresco": [5]

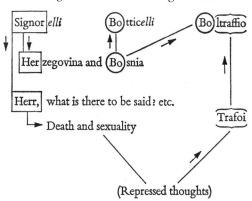

(Repressed thoughts)

Therefore, something that Freud left unsaid brought on this complex play of displacements and substitutions. But what, exactly, was it? "Repressed thoughts," Freud contents himself with saying—leaving us the trouble of guessing that they had to do with some guilty wish, irreconcilable with the conscious ego. A death wish regarding his patient, perhaps? Was he afraid that the phantom would return, revive—like the chosen ones in the fresco of Orvieto—to judge him? We will never know: Freud, in this auto-analytic fragment, ultimately unveils himself very little (unlike *Signorelli,* *Sigmund* does not leave us his self-portrait).[6]

But at least we know that the repressed (Hell) is formed of "thoughts," of *Gedanken*—in short, of *cogitationes,* of representations. This conforms to Freud's established theory: repression is not carried out on the drive (*Trieb*), but only on the drive's psychic "representatives" (*Repräsentanten*), "representations" (*Vorstellungen*)—"ideas," "thoughts," "phantasies," "memories," and so on. A drive as such (or "instinct," as Strachey prefers to translate), Freud says in a famous passage, escapes from the opposition "conscious/unconscious": "I am in fact of the opinion that the antithesis of conscious and unconscious is not applicable to instincts. An instinct can never become an object of consciousness (*Objekt des Bewusstseins*)—only the idea that represents it (*die Vorstellung, die ihr repräsentiert*) can. Even in the unconscious, moreover, an instinct cannot be represented (*repräsentiert sein*) otherwise than by an idea."[7] In other words, only the representation can be shown to *or* hidden from consciousness (in the manner of an object, *Objekt*), and that is why repression, according to Freud, has no other prey. Unable to repress the drive (or, if you will, the affect that is its non-objectal, non-representational "representative"), repression, for lack of anything better, falls back on the "thoughts" attached to the drive. In a word, repression is carried out on a "wish," but in the sense that this *Wunsch*, as Lacan insists, is a "wish" (*vœu*), a desire that is *formulated* ("conceived of," "represented") in the unconscious (1977a, 256/620 ff.).

Since the repressed wish belongs to the order of representation, we can see by the same token that its unconscious statement, as Freud often says, can be "translated" into a conscious representation. Thus, in our example, the "repressed thoughts" have actually been hidden/replaced by other representations (by the name Signorelli, and then by what Freud calls a "sequence of letters").[8] But nothing in Freud's theory opposes the final unveiling of these thoughts to consciousness—once it is actually a question, "even in the unconscious," of "thoughts." In short, what has been silenced (the desire, the "thoughts-of-desire") should be able to be spoken; and, according to Freud, this is exactly what happens in a successful analysis (or interpretation).

Is it the same in Lacan's theory of desire? Not at all. Not, of course, that Lacan questions Freud's having made the connection between desire and representation (or, if you will, between the unconscious and discourse); on the contrary—in Lacan, this connection excludes all others. Whereas Freud, in spite of everything, did not neglect to leave room for a non-representational unconscious ("unconscious feelings" or a non-repressed "Id," for example), Lacan settles the matter more roughly: there is no drive that is not always already represented, no desire that is not always already articulated in *Vorstellungsrepräsentanten*—that is (the equivalence is invariable in Lacan), in statements, in "signifiers" (1966, 714). In Lacan, however (and this changes everything), this articulation in discourse is also the very thing that makes desire "inarticulable" and "inexpressible" (1977a, 253/616). In contrast to what happens in Freud, desire is now what can never be (*un*)said—necessarily so, because to speak is to speak (of) death—that is, of what "negates discourse" (1966, 379).

Indeed, this is the interpretation of Freud's forgetting that Lacan proposes in the first seminar (1977b) and elsewhere: the last word of Freud's desire is death, and thus there is no last word of desire, any more than there is a definitive interpretation or final unveiling of truth. What does Freud repress by forgetting the name Signorelli? "*Signor* along with *Herr*, the absolute Master, is sucked up and repressed by the apocalyptic wind that arises in Freud's unconscious, on the echo of the conversation he is having: the disturbance . . . of a theme that has just emerged by way of an earlier theme—which, indeed, is that of accepted death" (1966, 447; see also 1977b, 27/29).

"Absolute Master," "accepted death": the "return to Freud," as we see, once again takes place through Kojève and the "fight to the death for pure prestige." The truth of Freud's forgetting is certainly a desire, but this desire in turn has no truth other than suicide and the sovereign acceptance of death. If Freud is guilty, it is not (as we might have expected, following Freudian doctrine) because of some unspeakable "Oedipal" death-wish, but rather because he "gave up on his desire" (1986, 368)—his desire of nothingness.

What Freud had to say, and did not say, was speech[9] at the level of death, a "veridical speech" that would speak his desire and the "deepest secret of [his] being": "God knows that it can reverberate a great deal, this veridical speech. What is at issue?—if not the absolute, namely death, which is present in it, and which Freud tells us that he preferred . . . not to confront . . . too closely" (1988a, 48/59). And so he alienates his desire in the other, by identifying with his companion and with what he imagines the other's desire to be. Rather than carry death in speech, he keeps silent for propriety's sake (What will *he* think of *me*?):

The impossibility in which Freud finds himself, the impossibility of citing the name Signorelli in the dialogue he is pursuing with his colleague (in this case, his fellow traveler), is due to the fact that by censoring, in his prior conversation with the other, everything that the latter's words suggested (as much by their content as by the memories that they trailed along with them) about the relation of man and doctor with death, and thus with the absolute Master, *Herr*, *signor*—by censoring all this, Freud literally left behind in his partner (and thus cut off from himself) the broken half (let this be understood in the most material sense of the term) of the sword of speech; and for a time, precisely the time during which he continued addressing his partner, he could no longer use that term as signifying material, because it remained attached to the repressed signification [1966, 379].

Repression = Return of the Repressed

So far, so good. Freud, we could say, *forgot* his desire in the other, *repressed* in him the "truthful" point of his speech—and this is why, instead of the sovereign *Signor*, he has only the debris of desire, halves of words: *bo* . . . , *elli* . . . , *traffio*. . . . In Hegelian terms, the slave defers and alienates his desire by entering into the mediation of labor and is thereby reduced to picking up the master's crumbs. In Freudian terms, desire, once social censorship has been internalized, can express itself only through "formations of compromise"—symptoms, slips of the tongue, forgetting, and bungled actions.

There is just one problem: Could the desire in question have been expressed *before* its repression? Above all, "can we content ourselves here with speaking of repression," as Lacan immediately asks himself (1966, 379)? A very interesting question indeed, and the answer is no less interesting: yes and no.

Yes, Lacan begins, this forgetting of the "Lord" (*Seigneur*) is a true repression, in the sense that repression is equivalent to not (being capable of) speaking the truth: "We can certainly affirm that [repression] is there, simply by Freud's overdeterminations of the phenomenon. We can also, by the actuality of its circumstances, confirm the range of what I want you to understand in the formula: the unconscious is the discourse of the Other. The man who, in the act of speaking, breaks the bread of truth with his counterpart, shares the lie" (1966, 379). Indeed, to speak to the other is first of all to defer desire, to not say it, and therefore to not *be able* to say it: thus it becomes unavailable to the subject, "unconscious," "repressed" as it is in that Other (capital O) which is the discourse addressed to the other (small o). To speak, in this first sense, is equivalent to not speaking the truth: it is to break the *sword* of speech, come to terms with the "counterpart" instead of fighting with him; therefore, in its sharing of bread rather than death with him, it is to lie, to hide the nocturnal truth of desire. Every society, insofar as it rests on such a symbolic exchange, Lacan says (1977a, 61–62/ 272 ff.) following Lévi-Strauss, presupposes the "breaking" that transforms the sword into a tessera, into a *sumbolon* (1966, 380)— and, by the same token, it presupposes the "sharing of the lie" that is repression and the forgetting of desire.

But, Lacan says, *no*—repression is still something other than lying, and forgetting is not simply a mistake. As for "the speech omitted here, how could it not be extinguished in the presence of being-toward-death?" (1966, 379). The truth of desire cannot actually be spoken, since it is precisely what cuts off speech. Consequently, repression can no longer be reduced to a lying by omission, a "not saying the truth." On the contrary, it must now be conceded that *this lie is the truth*, insofar as truth is literally unspeakable. Indeed, repression represses and forgets *nothing*; thus, strictly speaking, there is no longer any question of a dissimulating veil behind which desire could *hide*.

Desire, Kojève says, is the nothing (the negation) of everything that is. Thus, Lacan concludes, repression (which negates, denies, reneges, and so on) constitutes its paradoxical "presentation," for (as he writes here, in extremely condensed formulations) death, which is certainly "what negates discourse," is also what "introduces negation" into discourse (an allusion to Kojève's theses about the roots of discursive negativity in human finitude).[10] "The negativity of discourse" (or of the "symbolic order," as Lacan still says) is thus its "manifestation," in the sense that it "causes to be what is not" (1966, 379–380). Indeed, how could desire—the "revealed nothingness" of which Kojève speaks—"reveal" itself, if not by negating everything that could present it, incarnate it, realize it, and satisfy it? Thus, for Lacan, desire "reveals" itself always and only through *Verneinung*, through the negation that makes a thing present by its absence. "That is *not* my mother," Freud's patient says about the content of a dream, thus presenting the void of his desire in the absence of his mother.[11] "Go away!" ("*Fort!*") says the little boy to the reel as he throws it away—and his desire is "there" ("*Da!*") in the distancing of its object.[12] "Botticelli? Boltraffio? *No*, that's not it," Freud says to himself—and there it is, death is "present" (1988a, 48/59) in its repression, in its forgetting.

In other words, repression is the "revelation" of that non-being: desire. "Repression and the return of the repressed," Lacan repeats after Freud,[13] "are merely the inside and the outside of the same thing" (1981, 21, 94; 1988a, 191/216), and for him this means that repression is the *truth* of desire, its one and only (re)presentation. To repress is undoubtedly to lie, to not speak the truth of desire (the "veridical speech" that Freud should have spoken, instead of saying something else to his traveling companion); but to repress is also to speak the truth—the empty, deadly truth that can only be (not) said, "half-said" (*mi-dite*), since all adequacy of discourse to the "thing itself" of desire is radically *forbidden* (*interdite*). It follows, in the strange "logic" established here, that there is only a lying truth, only repressed desire. The forgetting of the name Signorelli, far from being an "error of memory," is the very truth of Freud's desire.

"I, Truth, Lie"

Here, we feel that we are really "getting very warm," as Lacan says at the moment when he enters on "Freudian truth" and the "revelation" of the unconscious made to Freud (1977a, 158/509). What is this burning truth, which we reach only in blindness (or blindfolded, since there seems to be a game of hide-and-go-seek going on)? We need not look very far, since Lacan leads us by the hand, citing the "being-toward-death" in the presence of which Freud's speech could only "be extinguished." The allusion to *Being and Time* is clear: this "Freudian truth" is apparently none other than the *alētheia* of Martin Heidegger—to whom, by the way, Lacan's references become more and more insistent, and whose "sovereign word" (1977a, 175/528) begins to compete seriously with that of the "master," Kojève.[14]

Indeed, to say that repression (that is, forgetting) is the truth of desire amounts to saying that this truth reveals *nothing* ("causes to be what is not") and thus veils itself in its very unveiling. As we know, this is the principal characteristic of truth as rethought by Heidegger in terms of presentation/withdrawal of Being. "Truth," as Heidegger continually recalls, is called *a-lētheia* in Greek, which literally means "unveiling." In other words, what is "true" in this initial sense "is" what holds itself "unveiled" in the light, what presents itself in the "opening" of the "non-occulted," of the "non-hidden." Prior to any truth conceived in terms of "correctness" of gaze or "accuracy" of enunciation, "truth" is a pure offering *to* a gaze—and thus, by the same token, a pure withdrawal *in the face of* that gaze.

To see (to be ek-statically open to what opens itself, in what Heidegger calls the "dimensionality" or the "lightening" of Being) is always to see *something*, and thus not to see something else. Unless one is God, one never sees the *two* sides of the tree simultaneously, the *six* faces of the cube. The dimension of the transcendent exteriority (where philosophy has always placed the problem of truth) is necessarily the dimension of the shown/hidden, and the same is true of the transcendental and ek-static archispatiality of Heideggerian "dimensionality," although here the structure of the shown/hidden is thought in its essence. For Heidegger, the "revealing" (apophantic) essence of truth is to "hide"—what? Nothing, no being (for such a being, once unveiled, would in turn veil, and so on). The *alētheia* (according to Heidegger, still hammering away) inevitably carries a portion of occultation and forgetting (*lēthē*): nothing can unveil itself in the opening of presence except on condition of occulting—not this or that, but its own essential *disocculta-tion*. Unveiled, the being-present "veils" the unveiling itself—which is nothing, for it "is" the very thing that opens the possibility of everything that is (being, present, and so on). It follows that truth is essentially an unveiling (a presentation, an "offering" of being) that is equivalent to a veiling (since Being, in its very disclosure, withdraws into veiling).

A passage from Heidegger's article "*Logos*" will perhaps state the matter even more clearly, and it is worth the trouble of citing here, for it is probably one of the principal "sources" of what is, as we shall see, Lacan's rather peculiar Heideggerianism.[15] In this article, Heidegger closely ties *alētheia*, understood as (un)veiling, to *logos*, even going so far as to make the two terms synonyms. Note, however, that this in no way means that language "speaks" the truth; even less does it mean that language, by this very fact, is the condition of truth. Just as *alētheia* initially has nothing to do with truth (understood as adequate judgment or statement), so *logos* originally has nothing to do with language (understood as *phonē semantikē*, a sonorous emission "signifying" or "expressing" something). *Logos*, as Heidegger was already saying in *Being and Time*, is a "letting something be seen" (*apophansis*),[16] and here he says the same thing again, defining *logos* etymologically as a "gathering-presencing" that "lets lie before":

Λόγος lays that which is present before and down into presencing. . . . Because the Λόγος lets lie before us what lies before as such, it discloses [unveils] what is present in its presencing. But disclosure is 'Aλήθεια. This and Λόγος are the Same. Λέγειν lets ἀληθέα, the unconcealed as such, lie before us. . . . All disclosure releases what is present from concealment. Disclosure needs concealment. The 'A-Λήθεια rests in Λήθη, drawing from it and laying before us whatever remains deposited in Λήθη. Λόγος is *in itself and at the same time* a revealing and a concealing. It is 'Aλήθεια.[17]

Before any characterization of truth in terms of enunciation, propositional judgment, adequacy/inadequacy of discourse to things or to itself, we must think of truth *and* language as a veiling unveiling. This is also to say that, before any opposition of truth to error, we must think of truth and language as irreducible "errancy" (*Irren*). This, indeed, is the unavoidable conclusion of this whole line of reasoning. The *lēthē* inherent in *alētheia*, since it is the forgetting of *nothing*, is strictly insurmountable and can thus no longer be qualified as error unless we add that this "error" is "truth" itself: "The disclosure of beings as such is simultaneously and intrinsically the concealing of being as a whole. In the simultaneity of disclosure and concealing, errancy holds sway. Errancy and the concealing of what is concealed belong to the primordial essence of truth."[18]

With this brief recapitulation of Heidegger's doctrine of truth, it is certainly easier to see how Lacan came to make repression and forgetting the paradoxical "truth" of desire. Repression—insofar as it is, for Lacan, tied to the speech by which man breaks the bread of truth with his counterpart and shares the lie—is heir to all the formal characteristics of the *logos-alētheia*: the "lying" subject speaks the "truth" of his desire, to the extent that this desire, in its pure nullity, appears only by disappearing, and so on. In short, *logos*-repression is the *alētheia* of desire.

But all of this should not conceal the important modifications that Lacan simultaneously brings to Heidegger's concept of *alētheia*. Indeed, whatever their apparent formal kinship may be, Lacan's "truth" cannot be purely and simply reduced to Heidegger's (making the latter the "truth" of the former). Lacan's truth, no matter how unfathomable and repressed, remains none the less the truth of a desire—that is, of a *subject*. It could hardly be otherwise in psychoanalysis. Isn't the patient invited to recount *himself*—that is, to reveal himself to himself through autorepresentation and autoenunciation? Thus Lacan tirelessly recalls that Freud's "domain" "is that of the truth of the subject. . . . What is at stake is the realization of the truth of the subject, like a dimension peculiar to it which must be detached in its distinctiveness (*originalité*) in relation to the very notion of reality" (1988a, 20–21/29). Indeed, in analysis it is unimportant whether the discourse of the subject conforms to reality; what is important is that the subject speak himself in his truth. Consequently, for Lacan—agreeing, on this point, with Kojève's teaching—truth is essentially distinct from reality. Better yet, truth *is opposed* to reality insofar as it arises only in the discourse through which the subject speaks himself by negating or "nihilating" the "Real"—for example (an example par excellence), in the form of "error." [19] In a word, the subject "realizes" his truth only in the discourse of autorepresentation or autoenunciation, by reducing reality (including his own) to nothing—the classic move that we recognize from Cartesian doubt (or even the "path of doubt and despair" spoken of by Hegel). Formally, the Lacanian definition of the "truth of the subject" is nothing other than truth as subjective certainty—which, by the same token, takes us far from Heidegger, for in Heidegger's eyes nothing is more foreign to the original essence of truth than truth thought of as the certainty of a subject assuring himself of himself in his representations or discourse. On the contrary, truth as subjective representation is instead the total oblivion of truth's original essence, as soon as it makes truth (as the "saying"—or "thought"—*of Being*) the certainty of a subject who speaks and thinks *himself* as Being ("I think, I am").

Nevertheless, it is precisely this same concept of truth, as auto-representation or autoenunciation, that Lacan, in his irrepressible combinatory passion, bizarrely mixes with Heidegger's *alētheia*. For the Freudo-Hegelian that Lacan continues to be, the "truth" is the word by which a subject speaks *himself*, represents and exposes *himself*, through the mediation of the inter-subjective interlocution (whose model, let us stress once more, is furnished by psychoanalytic interlocution in its detachment from any reality). As for the "Being" thus unveiled, it likewise remains the "nucleus of *our* being" (1977a, 173/526, 228/587; my emphasis), just as, in the prosopopoeia of "The Freudian Thing," truth herself rather brusquely tells her "lover," Heidegger, "In any case, in order to judge your defeat, isn't it enough to see me escape, first, from the dungeon of the fortress where you are so sure of detaining me by placing me not in yourself, but in being itself? I wander around in what you take to be the least true essentially: in dreams," and so on (1977a, 122/410); translation modified).

Thus we see that Lacan wholly maintains the concept of truth as the autoenunciation of a subject while at the same time, in agreement with Heidegger's *logos-alētheia*, making it an enunciation of nothing (or, if you will, of desire: "Whatever animates, what any enunciation speaks of, belongs to desire"; 1977b, 141/129). The result of this strange montage is that, under Lacan's pen, the unveiling/veiling of Being becomes an unveiling/veiling of the subject to himself. The "auto" (that is, the subject) of the enunciation having been very literally reduced to nothing (to the nothing that "is" Being and/or desire as no-thing), we can deduce, and very logically indeed, that truth is a (dis)appearance of the subject of the enunciation into the subject of the statement.[20] The subject, in sum, heir to all the features of Heidegger's Being, is now considered to speak himself in every statement—but also to disappear in every statement, since the subject speaks himself as nothing and as pure *desire* of self. Truth/certainty, classically defined since Descartes by the statement's subject being identical to the subject of the enunciation, now becomes—once it has passed through the burning fire of *alētheia*—the non–self-identity of the "same" subject.

Therefore, this truth says, "*I*, truth, speak"—and not (a statement more in agreement with Heidegger) "*Logos* is *alētheia*." We know the famous prosopopoeia in which truth, through Lacan's voice (1966, 866–867), "speaks of herself" (of herself and all alone [*d'elle-même*]) "in Freud's mouth" (1977a, 121/408):

So for you I am the enigma of her who vanishes as soon as she appears, men who try so hard to hide me under the tawdry finery of your proprieties! But I am prepared to believe that your embarrassment is sincere, for even when you take it upon yourselves to serve as my heralds, you place no greater value on wearing my colors than your own, which are like you yourselves, phantoms that you are. Where, then, will I pass into you? Where was I before I entered you? Perhaps one day I will tell you? But so that you will find me where I am, I will teach you by what sign you will recognize me. Men, listen, I am giving you the secret. I, truth, speak [1977a, 121/408–409].

This is a fabulous statement, which we must certainly not construe in the sense of its presenting a determined subject (Freud and/ or Lacan) who speaks the "thing itself" and thus is *himself* (the same as) the truth. As Lacan writes, in an obvious allusion to Klossowski's *Le Bain de Diane* (Diana's Bath),[21] truth is "akin to death . . . Diana perhaps" (1977a, 145/436), and so no subject can claim to possess her. Actaeon will never rejoin the Virgin Hunter in the place where she is Her-Self, before the event of her mortal and impure appearance, and this means that the identity between subject and truth (between speaker and statement) is radically forbidden, impossible—as is the "real," where they would be at the "same place" (1977b, 49/49). Thus the "real," as Kojève taught, is abolished as soon as spoken, and this is equally (and even especially) true of the reality of whoever speaks *himself* in discourse. No one, *in reality*, can speak "those intolerable words: 'I, truth, speak . . .'" (1966, 867): "To hear those words as they should be spoken—in horror—think of the unnameable thing that, by being able to speak them, would reach the being of language" (1966, 867). It would be a sacred horror indeed, for this "thing," *if* it could speak itself in reality, would say, "I am dead" (as in Poe's "The Facts in the Case of M. Valdemar," discussed by Lacan in 1988b, 231/270, and in 1966, 486). But this thing without a name (the torn flesh that Actaeon became in the teeth of Diana's dogs, the foul carcass of Poe's mesmerized character): Just how could it say "I"?

Thus the statement "I, truth, speak," rather than saying what it seems to say, signifies just the opposite—that is, its essential and radical *inadequacy*—to the one who speaks it. The "I" in the statement is not the same as the "he" who, *speaking* himself in it, absents himself in the statement by presenting himself in it. The truth, she who says "I, truth, speak," speaks the truth—which is precisely that she can *only* be spoken (hence Lacan's rejection of any metalanguage claiming to speak the truth *about* truth: "No language can speak the truth about truth, since truth establishes herself by speaking, and by having no other means to do so" 1966, 867–868). And so she speaks herself mischievously—fictionally, mythically—because she "hides herself" as soon as she is spoken ("as soon as she has appeared") and because this is the only possible truth, separated from any reality that would come to vouch for her. Where will Actaeon ever see θεά, the Goddess,[22] in her splendid nudity, if not in the fable ("Diana's Bath," "The Freudian Thing") where he speaks her impossible theophany and tells her untellable revelation?

With these details clarified, the fact remains that this truth, when she reveals herself "in Freud's mouth" and through Lacan's "voice," says, "*I*, truth, speak." Like it or not, the Word that reveals only itself is the word of a subject who speaks *himself* in his truth; witness the shifter "I," which designates him in the statement. (What would become of Lacan's demonstration if the "I" were to disappear?) Even if this word is no one's word, it is still the word and the truth *of* (no) one—*of* the silent mouth of Freud-Actaeon, for example, through which it reveals itself in so fabulously loquacious a manner. In the fable of Diana, it is truly *himself* (the secret of his desire) that Actaeon seeks in the Goddess, just as it is the *Freudian* thing that (un)veils itself in the truth-who-speaks "in Freud's mouth." Here, *alētheia* is in reality (if one can use that phrase) the "nothing" (the "hole in the real"; 1988a, 271/297) that the inexpressible subject of the enunciation (or of "discourse," as Kojève would prefer to say) becomes at the very moment when he speaks himself. Abolished in his reality, he emerges into it in the truth of his *Being*, which is to be precisely nothing (nothing "real"), as Lacan says elsewhere, in one of his many commentaries on Freud's *Wo Es war, soll Ich werden*:

There where it was just now, there where it was for a while, between an extinction which is still glowing and a birth that is retarded, "I" can come into being and disappear from what I say. An enunciation that denounces itself, a statement that renounces itself . . . what remains here if not the trace of what *must* be in order to fall from Being? . . . Being of non-Being, that is how *I* as subject comes on the scene [1977a, 300/801−802].

Since truth, as unveiling/veiling of Being in beings, has been re-interpreted once and for all as an unveiling/veiling of the subject in his "auto"enunciation (or "auto"representation), the result is that truth, under Lacan's pen, reveals itself in *lies, mistakes, deceptions,* and *fiction*. This is the second important modification that Lacan brings to Heidegger's *alētheia*: its total (and, from a strictly Hei-deggerian point of view, aberrant) reformulation in terms of ade-quacy/inadequacy to the thing and/or to itself. Indeed, to the extent that Lacan continues (in the tradition of Kojève) to circulate in the problematic of (auto)enunciation (of *logos* as "discourse," "judg-ment," "reason," "concept," "representation," and so on), he is brought by the same token to reinscribe the unfathomable "logic" of *alētheia* into *logic* pure and simple, even if he must therefore constantly (and complacently) use paradoxes, aporias, and auto-destructive "formalizations." Thus, whereas Heidegger spoke of an initial "errancy" of truth, attempting to indicate a "truth" prior to the alternatives "true"/"false," Lacan, for his part, said that "error is the habitual incarnation of truth," that truth "emerges in the most clearcut representative of the mistake" (1988a, 263/289, 265/292), and that truth has a "fictional organization" or "structure" (1977a, 306/808; 1966, 17, 451, 742). Moreover, whereas Heidegger wrote that "*das Ding dingt*," patiently kneading language to make it say the truth of "the thing," outside any problematic of adequacy or in-adequacy of discourse to *res*,[23] Lacan abruptly announced that "the thing *speaks* of itself." Whereas Heidegger attempted to think of truth beyond any "representation" of a "reality,"[24] Lacan would immediately translate, saying that truth distinguishes itself from re-ality (1977a, 306/808; 1966, 740)—indeed, it sets itself against reality (1966, 351). And whereas Heidegger proposed understand-ing truth as a retracted gift of Being, Lacan quite simply said that the truth is spoken in cheating, trickery, and lying.

What does Truth—Woman and Diana that she is—say in the fabulous and fabling mouth of Freud-Actaeon-Lacan? She says that she is the "great cheater" (the "great show-off," as Klossowski wrote[25]):

If the cunning of reason, no matter how disdainful of you, stayed open to your faith, I—truth—would be . . . the great deceiver, since it is not only through duplicity that my ways pass but also through the crack too narrow to find without dissembling and through the inaccessible cloud of dreams, through the pointless fascination of the mediocre and the seductive impasse of absurdity. Seek, dogs that you become upon hearing me. . . . Enroll to my call, and howl at my voice. There you are, lost already, I give way, I defy you, I slip away: you say that I defend myself" (1966, 411).

Truth says, in short, "I am lying" (the well-known "liar's paradox"), which, strictly understood, in no way means that truth is an error (a bit earlier, Lacan has been railing against "the shoddy Nietzschean notion of the lie of life"; 1977a, 118/405); it means that truth, as truth, speaks itself and reveals itself in its own concealment. This would bring us back once more to *alētheia* except for Lacan's intentionally "logical" formulation and, especially, for his insistence on lying and cheating. Here, we see, truth is *all the more true* for being false and deceptive. There is in Lacan a sort of privileging of the lie, and this is because the lie, being inadequate to the thing it speaks about, is better able to reveal the truth of the subject as "speaking thing" (or as *res cogitans*, since Lacan also explicitly compares the "I lie" to the "I think"; cf. 1977b, 140–141/ 128–129). Indeed, by lying, the subject speaks his truth "most truly" (1966, 21), which is to be precisely nothing, no reality. "An *adequate* thought, [as a] thought," Lacan says, "always *avoids* . . . the same thing. Here, the real is what always comes back to the same place—to the place where the subject, as thinker (*res cogitans*), does not meet it" (1977b, 49/49; my emphasis). Once we concede, with Kojève, that the subject cannot speak himself (or think himself) in his truth except by abolishing himself as reality (which is exactly what happens to the Cartesian subject at the moment of the hypothesis of the Evil Demon), it goes without saying that truth will define itself as inadequate to reality, and that it will therefore be (this is Lacan's imperturbably logical conclusion) *all the more true and "adequate" insofar as it is inadequate.* Since the "thing" (the *res*) is irretrievably lost as soon as it "speaks of itself," then (according to a sort of "logic of the worst," which brings to mind certain Gnostic—or Klossowskian—schemas) the lie, the masquerade, and the simulacrum will, paradoxically, conform more closely to it than the accurate (conforming) discourse will: "Speech appears all the more truly to be speech the less its truth is founded on what is called adequacy to the thing; thus, true speech, paradoxically, is opposed to true discourse" (1966, 351). Truth, when it reveals itself, is forced to say, "I lie," because that is the only way to speak the truth in a fallen world (that of language) where inadequacy is the rule.

So here it is:

Two Jews met in a railway carriage at a station in Galicia. "Where are you going?" asked one. "To Cracow," was the answer. "What a liar you are!" broke out the other. "If you say you're going to Cracow, you want me to believe you're going to Lemberg. But I know that in fact you're going to Cracow. So why are you lying to me?[26]

Because it's the truth, of course! All Galicians, in the memory of Central European Jews, have been inveterate liars, and so in this universe where trains and words circulate indiscriminately in all directions, there is no other means of speaking the truth than to lie *truly*.

The Apocalypse of Speech

When will this train arrive at the station? When will speech arrive at its destination? We find ourselves once more (we have never left) in the train that is taking Freud from Ragusa to Herzegovina. We now understand that the speech addressed by Freud to his traveling companion is just as "true" as it is "false," just as revealing as repressive: "Truth is introduced along with [speech], and so is the lie. . . . Speech is in its essence ambiguous" (1988a, 228–229/254).

Speaking of this and that, instead of uttering the "veridical," fateful speech that would have placed him before his own nothingness (before his own desire), Freud misspeaks himself at the very moment he tries to speak the truth. Exactly who *did* paint the frescoes of the Apocalypse? The word is quite literally missing, (1975b, 295), and other words crowd into its place. The "sword of speech" remains fixed in his interlocutor, in the alter ego who inhibits him to the same extent that Freud uses him as a handy shield to avoid his own death. In short, Freud calls on the other "to bear witness" (1988a, 50/60–61); he leaves it to him to speak the true word of his desire ("But of course, *you know*, that painter . . . the one who did the famous frescoes at Orvieto . . ."), in return for which, Lacan comments, he *resists* the revelation of his desire, resists it through the mediation of the imaginary "ego" in which he alienates his speech, through which he speaks. Resistance, Lacan repeats after Freud, is a resistance of the ego (let us add: as it is incarnated in an alter ego; cf. 1966, 374), and it "makes itself felt in the guise of transference" (1988a, 46/57), when speech, as if possessed and hypnotized (1988a, 56/67–68; 1966, 377–378), swings entirely toward the other:

It is insofar as the confession of being doesn't come to term that speech runs entirely along the slope by which it hooks on to the other. . . . Resistance is produced at the moment when the speech of revelation is not said, when . . . the subject can no longer get himself out of it. He hooks on to the other because what is pressing towards speech cannot attain it. . . . If speech then functions as mediation, it is on account of its revelation not having been accomplished. . . . For resistance, in fact, is embodied in the system of the ego and the other. . . . But it emanates from somewhere else, namely, from the subject's impotence to end up in the domain in which his truth is realized [1988a, 48–50/59–61].

   And yet, from another angle, Freud's error really does reveal "the deepest secret of his being," the forgetting on which the null and mortal point of his desire must necessarily founder. Desire—which is nothing, or "being" as non-being—arises only in speech where the subject speaks himself while abolishing himself (that is also to say, while killing himself) as "real." Lacan states this more specifically in the last sessions of the first seminar, once more taking up Kojève's directions for the distinction between the real and the true: "Before speech, no-thing neither is nor is not [*rien n'est, ni n'est pas*]. . . . Truth hollows out its way into the real, thanks to the dimension of speech. There is neither true nor false prior to speech. . . . Symmetrically, the hole, the gap of being as such, is hollowed out in the real" (1988a, 228–229/254; translation modified). A bit farther on, with respect to desire in Freud, he says, "The repressed desire made manifest in the dream is identified with this register [in]to which I am trying to get you to enter—what is waiting to be revealed is being. . . . Depending on the way one envisions it, this hole in the real is called being or nothingness. This being and this nothingness are essentially linked to the phenomenon of speech" (1988a, 270–271/297). In other words, speech *is* the manifestation of desire as being-nothing, just as it *is* truth in opposition to reality. This is precisely why Lacan, speaking of the forgetting of "Signorelli," said that "the man who, in the act of speaking, breaks the bread of truth with his counterpart, shares the lie." Speech is simultaneously true and false—false in regard to the reality that it annuls, and all the more true in regard to the nothing that it evokes. Freud's "error"—the error he formulates in *speaking* to his traveling companion—is thus more "true" than any adequacy to the thing to be expressed, and this is what Lacan calls by a very strong name: the *revelation* of unconscious desire. In fact, shortly after having described resistance as the "hooking" of speech onto the imaginary alter ego, he continues:

But there is another side to speech—revelation. Revelation and not expression—the unconscious is not expressed, except by deformation, *Entstellung*, distortion, transportation. This summer I wrote *The Function and Field of Speech and Language*, intentionally without using the term 'expression', because the whole of Freud's work unfolds in the dimension of revelation, and not of expression. Revelation is the ultimate source of what we are searching for in the analytic experience [1988a, 48–49/59].[27]

And so verily (*en vérité*), verily, I, truth (*la vérité*), say unto you, it is in error, forgetting, slips of the tongue, bungled actions, deformation, and pretense that I reveal myself to you, you men who insist on pursuing me where I am not: "Our abortive actions are actions which succeed, those of our words which come to grief are words which own up. These acts, these words reveal a truth from behind" (1988a, 265/292). Such, according to Lacan, was the revelation made to Freud ("It is none other than Freud who had this revelation, and he called his discovery the unconscious"; 1977a, 159/509): faltering speech, false speech, is finally the true revelation, the only *apokalupsis* of desire—its Apocalypse, therefore, but in the precise sense that the Apocalypse takes place only in being avoided. *Signor, Herr*, the "absolute Master," everything that an "apocalyptic wind" swept from Freud's speech—none of it was true except as it was forgotten, covered over, transposed, failed, and there was nothing that could have been made conscious in order finally to unveil the unconscious desire. On the contrary, it was in Freud's mistake, in the ungraspable, fugitive moment of stammering, that the Apocalypse of desire had *already* taken place. In other words, the Apocalypse is not still to come; rather, it is we who, catastrophically, always come too late to receive it. The Apocalypse of desire is endless, as endless as the Word (*Parole*) in which it takes "place," for repression is absolutely the Last Judgment of desire, and the resurrection of the flesh of truth therefore takes place only halfway (*à mi-corps*)—amputated, castrated, divided in speech. And so, verily, verily, I say unto you,

There is no error which does not present and promulgate itself as truth. In short, error is the habitual incarnation of the truth. And if we wanted to be entirely rigorous, we would say that, as long as the truth isn't entirely revealed, that is to say in all probability until the end of time, its nature will be to propagate itself in the form of error. You don't have to go much further to see in this a structure constitutive of the revelation of being as such [1988a, 263/289–290].

But here, by the same token, we are truly "burning"—and not only because the Revelation is written in letters of fire; as Lacan immediately objects, "How, from within speech, will error ever be discerned?" (1988a, 263/290) In fact, if the absolutely last revelation of being, of desire, and of the subject takes place in erroneous speech, *what distinguishes it from that other "error": the alienated and "miscognizing" speech of the imaginary ego?* In other words, what distinguishes *repression*, as the revealing-absenting of desire in speech, from *resistance*, as the presenting-avoiding of desire in that same speech? Indeed, it is one thing to strictly separate the domain of the real (which is neither true nor false) from the domain of speech (which is simultaneously true and false); it is something completely different to separate, with equal precision, two types of speech—one of which, now baptized "symbolic," is supposed to be more true than the other, which is reputedly "imaginary." This famous distinction between the symbolic and the imaginary cuts across the domain of speech, and thus we cannot be content with simply relegating the imaginary to the domain of specular vision: as we have seen, Lacan actually does describe the resistance of the imaginary ego in terms of alienated *speech*, just as, inversely, it is actually in terms of *alienation* that Lacan continues to describe true and revealing symbolic speech: "Speech is founded in the existence of the Other [capital O]" (1988b, 244/286), particularly when this speech lies, since then it "speculates on faith in testimony" (1977a, 43/252), on "the Other witness," which permits it to "present itself as Truth" (1977a, 305/807). In short, truth still speaks itself through the mediation of the Other.

From that point on, from the perspective of truth, what difference is there between these two types of speech (speech of alienation, speech of mediation): between the speech of imaginary resistance, in which the subject avoids his desire by calling on the other (small o) "to bear witness," and the speech of symbolic revelation, in which he manifests his desire in its absence by lying to "the Other [capital O] witness"? For instance, what is the difference between well-mannered speech, which permits Freud to forget the "absolute Master" (thanks to the alibi provided by his interlocutor), and apocalyptic speech, in which death reveals itself to him *in* his forgetting? Isn't it the same speech in either case, still just as deceitful, still just as true? And is it enough, in this respect, to invoke the insidious violence of imaginary speech as opposed to the contract supposedly instituted by symbolic speech?

Indeed, Lacan alleges that imaginary speech avoids (the fight to the) death only at the price of an envious submission to the little master in whom the subject alienates his desire, and the peace that this seems to institute is therefore always pregnant with an "implicit violence," a "degradation . . . of speech" (1988a, 51/62). Symbolic speech, by contrast, seals a pact with the other—a pact that Lacan calls "symbolic" because the subject, by agreeing to *exchange* speech, agrees to break the "sword" and transform it into a sign of recognition, a symbolic tessera, a *sumbolon*. Through speech, I recognize the Other (who is not me) as the very locus of truth (and of *my* truth), since it is actually necessary for me to call on him to witness the truth of my speech, even if I do this to lie to him and fool him. In other words, the game of truth presupposes a law, a rule of the game—and that, as Lacan clarifies in an astonishing rereading of the dialectic of master and slave, is why mortal violence is avoided here. Why does the slave accept submission to the master? From fear of death, according to Hegel; and yet, Lacan adds,

It is not sufficient for him to plead for mercy, he has to go to work. And when you go to work, there are rules, hours—we enter into the domain of the symbolic. If you look at it closely, this domain of the symbolic does not have a simple relation of succession to the imaginary domain whose pivot is the fatal intersubjective relation. We do not pass from one to the other in one jump from the anterior to the posterior, once the pact and the symbol are established. In fact, the [Hegelian] myth itself can only be conceived of as already bounded by the register of the symbolic. . . . In the Hegelian myth, death is not even structured like a fear, it is structured like a risk, and, in a word, like a stake. From the beginning, between the master and the slave, there's a rule of the game [1988a, 223/248–249].

The origin of truth, in other words, is not imaginary violence but the symbolic contract (which also means that this origin, for Lacan, is no genesis: from the real to the symbolic, the imaginary inference is no good, for we get from one to the other only by way of a leap—the pact of truth—which *hollows out* the abyss that it straddles).[28]

Let us concede for a moment that this may be so, and that the pact of speech precedes its violent and imaginary degradation. Will we have solved the problem of the difference between the two types of speech—*from the perspective of truth?* Not at all. In fact, whether death is avoided in speech because of the slave's fear or, on the contrary, because a preexisting code of chivalry structures the fight, death is still avoided. And yet for Lacan this is precisely the ultimate criterion of truth, the one that should have allowed the two types of speech to be distinguished: Is death as such confronted? Yes or no? Does the nothingness of the subject's desire reveal itself to him as "the deepest secret of his being"? Yes or no? But this singular criterion, such as it is, does not allow us to separate the grain of truth from the chaff of error: Death will never reveal itself, except in its avoidance, in the speech that presents it while absenting it as desire. From this point of view (which is the vanishing point of truth), it needs no great genius to notice that so-called true speech and so-called imaginary speech are in the same boat. How, then, can Lacan claim to distinguish between them? Above all, how can he *certify* the difference between them, since the criterion of truth cannot be exhibited—since the truth about truth is that it shows itself only in its retreat? Indeed, we may grant that the subject fools himself, enviously seeking the truth of his desire in another (who, he believes, possesses it). Nevertheless, by Lacan's own admission, only by fooling himself and the other can the subject, at best, be given the shattering revelation of that truth's concealment. In other words, truth "reveals" itself at the *same* level as imaginary speech, in the *same* "miscognizing" speech. "Authenticity," exactly as in Heidegger's *Sein und Zeit*, is finally nothing but the paradoxical revelation of "inauthenticity"; therefore, strictly speaking, the two should not be opposable.

Lacan, moreover, did not neglect to indicate this himself in the first seminar, where his approach, still rather open, attempts to capture the reality of analysis. Thus we read that the speech of revelation is "another side" of the speech of mediation (1988a, 48/59); and, a bit farther on, "Between these two extremes, a whole gamut of modes of realization of speech is deployed" (1988a, 50/61). It could not be clearer that the difference between these two "types of speech" is less a difference in nature than a difference in degree, within a single, fundamentally two-faced, enduringly ambiguous speech. Transference-resistance, the "swinging" of speech toward the other, its revealing stagger—all of this *is* inextricably the "approach" or, as Heidegger would say, the "de-severing" [*Entfernung*] toward truth: "The moment when the subject interrupts himself is usually the most significant moment in his approach toward the truth. At this point we gain a sense of resistance in its pure state, which culminates in the feeling, often tinged with anxiety, of the analyst's presence" (1988a, 52/63). And the analyst, correlatively, is always simultaneously in the place of the imaginary alter ego and the symbolic Other—hence the "paradox of [his] position" (1988a, 51/61), since he cannot serve as a prop for the speech of the subject's truth except at the price of simultaneously alienating him (1988a, 51/61–62). Between/among these two/four poles—subject/ego, other/Other—the interminable spiral of analytic speech is instituted (1988a, 283/312),

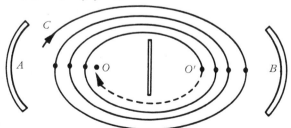

where A is the subject, B is the analyst, O is the "unconscious no-tion of the ego," and O' is the "specularity of the image." Between the poles, simultaneously separating and joining them, is a flat mir-ror. Finally, C is the arrow of speech that flies toward the imaginary other. Propelled by what has never been said or recognized in O (the "imaginary fixations which were unassimilable to the symbolic development"), the arrow lodges itself in O', the counterpart, where it repeats the same *méconnaissance* of desire: "What is on the side of O passes over to the side of O'. Everything which is proffered from A, from the side of the subject, makes itself heard in B, on the side of the analyst." In other words, the subject speaks *himself* in the other, speaks the zero, O, of his desire in the double, O', in whom he recognizes/"miscognizes" himself. And sure enough, when the analyst approaches O', "a critical phenomenon takes place . . . re-sistance in the most acute form in which it manifests itself—si-lence" (1988a, 284/312–313). A critical moment indeed, since by trying to push through this resistance—as if the silence hid some-thing—the analyst would actually only reinforce it (as Lacan says elsewhere, "In analysis, the only resistance is the analyst's"; 1966, 377). But the analyst also returns this revealing silence to the sub-ject, since the subject speaks himself through the analyst. "Every-thing proffered by A . . . makes itself heard in B," and the arrow goes flying back again:

The analyst hears it, but, in return, so does the subject. The echo of his discourse is symmetrical to the specularity of the image. This revolving dia-lectic, which I represent on the schema by a spiral, binds O' and O more and more tightly. The progress of the subject in his being must finally bring him to O, via a series of points spaced between A and O. On this line, the subject, settling down to his labor, over and over again . . . makes progress into the order of fundamental symbolic relations in which he has to find the time, resolving the halts and the inhibitions which make up the super-ego [that is, the imaginary master]. You need time for that" [1988a, 284/312; translation modified].

And so it really is one and the same speech, simultaneously imaginary and symbolic, turning and returning around the empty center of desire, opening "the subject to [that] fertile mistake through which genuine speech joins up once again with the discourse of error" (1988a, 282–283/311). *Joins up* with it—by catching up with it, joining itself to it, and certainly not by passing it, for, if "you need time for that," it is really because the arrow of speech never arrives at its target, O—except by missing it, in the O', where it breaks (hence the broken line of the diagram).

Anyway, why O and O'? Lacan answers this question by referring to an early presentation of this diagram: "A little girl . . . one day came up with this pretty phrase—*Oh, you mustn't think I'll spend my whole life in O and O'*. Poor thing! Of course you'll spend your life in O and O', the same as everyone else" (1988a, 165/187; translation modified).

How to Do Nothing with Words

> Speech in the sense of empirical language—that is,
> the opportune recollection of a pre-established sign—
> is not speech in respect to an authentic language. It
> is, as Mallarmé said, the worn coin placed silently
> in my hand. True speech, on the contrary—speech
> which signifies, which finally renders "l'absente de
> tous bouquets" present and frees the meaning captive
> in the thing—is only silence in respect to empirical
> usage, for it does not go so far as to become a com-
> mon name.   —Maurice Merleau-Ponty[1]

Let's not get the wrong idea. The waverings and
stammerings that we have been considering, important as they may
be, are nevertheless only *hesitations* within a discriminatory project, which remains constant. In spite of everything (despite clear
recognition of the problem), Lacan wants at all costs to differentiate
between "miscognition" and recognition of truth, between "empty
speech" and "full speech," between the "small other" and the "capital Other," between the imaginary and the symbolic. In this respect,
the evolution of the seminars is very clear: all these distinctions,
which can be understood at first as simple didactic indicators within
a freewheeling oral teaching, progressively solidify into "registers,"
"categories," and entities, fabulously proliferating in ever more
complicated schemas and "graphs." One step more, and the distinction itself between the two types of speech will disappear, giving way
to a quasi-exclusive celebration of language and the signifier, by
means of which the very problem that this distinction had denoted
will disappear, overlaid as it will be by its successive "solutions."

Why Do We Need Truth?

Before we examine these distinctions in their own right, it may
be useful to look briefly into the critical (discriminatory) will that

oversees their establishment. After all, why did Lacan feel the need to introduce these distinctions, which everything in his own discourse should have prohibited (or at least nuanced)? There were probably several reasons, all inextricably intertwined.

1. The first, seemingly trivial, reason is connected with the institutional context of Lacan's teaching. Let us recall that Lacan was not only a well-known psychoanalyst but also at this time a didactician engaged in heated battles to control the French psychoanalytic institution.[2] To profess, as Lacan did, that repression is the truth of desire was not only to call into question one of the most firmly anchored certainties of Freudianism; it was also, ultimately, to challenge the analytic cure itself, at least as it had been conceived until Lacan, for wasn't this fundamentally the same as promising the patient that he would never be cured and that his analysis would be endless, as "interminable" as his neurosis? There is no point in saying that the philosophical radicalism of the Kojèvian-Heideggerian reversal effected by Lacan rendered the very terms of such a question null and void; the fact remains that it was just this philosophical radicalism that could not fail to cause problems for Lacan's colleagues. Was it really possible to completely superimpose the thesis of radical finitude onto the practice (mildly therapeutic, after all) of psychoanalysis? To put it succinctly, Heidegger, reflecting on the transcendental mode, could well afford to go searching for *Dasein*'s "authenticity" in the abyssal experience of *anxiety*, just as Kojève could afford to make *suicide* the most radical manifestation of human desire. But was it really a psychoanalyst's role to transform his office into the scene of a grandiose Greek tragedy? Wouldn't this completely belittle patients' request for solace and finally drive clients to despair (just as others had done to the workers at Billancourt)?[3]

Lacan, struggling as he was for recognition from the psychoanalytic community, clearly could not afford to ignore such objections. It was necessary to give the client some glimmer of improvement or progress, just as it was necessary to find some criterion for favorably distinguishing oneself from the practices of rivals on the other side. And where is such progress, such a criterion, to be found, if not in *truth?*—if not, more precisely, in the "truth of Freud," finally restored, out of reach of the errings and falsifications of his unfaithful heirs—"this truth," as we read in the conference/manifesto on "The Freudian Thing," "without which there is no way of discerning the face from the mask, and outside of which there appears to be no other monster than the labyrinth itself" (1977a, 118/406)? This partially explains why the "return to Freud" trumpeted in those celebrated pages was so insistently presented as the return to truth *itself*—to the truth that, several lines later, is nevertheless put on stage as "Deceit itself," she "who vanishes as soon as she appears" (1977a, 123/411, 121/408). This great insistence on truth clearly corresponds, in Lacan, to the will to pose oneself as the sole bearer of "Freud's discovery." Since nothing, finally, can be opposed to the "error" and "lure" of the imaginary—nothing but the unpresentable *nothing* of death, deferred in resistance—only a forced and fundamentally equivocal emphasis on the motif of truth allows one to distinguish between authentic analysis and the "analysis of resistances" advocated by one's rivals and, especially, to attribute to authentic analysis the exclusive monopoly on the cure.

We can judge for ourselves:

The meaning of a return to Freud is a return to the meaning of Freud. And the meaning of what Freud said may be conveyed to anyone. . . . To make this clear, one has only to remember that Freud's discovery puts truth into question, and there is no one who is not personally concerned by the truth. . . . Yet is it [the word of truth] not inscribed at the very heart of analytic practice, since this practice is constantly re-making the discovery of the power of the truth in ourselves, in our very flesh? How is the unconscious more worthy of being recognized, in fact, than the defenses that are set up in the subject against it, with such success that they appear no less real? . . . I am asking where the peace that follows the recognition of an unconscious tendency comes from, if it is not more true than that which constrains it in the conflict. Indeed, for some time now, this peace has proved to be an illusory one, for, not content with recognizing as unconscious the defenses attributable to the ego, psychoanalysts have more and more identified their mechanisms—displacement from the object, the turning against the subject, regression of the form—with the very dynamic that Freud had analyzed in the tendency, which thus seems to continue in them with little more than a change of sign. Have we not overstepped the limit when we admit that the drive itself may be led to consciousness by the defense in order to prevent the subject from recognizing it? [1977a, 117–118/405–406; translation modified]

To all appearances, nothing could be more Freudian than these lines, which introduce the vast movement of the "return to Freud." Indeed, wasn't it from just such recognition of the unconscious, beyond the ego's defenses and resistances, that Freud expected relief from symptoms? Yet there is nothing more ambiguous, nothing more wily, than this emphatic (not to mention pompous) appeal to the Freudian truth. But let us make no mistake: here, all the words are traps, masks for other masks. On the one hand, as we have already confirmed, the "truth" that Lacan has in mind actually has nothing unveilable or unmaskable about it, since behind the intrapsychic conflict, in Freud's sense of the word, looms the menacing profile of that other, much more insurmountable, conflict: the fight with the "absolute Master, death." And yet, on the other hand, Lacan could not have been unaware that his colleagues' alleged misunderstanding of the unconscious "defense mechanisms" had some very solid Freudian references. Indeed, as Freud himself had recognized in *The Ego and the Id*, "A part of the ego, too—and Heaven knows how important a part—may be *Ucs.*, undoubtedly is *Ucs.*,"[4] just as it was Freud who emphasized, in *Beyond the Pleasure Principle*, the unconscious and "driven" character of the transferential resistances,[5] going so far as to speak, in "Inhibitions, Symptoms, and Anxiety," of a "resistance of the unconscious."[6] And so why grow so vehemently indignant over a perfectly orthodox doctrine, which, moreover, was not really so far from Lacan's own, since it also emphasized the indistinguishability of repressed from repression (of truth's "revelation" from its concealment)?

The answer, at least in this context, leaves little room for doubt: it was for the purpose of emphasizing, through this feigned indignation, an otherwise nonexistent and unlocatable difference. Lacan emphasizes the Truth with a capital T, the better to shatter the "adversary" and *appropriate the "Truth"* by reserving for himself the exclusive right to emphasize its abyssal, evanescent character. If we stay on the surface of his argument (his offensive "mask"), we find that everything ultimately depends on the perfectly peremptory assertion of a "truth," about which we are told nothing except that it *heals*. If it is proper to "recognize the unconscious tendency" (that is, desire as desire of recognition), rather than analyze the resistances opposed to it "in the conflict," it is because this is "more true." Why is it more true? Because recognition heals, it procures "peace" (that is, recognition of desire puts an end to the fight for recognition).

Yes; but what if such a cure, even from Lacan's point of view, is problematic, to say the least? What if desire, in its unrevealable vacuity, can really be approached only in the anxiety of death—and thus, necessarily, through an "*imaginary* fear" and fight (1988a, 223/249)? What if truth, far from bringing reconciliation and well-being, aggravates irreconcilability, conflict, *agony*?[7] All these disturbing questions Lacan addresses later (especially in his seminar on the ethics of psychoanalysis), but here they are carefully deferred, circumvented, for reasons that ultimately owe nothing to truth "herself," since they owe everything to a far from peaceful *rivalry* for truth. In its ambiguity, the prosopopoeia could just as well be understood in this way: "Verily, verily, I, Jacques Lacan, say unto you, *I* speak the truth."

2. But that is not all. To these rhetorical/strategic preoccupations are added others of a philosophical/political type, which specifically concern rivalry, battle, and war. If Lacan insists so on truth and its "power," it is also because he attempts to oppose truth to what he perceives as a violence fundamental to the imaginary relationship with the other. From this point of view, it is no accident if he asserts that, with the recognition of truth, "*peace*" is established. The peace he refers to is not only the peace procured by the cure; it is also, and much more literally, what pacifies human relationships and makes properly social ties of them. Indeed, Lacan says, only the truth allows us to arrive at a consensus, and we have already seen why: it institutes a "pact," an "agreement," a "law," a "regulation" (1977a, 61/272, 140/430−431; 1988a, 157/179; 1981, 50), where otherwise discord and imaginary rivalry for the object of the desire of the other would reign. Better yet, truth *is* this very pact, insofar as truth corresponds to the emergence of the speech in which the

reality of the object of rivalry is abolished by convention (1981, 279), and this for the sake of a symbolic exchange through which the interlocutors mutually recognize each other as witnesses and guarantors of a contract, that of truth itself: "Full speech is speech which aims at, which forms, the truth such as it becomes established in the recognition of one person by another" (1988a, 107/125). In other words, truth is not simply the "agreement upon the object" of discourse—the old Platonic theme of *homologia*, which, as Lacan emphasizes, did not prevent Thrasymachus from making "his stormy exit" in the *Republic* (1977a, 12/106); it is also (and much more) the agreement of speech by which truth is guaranteed in "sworn fealty" (*foi jurée*; 1966, 353): *Let us agree* that I am X and you are Y; *let us concede* that this is yours and that is mine; *let us swear* to speak the truth. And here we do not mean violent speech, destructive of all truth as of all good faith: You are me (*tu es moi*); I commune with you, who kill me; I kill you (*je te tue*)—dead (*tué*) [in French, *tué* evokes *tu es*] (1981, 341). "This rivalrous, competitive base at the object's foundation is precisely what is surmounted in speech, insofar as it interests a third party. Speech is always a pact, an agreement; people understand each other, they agree—this is yours, that is mine, this is one thing, that is another" (1981, 50). Truth, as "founded" in speech, is therefore the authentic social contract, the one and only contract that "links human beings to each other" (1988a, 142/162).

All of this, to which we will return, is already enough to show the extent to which the distinction established by Lacan between "true" speech and imaginary speech is controlled by a preoccupation that could very well be termed "political" (in the sense of the Greek word *polis*, and not in the sense of the politics of politicians). In Lacan, the appeal to truth must be understood on the basis of a threat that goes far beyond the analytic relation, since it touches on the very possibility of the social tie. In fact, for Lacan, behind this "affliction"—the ego's resistance to the recognition of its desire— lies the political "affliction" par excellence: imaginary violence (mimetic violence, to speak René Girard's language). Even more precisely, it is that "discontent of civilization" and the strictly modern crisis of identification (of the Oedipus) whose devastating (neurotic and psychotic) effects Lacan had already diagnosed in his article on the family: the insolvency and "narcissistic bastardizing" of the father figure, the growing indistinguishability of the paternal function from the "specular double," the "tangential movement toward incest" in our societies (1977a, 66/277), and so on. In short, it is the competitive, rivalrous world, revealed as the great traditional ordering principles retreat, a world of doubles all the more identical for asserting their autonomy, all the more racked by guilt for declaring their emancipation from every law: "God is dead, so everything is permitted"; "Nothing is permitted anymore" (1966, 130). "In this way," Lacan notes in his article on the function of psychoanalysis in criminology, "the criminal tensions within the family situation . . . become pathogenic . . . in the societies where this very situation disintegrates" (1966, 136), and it is also in this way that the "man of today, abstracted from his social consistency, *is no longer believable*" (1966, 136)—in other words, no longer *reliable* (*fiable*).

With this diagnosis made, we understand that Lacan, the man of order,[8] would have felt the need to find a remedy for the social affliction that he denounced with such acuity and vigor. In fact, it was as such a therapy of the *socius* (such a "medicine of civilization") that Lacan dreamed of analysis (as we clearly see in an article like "Situation of Psychoanalysis in 1956," where the demonstration is carried out on the example of the analytic community itself, which is said to be resisting the imaginary "forces of dissociation" simply by virtue of the "Word" of the "Master" and the dead "Father"; cf. 1966, 486).[9] In that case, however, in the name of what can we stop the fatal spiral of identificatory violence, since here the very foundation of the social tie is undermined (the *alliance* of "Father" and "son," the *responsibility* of witnesses to truth), and since every dialectical solution to the narcissistic conflict of the ego and the alter ego (Kojève's universal and homogeneous State, for example) turns out to be illusory?

In the name of truth, Lacan declares in his "new alliance with the meaning of the Freudian discovery" (1977b, 126/115–116). This solemn assertion, supposed to seal a new social contract, corresponds to the necessity that Lacan obviously found himself in— that of opposing (even artificially and fictitiously) "truth" to the "error" of the imaginary. Certainly, to recognize the only, and paradoxical, "revelation" of desire (of the "absolute master") in resistance and the imaginary struggle would be tantamount to challenging once more any possibility of peaceful coexistence between the ego and the other (between the slave and his envied master). More precisely, it would ruin beforehand any possibility of a pact or contract, since the contractual parties would be simultaneously rivals, "equal" egos (*égos égaux*) (1977a, 231/550)—and how, then, cut through that inextricably tangled web of hatred and death? Thus it was necessary to be able to set an *alternative* against the vicious circle of imaginary violence (against the impasse of dialectic), and this too is hidden behind the peremptory assertion of a "true speech" that would not be the *same* as undecidable, unverifiable "empty" speech.

This assertion conceals a decision—unjustifiable, as all decisions are. What is really at stake is an attempt to install (or reinstall) a rule of the game in the absence of any rule, at a time when truth, precisely, is no longer "believable." "Truth *exists*"—which, again, should be understood as "*Let us agree* to speak the truth," "*Let us play* the play of truth," "Let us act *as though* we can have a dialogue instead of taking the words out of each other's mouth." Exactly as in Plato's *Republic*, where the question of the bad or good (mimetic or non-mimetic) enunciation is inextricably tied to the question of the good political constitution, the assertion of truth by Jacques Lacan coincides with the elaboration of a *myth* of truth—a foundational myth equal to the myth of the Cave, expected all the more to win the adherence of the incredulous for explicitly and ironically presenting itself as a myth: "I, truth, speak"—and I say that I am lying; or "I always speak the truth. Not the whole truth, because there is no way to say it all" (1990, 3). In other words, it scarcely matters that truth is a fiction; what is important is only that we agree on that fiction, and that its enunciation should simultaneously confer *authority*—the obscure authority of the word that Lacan so ably incarnated, and without which peace would be inconceivable: "Thus it is from somewhere other than the Reality that it concerns that Truth derives its guarantee: it is from Speech. Just as it is from Speech that Truth receives the mark that establishes it in a fictional structure. The first words spoken (*le dit premier*) stand as a decree, a law, an aphorism, an oracle; they confer their obscure authority upon the real other" (1977a, 305–306/808).

Verily, verily, I say unto you, I speak the truth, and I say unto you that I speak it, and that it is nowhere but in my Speech— apocalypse of Jacques, oracle of Lacan.

3. Finally, the statement that it is necessary to tell the truth should be understood, very simply and quite tautologically, as "There must be truth." Our earlier considerations inevitably bring us back to this unforfeitable demand for truth, which is the philosophical demand par excellence. It is the demand for *manifestation*, meaning precisely that the "thing itself" must be *ex*hibited in broad daylight, in public, for agreement to be reached on it and for the matter at hand (the *Sache*) to be decided. In this respect, it should not surprise us that truth in Lacan is so often expressed in an "agora" or "forum" (1977a, 140/431), "before its assembled citizens" (1977a, 47/255), or at the "place of the Other." This is because truth, in fact, must always take (a) *place*. There is no truth, in the philosophical sense, that does not imply and exact an "opening," an "openness" into which it can unfold and where everything comes to light. To unveil, reveal, show, demonstrate, attest to, prove, certify, witness, swear—the whole lexicon of truth invariably leads back to a requirement for phenomenalization (that is, for exteriorization: "Show me"). As for speech, as Heidegger (following Aristotle) recalls in *Sein und Zeit*, it is true (or false) only insofar as it accomplishes (or does not accomplish) that apophantic demand:

The λόγος lets something be seen (φαίνεσθαι), namely, what the discourse is about; and it does so either *for* the one who is doing the talking (the *medium*) or for persons who are talking with one another, as the case may be. Discourse "lets something be seen" ἀπό. . . : that is, it lets us see something from the very thing which the discourse is about. In discourse (ἀπόφανσις), so far as it is genuine, *what* is said [*was* geredet ist] is drawn *from* what the talk is about, so that discursive communication, in what it says [in ihrem Gesagten], makes manifest what it is talking about, and thus makes this accessible to the other party. This is the structure of the λόγος as ἀπόφανσις. . . . Because the λόγος is a letting-something-be-seen, it can *therefore* be true or false. . . . The "Being-true" of the λόγος as ἀληθεύειν means that in λέγειν as ἀποφαίνεσθαι the entities *of which* one is talking must be taken out of their hiddenness; one must let them be seen as something unhidden (ἀληθές); that is, they must be *unveiled*.[10]

However specific the Lacanian doctrine of truth may be (truth as unveiling/veiling of the *subject* in speech), the same fundamental demand for manifestation is what, in Lacan, actually governs the call for a "full" and "true" speech. Indeed, if there must be truth, it is not only because truth heals and pacifies; it is also, and more profoundly, because desire (of the subject) must be and wants to be recognized *as such*—that is, to be exhibited, explained, expressed, exteriorized—in speech. And, inversely, if desire must be and wants to be recognized, it is because this recognition in speech is the only truth of desire (of the subject). There must be truth because desire (the subject) wants to be spoken publicly, just as it is, and because this will to manifestation is its ownmost essence: it wants to (re)present itself, pose itself before itself, know/see ([*sa*]*voir*) itself by showing itself—itself, "thing" and "cause" itself.

And so, Lacan asks himself in "The Freudian Thing," why is the "unconscious tendency" "more deserving of recognition than the defenses that oppose it in the subject" (1966, 405)? Because, we read, it is "more true"; but let's not get the wrong idea: this does not at all mean that it is "true" *before* it is recognized. On the contrary, it is true only insofar as it is recognized by the other in the pact of speech. Indeed, Lacan says again, desire is a "desire to have one's desire recognized" (1966, 343): "Man's desire finds its meaning in the desire of the other, not so much because the other holds the key to the object desired as because its first object of desire is to be recognized by the other" (1977a, 58/268)—that is, to be manifested. Here, as in Hegel, the desire for recognition is a desire for manifestation or, again, a desire for truth. Desire wants to know itself, excise itself from its night in order to appear "in the light of day,"[11] and this is why it can be fulfilled only through the reflecting mediation of the other, by making itself recognized outside, in a common speech where "the intersubjectivity of the 'we'" is sealed (1977a, 86/299). This is also why, for example, the desire fulfilled in a dream is always the desire of an other: the dream is an "oneiric *discourse*," just as "every [bungled action] is a successful . . . *discourse*" (1977a, 58/268), or just as every symptom "is speech functioning to the full" because the desire fulfilled in it "includes the discourse of the other in the secret of its cipher" (1977a, 69/281). Desire, as Lacan goes on to stress, *is* its interpretation, and this means that the essence of desire is to manifest itself in the speech where it makes itself recognized, where it *truly* appears.

This is a huge presupposition, if we think about it. Is it really so obvious, after all, that the unconscious *Wunsch* wants to be revealed outside, wants to speak? Does the hysterical body speak, the same body that "somatizes" desire and refuses to speak it? And do we dream only to be able to tell our dreams? It is true that Freud's whole message in *The Interpretation of Dreams* is that the "dream narrative" *can* be interpreted, but in no way does this prevent him from asserting elsewhere that the dream is "asocial," "narcissistic," [12] and "completely egoistic" [13]—certainly not because the other does not intervene in the oneiric scenario, but because desire is "fulfilled" in the dream through an identification that takes no account of *distance* from, and therefore of all speech with, the other. [14] "The dream work does not think": this famous formula means precisely that the dream *does not mean, does not want to say, anything (ne veut rien dire)*, because the "other scene" where it takes place is not the place of truth, is not the *agora* "in which is constituted the I who speaks with the one who hears" (1977a, 141/431; translation modified). Granted, it is the "other scene," the "other place"—but precisely because there is no question of a place or a scene. The desire fulfilled here in no way seeks to be manifested before itself, in the footlights, for the good reason that it does not *desire* to manifest itself: it is already manifest ("fulfilled") in a completely different way, before the ob-positive space of the visible-speakable and the time of reflection even open. Besides, wasn't Freud already saying that the unconscious knows nothing of contradiction, it contains "no negation, no doubt, no degrees of certainty"? [15]

But this is not Lacan's doctrine. For him, desire resides in desire of self; it wants to (and therefore must) manifest itself as it is, in its truth—which is the whole trouble with this discourse on desire, truth, and discourse, for this desire that seeks recognition is simultaneously described (after Kojève) as a desire of nothing (as a desire of the pure *desire* of the other). Now, under these conditions, how can this desire ever be manifested? How can the subject of desire, in his radical negativity, recognize himself (or make himself recognized) for what he really is: nothing, nothing at all, nothing of what is (present, subsistent, "given," "real," and so on)? What speech could ever exhibit desire in its vertiginous, mortal transcendence, in the ek-stasy that carries it beyond any object of satisfaction— except, precisely, by exhibiting it, "showing" it, and therefore failing it, missing it, dissimulating it; except by masking the black opening of desire while carrying it into the light of openness?

And yet there *must* be truth. The subject *must* speak himself as he is. Lacan stubbornly continues to define desire as desire for recognition, and this is the sign of his perfect adherence to the demand for manifestation: the subject of desire must unveil himself (decipher himself) outside, openly, *even as the nothing (the gaping hole) that he is.* Hence the inextricable double bind where Lacan is caught (dragging his patients and followers along with him): "Present your absence," "Announce your desire," "Manifest your nothingness," "Speak your death." These are all strictly paradoxical injunctions ("schismogenic," as Bateson would say), which the impossible distinction between "true speech" and "empty speech" attempts to address by exacerbating them. In the end, if the two types of speech have to be opposed, it is precisely because there must be, in accord with the demand for truth, a speech that manifests desire, not forgetting it or concealing it in any way and leaving nothing to be desired. Such is the "demand, presupposed by psychoanalysis, for 'true speech'" (1977a, 71/283). But at the same time, since it is a question of manifesting desire as such in its unsaturable vacuity, only a speech that shows the impossibility of such manifestation will do. Where will we find this kind of speech, *if not in "empty speech,"* constantly exposed in its guilty impotence to answer the exorbitant demand for truth that torments it? How can we speak the truth, if not by speaking its perpetual retreat into speech and revealing the double bind for what it is? But this is precisely what is impossible, and it puts us right back on the merry-go-round. It is a lifework, dedicated to the impossible possibility of death—that "possibility," Lacan writes, bootlegging a (mis)quotation from Heidegger, "of the subject, which is absolutely one's own, unconditional, unsurpassable, certain, and, as such, undetermined" (1977a, 103/318; translation modified).[16] If desire is desire of death, how can we speak the silence of that death(-instinct)? To speak it is inevitably not to speak it, and so only by not speaking it can we speak it: if yes, then no; and if no, then yes.

In short, we can never respond to the paradoxical demand for truth except by ceaselessly reproducing the implacable dilemma: if "true speech," then "false speech"; and if "false speech," then "true speech." Truth is (the) impossible—and yet, verily, verily, I say unto you: the impossible must *be*.

You Are

With these clarifications, we will now consider the impossible doctrine of "full speech" itself. What, finally, is this authentic speech in which the "psychoanalytic realization of the subject" is believed to be sealed (1977a, 40/247)? Can we give it a positive, *fully* positive, definition? Already we suspect formidable difficulties on the path ahead, and so it will be better to advance cautiously, proceeding at first by elimination. Knowing what full speech must be—a speech in which the subject of desire speaks himself and makes himself recognized as the nothing that he is—let us start by establishing what it must *not* be.

First of all, it must not be *language* (or at least not exclusively). This may seem astonishing, since all speech necessarily uses language, if only the coded "language" of dreams or symptoms. But, Lacan says, it is from precisely this language that "speech must be delivered" (1977a, 59/269). Why? Because what is at stake in analysis is the truth of the subject, and such a truth necessarily takes the form of an autoenunciation (the autoenunciation of a nothing, in this case). In this respect, language is particularly ambiguous, since at first sight it seems pledged to refer, "to signify something" (1966, 82). Lacan certainly knows—and is already repeating after Augustine, Hegel, Kojève, and Saussure—that the linguistic sign does not represent any reality. Nevertheless, he concedes that language, from the point of view of its users, is essentially turned toward the world: it expresses the state of things, names realities, represents events, signifies concepts and ideal objectivities, and so on. In a word, it *objectivizes* what it speaks about, even and especially when it deals with a subject ("Peter, *of whom* I speak," "I, *who* am speaking to you" ["*Moi qui* vous parle"], and so on). In this way, it constitutes an obstacle to strictly autoenunciative speech, in which a subject speaks himself to another subject, on the other side of what Lacan significantly calls the "wall of language" (1966, 282, 308) (here translated as the "language barrier"; 1988b, 244–245/ 285–286).

Language, of course, is not the imaginary; but, Lacan believes, language lends the imaginary the appearance of consistency insofar as it tends irresistibly to reify the interlocutor (and, on the rebound, the "locutor"). For example, it transforms the interlocutor into an object of knowledge and simultaneously divests him of speech (and this is why the planets are mute: Newton's law of gravitation silenced the music of the spheres; cf. 1978a, 280). But this goes against authentic speech, within which it is a question of recognizing—and making oneself recognized by—the interlocutor as an unrecognizable and unpredictable subject (that is, as Other):

> The imaginary gains its false reality, which nonetheless is a verified reality, starting off from the order defined by the wall of language. . . . When the subject talks to his fellow beings, he uses ordinary language, which holds the imaginary egos to be things which are not simply *ex-isting*, but real. . . . If speech is founded in the existence of the Other, the true one, language is so made as to return us to the objectified other. . . . In other words, language is as much there to found us in the Other as to drastically prevent us from undestanding him. And that is indeed what is at stake in the analytic experience [1988b, 244/285–286].

Hence this little diagram, where the arrow of speech (the one that starts from the Other, *subject*, to found the truth of S, *subject*) is broken and refracted while passing through the "wall of language," where the imaginary relation of the ego, *a*, and its alter ego, *a'*, is objectified (1988b, 243/284). [Here it should be recalled that *a* has some relation to *autre*, the "other."—Trans.]

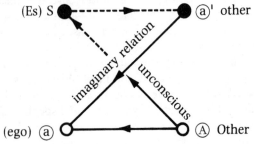

In other words, language is simultaneously the site of truth (of speech) and the site of a fatal illusion, which Lacan never ceases to denounce: *representational illusion*. Irresistibly, it makes us believe in the reality of which it speaks, a reality that it then purports to represent (adequately, correctly, precisely, and so on), just as it makes us believe in "the reality of the subject beyond the wall of language" (1977a, 94/308; translation modified), as if this subject had already been something before the speech in which he makes himself recognized. This is what Lacan calls the "mistaken notion of 'language as a sign'" (1977a, 83/296); whereas "the world of words . . . creates the world of things" and the symbol "makes [the] man" (1977a, 65/276), language presents itself as a sign that represents, communicates, signals, facilitates something for someone (1977a, 83–84/296). And this is why it creates a "wall": not at all because it would prevent anyone from attaining the thing itself but, on the contrary, because it makes us believe that there are objects and/or subjects "behind the wall" (1977a, 93/307; translation modified), *whereas it is actually the wall that is the thing itself.* Therefore, language as such cannot speak the subject's empty truth. Only speech, properly speaking, can do that, insofar as it replaces discourse's goal of adequacy with the unsecured certitude of the intersubjective pact:

Speech appears all the more truly to be speech in that its truth is founded less on what is called "adequacy to the thing": thus, paradoxically, true speech is opposed to true discourse; their truths are distinguished by the fact that true speech constitutes the recognition by the subjects of their beings, in which they are inter-ested,[17] whereas true discourse is constituted by knowledge of the real, insofar as the subject aims for it in objects [1966, 351].

But speech in turn must not be "*empty.*" Indeed, to "speak truly," to speak fully, it is not enough to speak to the other. On the contrary, while speaking to the other in order to speak himself, the subject usually speaks *himself* in the other, (re)cognizing himself in the alter ego instead of making himself authentically recognized as and by an Other-than-himself, beyond every possible cognition (1981, 48): an imaginary speech, whose mad dialectic we already know, one that, according to Lacan, is always fundamentally inclined to tumble into the compact certainty of those delirious "voices" in which the subject *hears himself say* who he is—a sow, a wreck, a whore (1981, 60–64). Or, speaking of one *thing* or another, the subject mixes speech and language in the style of what Lacan calls "intermediate discourse" (1966, 352), losing, by the same token, "his meaning in the objectifications of discourse" (1977a, 70/281). In every case, speech remains desperately "empty"—not because it says nothing,[18] but, on the contrary, because its unstoppable babbling fills—and, by the same token, occults—the void of the subject.[19]

Now, as we know, it is this void that is supposed to be revealed. Here we are, then, reduced to searching for authentically revelatory speech in a speech that would say nothing ([*ne*] *dirait rien*)—neither an object nor an ego—and thus speaks the subject in his abyssal vacuity. And this, indeed, is precisely what Lacan calls "full speech." This speech, in contrast to so-called empty speech, is full of nothing (*n'est pleine de rien*). In particular, it communicates no message, no information, no meaningful content. On the contrary, it communicates nothing—nothing, Lacan says, but "the existence of communication." Does this mean that it is *actually* different from empty speech? Not necessarily, and later we will see the importance of this concession. Lacan willingly admits that speech can be both "empty" and "full." (And, really, how could it be otherwise, if no speech can avoid also being language, language that always says something?) Lacan proposes quite simply to distinguish between what speech says (its "statement") and speaking itself (its "enunciation"). As the theoreticians of the pragmatics of language would say here, to the "meaning of the statement" is necessarily joined the "meaning of the enunciation" (Grice), or its "illocutionary force" (Austin), and every message must therefore be analyzed in terms of both communicated "content" and "meta-communicated context" (Bateson). Thus, Lacan notes, one never communicates anything without communicating *that* one is communicating and *how* one is communicating. It is this second dimension of speech that characterizes it as "full," even when it is otherwise perfectly "empty":

Indeed, however empty this discourse may seem, it is so only if taken at its face value: that which justifies the remark of Mallarmé's, in which he compares the common use of language to the exchange of a coin whose obverse and reverse no longer bear any but effaced figures, and which people pass from hand to hand "in silence." This metaphor is enough to remind us that speech, even when almost completely worn out, retains its value as a *tessera*. Even if it communicates nothing, the discourse represents the existence of communication; even if it denies the evidence, it affirms that speech constitutes truth; even if it is intended to deceive, the discourse speculates on faith in testimony [1977a, 43/251–252].

Full, true speech, in this sense, says nothing other than what empty, lying speech says. But it *says* that it says (it). And, saying that—saying *nothing but* that—it carries speech to *speech itself*, in its essence of pure speech decontaminated of all language. Under these conditions, we understand why Lacanian analysis is a long (very long) speech. It is because the subject must be induced to cross over the objectifying-representing "wall of language" in order to speak, period—that is, literally, to speak in order to say nothing: "Words, words, words. . . ."[20] Speech, instead of saying something, now speaks itself and thus speaks the truth, which is precisely that speech says nothing—nothing other than the "hole in the real" (1988a, 271/297) that is the subject at the moment when he speaks.

Have we now reached the limit of our troubles? No; for on this count, every speech—even (and perhaps primarily) the most empty—could be called "full." Again, the emptiest, most idle talk still communicates *that* it communicates. (And isn't this "phatic" function, as Jakobson would say, what our daily conversations are very often reduced to? "Hello, are you there?" "Stay in touch," and so on.) From this perspective, we could very well claim that it is precisely this sort of speech that best shows speech's essential vacuity. After all, how are we to distinguish between the insipid "blablablah" of empty speech (empty because it is stuffed with meaning) and the pure and authentic "blablablah" of full speech (full because it is stripped of meaning)? Now, from Lacan's point of view, it is still very necessary that we be able to make this distinction. It is necessary because the truth must be spoken in the end, spoken in a speech that says explicitly that it says (nothing)—and thus shows, manifests, its own emptiness. In other words, there must be a speech that speaks itself as pure speech—and that does not speak it simply in the form of a metalanguage that would speak the "truth about truth" (1966, 867–868) or the "meaning of meaning" (1977a,

61/271, 150/498; 1966, 351, 353), since then it would still say
something, namely, "I say, /I say/."

Where, then, can we find such a speech, perfectly sui-referential,
auto(re)presentative, and autoenunciative? In the *given* word.²¹ If
speech, in Lacan, is said to be "full," this is because he understands
it in a quasi-feudal sense: ²² full, authentic speech, which is supposed
to manifest itself as such at the interminable term of analysis, is the
speech in which one gives one's word, one's fealty (from the same
root, *fides*, as "faith"). When I sign a contract, when I say "I do"
before a justice of the peace, or when I recognize someone as my
master (or my disciple), I neither communicate nor give anything
but my word, and yet that word binds me, it "performs" (1988a,
107/125−126). In fact, the rare examples of full speech that Lacan
gives are all of this type: "You are my wife." "You are my master"
(1977a, 85/298; 1966, 351; 1981, 47−48). "You are the one who
will follow me" (1981, 315 ff.). They are words that not only have
no referents before their enunciation but also have no signified
other than themselves. In Lacan's terms, they "are first and fore-
most signifiers of the pact that they constitute as signified" (1977a,
61/272). Indeed, the given word does not represent the pact of
speech, any more than it contents itself with being its secondary and
exterior sign or record. It is the pact itself, insofar as its utterance
(the act of giving one's word) accomplishes the act that it designates
or enunciates (that is, the act of giving one's word). The *act* of
swearing in, of taking an oath, or of committing oneself is here
strictly identified with the fact of saying "I swear" or "I promise."
Thus, here we stand before the remarkable case of a perfectly sui-
referential speech, since it says nothing other than itself ("mentions" nothing other than its "use," to use Quine's famous distinction, here completely turned on its head) but nevertheless performs,
performs the act of full speech. It is a speech that "constitutes,"
effectuates the pact that it itself is—a pact that Lacan calls "symbolic" because it is not bound to any reality (the term "symbol"
must be taken here in the sense used by Peirce and Lévi-Strauss) and
because it acts as a sign of recognition (as *sumbolon*).

On the one hand, before its enunciation, the given word represents nothing, whether an "objective" reality *or even a "subjective"
reality*. To sign a contract, for example, is not the same as to ratify

or express an interior resolution after the fact, for I am indeed not the one who commits myself, until the moment when I sign my name. By the same token, my signature does not represent my interiority (strictly speaking, it does not represent anything); on the contrary, it institutes me as a contractual party (even if I have no intention of honoring the contract). Here there is no inner voice, since it is the exterior voice that constitutes and manifests me for the first time, by transforming me into a debtor of this or that. As Lacan says, to give one's word is equivalent to becoming *other* than one was before; witness the "gestalt philosopher" who signed a contract with a New York publisher: "In fact, from the moment that M. Keller receives the order, has replied *yes*, has signed a contract, M. Keller is not the same M. Keller. There's another Keller, a contracted Keller, and also another publishing house, a publishing house which has one more contract, one more symbol" (1988a, 156/179; see also, 1988a, 107−108/125−126; 1981, 315; 1977a, 83/296). In the same way, I become a (symbolic) "father" in recognizing my child, a "disciple" (and not a rival) in publicly recognizing my intellectual debt, a "husband" (and no longer simply a sex partner) in ceremonially recognizing my spouse—all things (or rather symbols) that I was not before these various recognitions.

With this, we come to touch on the second characteristic of the given word—namely, that it presupposes the recognition of the one to whom it is addressed. It is not what it is—a word that binds—except on condition of being given to an other who is not *me*. In this respect, it does not matter whether the other accepts this gift or not, whether he in turn gives his word or not; the given word institutes in any case, by the very fact of its enunciation, a relationship that defines me in my relation to an other, just as it defines the other in his relation to me: he is forced to respond, even if in silence (1977a, 40/247); and if he absolutely cannot respond, as in the case of a newborn infant, the relation is ipso facto considered to have been accepted (1966, 354). In other words, the given word implies that I recognize the other as this or that (master, creditor, or coconspirator), in order to recognize myself or make myself recognized as this or that (disciple, debtor, or coconspirator).

This is also why Lacan always formulates his examples of full speech in the second person singular (which, strictly speaking, is not at all necessary, since one most often gives one's word in the first person). "This *you*," he says, "is absolutely essential in full speech" (SV, 8 January 1958). What Lacan means to emphasize here is the necessary co-relation or co-respondence between the *you* and the *I*, the latter instituting its identity only by investing the former with the power of responding (or not); *you* are the one *I* am speaking to, *I* am the one *you* are speaking to. Thus, I am not an *I*, according to this purely linguistic analysis, except by speaking to *you* (1977a, 85/298). Here again, we see that what is said (*I*) coincides with the act of saying it (to *you*). The enunciation (the gift) of speech is what institutes and very literally gives being to what is uttered (given to be heard). As Benveniste (to whose analyses Lacan's implicitly refer) has said, "'Ego' is he who *says* 'ego'" and he who says it to a *you*.[23] Benveniste asks, "What, then, is the reality to which *I* or *you* refers? It is solely a 'reality of discourse,' and this is a very strange thing. . . . *I* signifies 'the person who is uttering the present instance of the discourse containing *I*.'" Likewise, "we obtain a symmetrical definition for *you* as the 'individual spoken to in the present instance of discourse containing the linguistic instance *you*.'"[24] And that, Benveniste adds, is why verbs of the type *swear, promise, guarantee, certify,* and so on, perform (are effectively binding) only when pronounced in the first or second person ("he swears," by contrast, commits *no one*):[25] only the sui-referentiality of this "personal" enunciation is capable of instituting the singular "reality" that it speaks of, which in this case is that of *speaking* subjects, speaking *among themselves*. "Subjectivity," Benveniste rashly concludes, is founded on language[26] and on "*intersubjectivity*, which alone makes linguistic communication possible."[27]

This theory was bound to please Lacan, since it reduces the subject to the pure fact of saying (nothing): a subject of speech constituting itself through the mediation of *you*. The given word, in itself perfectly empty of meaning, is a "password," Lacan says, for getting to recognition of self via recognition of the other:

In order to conduct us from the pole of the *word* (*mot*) to that of *speech*, I will define the first as the crossover point of the material most empty of sense in the signifier with the most real effect of the symbolic, the place held by the password, under the double face of non-sense to which custom reduces it, and of the truce that it brings to the radical enmity of man for his counterpart.[28]

Thus, by saying "You are my wife" (a perfectly senseless statement, according to Lacan; after all, what do I know about it? 1981, 48), I recognize and institute you as such while simultaneously recognizing myself as "your husband." In short, as Lacan says, taking up a formula suggested by his friend Lévi-Strauss, I receive "[my] own message back from the receiver in an inverted form" (1977a, 85/298). I institute myself as subject (I manifest myself publicly, in the luminous center of the *agora*), by becoming *other* than I was the moment before. Here I am, at present, "your husband," from now on submitted, for better or for worse, to a symbolic and differential order in which I am no longer anything but the symbol (or the "signifier," as Lacan says) that represents me for another symbol (for another signifier).

To Perform Nothing?

At this point, the reader will no doubt be unable to fend off a disquieting feeling of déjà vu, and with good reason: Is what Lacan here calls "full speech" really anything other than what Austin, at about the same time, called "performative" speech, the speech that "does things with words"?[29] Moreover, didn't Austin enlist the same example of marriage to illustrate his thesis? Readers can judge for themselves:

> One of our examples was, for instance, the utterance "I do" (take this woman to be my lawful wedded wife), as uttered in the course of a marriage ceremony. Here we should say that in saying these words we are *doing* something—namely, marrying, rather than *reporting* something, namely *that* we are marrying. And the act of marrying, like, say, the act of betting, is at least *preferably* (though still not *accurately*) to be described as *saying certain words*, rather than as performing a different, inward and spiritual, action of which these words are merely the outward and audible sign.[30]

Isn't this exactly what Lacan also says? In fact, it does not take long to perceive that Lacanian "full speech" has all the essential characteristics of Austinian "performative" speech:

1. It is a non-"constative" speech, in Austin's sense, one that does not represent or describe or report anything that would predate its utterance, whether concerning a state of affairs or an interior event ("*Our word*," Austin writes, "*is our bond*").[31] It is therefore

opposed to empty speech and to language, exactly as the performative utterance, in Austin, is opposed to the affirmative statement of the constative type.

2. It is, by virtue of this very fact, neither true nor false—at least if we understand these terms, as Austin does, in the sense of a statement that "corresponds with the facts"[32] (of "adequacy" and "exactitude," as Lacan would say). In this respect, Austin attacks the "'descriptive' fallacy"[33] (which consists in analyzing all statements in terms of truth or falsity) no less than Lacan denounces the "mistaken notion of 'language as sign'" (which purports to be the adequate or inadequate representation of some thing). The *I do* of marriage, for example, has nothing to do with the alternatives "true/false," but rather with the purely pragmatic ones of "happiness" or "unhappiness," "felicity" or "infelicity."

3. Lacanian full speech commits, acts, institutes, and transforms, just as Austinian performative speech performs an action in the simple fact of its utterance.

4. More precisely, Lacanian full speech engages a subject, and this corresponds to Austin's remarks on the necessarily "subjective" character of the performative: "The 'I' who is doing the action does thus come essentially into the picture,"[34] since "there is something which is *at the moment of uttering being done by the person uttering*"[35] (Austin thus explains his initial—and, as he adds, by contrast to Benveniste, finally unjustified—preference for examples of performative speech formulated in the first person singular of the present indicative active).

5. Full speech presupposes and "calls for a reply," which in turn defines it, just as the effect of performative speech (called "illocutionary" by Austin, since it is produced *in* speaking) presupposes its being grasped (its "uptake") by the addressee.[36] The *I do* of marriage can be performed "happily," as Austin says, only if the woman responds *I do*,[37] just as speech, according to Lacan, remains "held up" (*en souffrance*; 1966, 29–30) for lack of "a *happy* punctuation that gives meaning to the discourse of the subject" (1977a, 44/252, my emphasis; translation modified; see also 1977a, 95–99/310–314).

6. Finally, the efficiency or effectiveness of full speech is purely symbolic, just as in Austin the illocutionary effect of performative speech is purely "conventional"[38] (contrary to the so-called perlocu-

tionary effect of an utterance, which for its part is unpredictable and uncodable). As Austin writes, the "happiness" of performative speech requires, among other essential conditions, the existence of "an accepted conventional procedure having a certain conventional effect, that procedure to include the uttering of certain words by certain persons in certain circumstances." [39] Now, this code is not the strictly linguistic one used by locutors in order to convey their "messages"; it is the extralinguistic one, Austin seems to say (but, in reality, "linguistic" in the larger sense, as Lacan asserts, inspired by Lévi-Strauss [40]), that rules the utterance or enunciation of certain statements by conventionally determining the locutors in their "symbolic" or "pragmatic" interrelations. Full and/or performative speech is a "speech act" because to the regulating code of the statement is added the code regulating utterance or enunciation; the very fact of speaking institutes ipso facto such and such a condition of discourse: an order necessarily entails the obedience (or disobedience) of the interlocutor, a question necessarily calls for a response (or silence), a request is necessarily gratified (or frustrated), and so on. [41]

Did Lacan know of Austin's work? It seems that he did not, if only because, had he known of it, he would have been able to save himself (and us!) the painful task of formulating his hypothesis in the vocabulary of a structural linguistics bound to be allergic to it. [42] But the fact remains that full speech as described by Lacan is, from the formal point of view, nothing but explicitly performative speech, in Austin's sense. And, by the same token, haven't we discovered what we were searching for—a finally *positive* characterization of full speech? Full and/or performative speech, under this hypothesis, would be the speech that, by contrast to empty and/or constative speech, represents no reality before its enunciation and is thus all the more "true" for manifesting the subject in his pure and null "reality of discourse." Analytic speech, by returning speech to its performative essence, therefore brings about the paradoxical "realization of the subject" (1977a, 40/247): it creates him ex nihilo, by bringing that nothing into existence solely through the power of the Word (*Parole*). As Lacan says, refuting Goethe's interpretation of the first verse of the Gospel according to John, "It was certainly the

Word (*verbe*) that was in the beginning" (1977a, 61/271)—the Word, certainly, but as an *act* of speech, as a creative "speech act." The true and authentic Word (*Parole*) of revelation is the Word that creates nothing (except) by speaking, thus unveiling its own "emptiness."[43]

In reality, however, this only perplexes us more. In the end, we really must ask whether such speech ever exists in a pure state and whether analysis can seriously propose to bring it to light as such. Does Lacan really mean that analysis ends with explicitly performative speech? Such a hope courts grave disappointment. Indeed, Lacan himself recognizes that true speech is extremely rare: "This speech, which constitutes the subject in his truth, is nevertheless always forbidden to him except for those rare moments of his existence when he tries, however confusedly, to grasp it in sworn fealty" (1966, 353). If this is the case, it is because "true [that is, performative] speech" tends to be irresistibly confused with "true [that is, constative] discourse": "Each of the two truths distinguished here is altered through its intersection with the other in its path," in the form of an "intermediate discourse" (1966, 351–352).

This is another way of saying that the difference between the two types of speech may once more be revealed to be perfectly imperceptible. Indeed, as Lacan explains, just as "true discourse" can produce nothing but a simple sign as proof of its adequacy to the real (therefore invoking the performative "good faith"), so does the purest promise still refer to a state of the world, even if it is non-"constatable" at the moment of enunciation. "I promise to marry you" *also* means "We shall be married in two months": "True discourse, if we extract from the given word what is given in the promise, makes [the promise] appear a lie, since it engages the future, which, as they say, belongs to no one" (1966, 351–352). Isn't this the same as admitting (as Austin also had to do) that the distinction between performative and constative is not nearly so well decided, so clear-cut, as we might have believed at first? As we know, this was the problem that led Austin to substitute a second distinction for this first one between two types of utterance, a much more encompassing distinction (and therefore much more vague as well, for which Benveniste reproaches him)[44] between the "locutionary" and "illocutionary" dimension of *all* utterances. Indeed, as Austin remarks, not only are performative utterances often formulated in the constative mode ("The meeting will begin," "You are fired," and so on), every constative utterance also (and inversely) has an implicit or "primary" performative dimension. The assertion "*s* is *p*," for example, always implies an "*I assert* that *s* is *p*," which defines the "illocutionary force" or "value" of the utterance: "Statements do 'take effect' just as much as 'namings', say: if I have stated something, then that commits me to other statements."[45]

Now, as we have already seen, Lacan returns to a completely analogous train of argument when he is confronted with the notable rarity of full speech. It does not really matter, he tells us, that such speech cannot be found in analysis (or anywhere else), since even empty speech is always simultaneously full: to lie is still to say (that one is speaking) the truth; to communicate inanities is still to communicate that one is communicating, and so on. It does not even matter whether the pact of speech is explicitly sealed during an analysis, since the very fact of speaking from the couch presupposes a "*secret*" pact (1977a, 79/291; my emphasis). In other words, there is no need to make the pact explicit, for "secret" speech is just as effective—a train of argument ("The kettle already had a hole in it when I got it from him") that, if it does not at all suppress the legitimate distinction between the two dimensions (locutionary and illocutionary) of all speech, nevertheless threatens to make the effective distinction between empty speech and full speech pointless. After all, if full speech is so rare, why assign analysis the goal of attaining that almost unattainable ideal (that "fiction . . . of speech," as Lacan himself says later; 1973a 18)? Why, indeed, *if empty speech is just as effective in any case?* Wouldn't it have been much better to recognize that the speech encountered in analysis is always both empty *and* full (resisting *and* revealing, imaginary *and* symbolic)—and, once and for all, to lay to rest the dream of a "true" speech, which would finally speak the truth by speaking itself as "empty"?

But worse is still to come, even from Lacan's perspective. We could object that full speech, perhaps inaccessible in fact, still functions as a very legitimate "ideal regulator" for analysis. And why

should we forbid ourselves to stretch toward that ideal? Let us concede this, then, and behave for a moment *as if* such a speech existed,
a speech that would be exclusively and explicitly performative. Will
it then render the services that Lacan expects of it? Not at all, for we
must remember that it is a question of finding a speech that speaks
the truth of the subject (of desire) by saying *nothing*. Now, from
this perspective, it actually is true that purely performative speech
(which, for the moment, we are pretending exists) does not represent or state anything. But can we conclude from this that it *manifests the nothing as such* (the pure abyss of a desire perpetually
ek-stasized in the no less abyssal desire of the other)? This is what
Lacan implies (and if he did not, why would he *privilege* full speech
in relation to empty speech?). But there is a very obvious sophistry
here: from the fact that performative speech does not re-present
anything, it does not at all follow that it does present (the) nothing.
On the contrary, this speech really does present something—that is,
itself. It is an "autoapophantic" speech, which speaks itself by saying what it does and doing what it says. Better yet, it is a speech that
shows (*zeigt*, to use Wittgenstein's terminology)—and, according
to Lacan, *shows the subject*: he is henceforth exhibited in his pure
"reality of discourse," frozen for eternity in his compact identity of
"husband" or "disciple."

Therefore, fully performative speech does not escape the apophantic fatality of *logos*. In exhibiting itself, it still causes something to be "seen"—something (a subject), not nothing. How can it
henceforth be invested with the exalted power of presenting the
nothing, that null and non-being transcendence that is supposed to
"be" the subject of desire? If it does "present" this, it can do so only
by occulting it, the same as any other speech. In reality, nothing
allows performative speech to subtract itself any better than any
other speech from the implacable "double bind" of the *logos-
alētheia*: if you show, you hide, and if you hide, you show. From the
moment when language is assigned the formidable task of saying
(the) nothing, *any* speech serves equally well, since *none* will serve.
Full speech does not perform the nothing any better than empty
speech does, for the latter does it just as well: everywhere, it is all
one and the same *clamor* of nothing.

The Unconscious Is a Myth

We can now recapitulate and conclude the problem of the analytic cure. At the beginning of the preceding chapter, we were asking ourselves what was the objective of a cure conducted according to Lacanian principles. Is it, as in Freud, a question of speaking the truth of unconscious desire? Yes, except that for Lacan it can no longer be a question of unveiling, in broad daylight, the thoughts, memories, or phantasies hidden from consciousness by repression and internalization of the prohibitions demanded by society. Even less is it a question of provoking the "abreaction" or "working through" of affects that until then have been displaced, transferred, "cornered," "repressed," or converted into anxiety or somatic symptoms. For Lacan, disciple of Kojève, the desire of man is not a drive, not a "pressure" arising from the biological body, not an immediate affect or feeling of self;[46] it is (a desire of) nothing. Correlatively, the human subject has no interiority, no interior in which to store or save for himself the so-called unconscious representations. A pure and null ek-stasized transcendence in the desire of the other, he is always already "ek-sistant" (1966, 11), always already projected outside, into the openness of a public space. He is, as tradition proclaims, a speaking animal (*zōon logon ekōn*), rational (*animal rationale*) and social (*zōon politikon*)[47]—to which we need add only that this singular "living creature," from the moment that it speaks, "lives a life that is dead" (1988b, 232/271): the *"parlêtre,"*[48] as Lacan also defined it, is a "being-toward-death," and its desire is a desire of death (1977a, 101–105/316–321). This desire, therefore, is no more a vital instinct "from before consciousness" (a pre-Freudian definition of the unconscious, according to Lacan; 1977b, 24/27; translation modified) than it is something represented in the "private theater" of an unconscious receptacle (a definition closer to Freud's). Since, strictly speaking, desire is nothing outside its public, linguistic ek-sistence, it is (like Poe's famous "Purloined Letter") in fact never *hidden*, in the sense of being concealed behind something else. On the contrary, it is always already *said*, as openly as can be, and this, paradoxically, is what Lacan calls the "unconscious": "At the level of the unconscious . . . this thing (*ça*) speaks and functions in a way quite as elaborate as at the level of the conscious, which thus loses what seemed to be its privilege" (1977b, 24/27).

So here we are, at Lacan's famous thesis: the unconscious, the "manifestation" of desire, is a "discourse," and it is "structured as a language." This is a highly ambiguous formula, which we really must avoid understanding in the sense of a subject's expressing his desire in symbolic form, in the sort of idiom that we need only decipher to find its proper, nonfigurative meaning. Lacan's formula must actually be interpreted literally: the unconscious "as" language is not a symbolic or metaphorical language, it *is* language. Even more precisely, it is *the* "symbolic" in the sense of the structural anthropology of Lévi-Strauss. It is "concrete discourse, insofar as this is the field of the transindividual reality of the subject" (1977a, 49/257)—that is, as Lévi-Strauss would have it, the regulated system of exchange, communication, and kinship, which imperatively defines everyone's place, within a social structure assimilable to language ("Like language, the social *is* an autonomous reality [the same one, moreover]")[49] and removed from the conscious mastery of individuals ("The unconscious would thus be the mediating term between self and others").[50] Therefore, that the unconscious is language means first of all that the subject of desire is nothing (cannot be the nothing that he "is") outside the "discourse of the Other," in which he is always already said, named, preinscribed, "if only by virtue of his proper name" (1977a, 148/495). The subject is now defined by Lacan as the subject *of* the unconscious, because the subject never appears anywhere but in a discourse that is not his and therefore escapes from him (1988a, 54/65; 1988b, 261/303); and yet he *is* himself, "beyond the ego" (1988b, 175/207): "The subject goes well beyond what is experienced 'subjectively' by the individual, exactly as far as the truth he is able to attain" (1977a, 55/265).

Nevertheless, the problem is that this truth of the subject, if it is always already said, is not necessarily recognized; and it is very often in this second sense that Lacan *also* intends his formula: "Translating Freud, we say that the unconscious is a language. Just because it is articulated does not mean that it is also recognized" (1981, 20). The reader will have understood that this definition already goes much farther than the one borrowed from Lévi-Strauss, according to whom, in fact, the unconscious simply designates what goes beyond the individual, what he cannot grasp: it is the "trans-individual" discourse that imperatively defines me as this or that, without my being able to do anything but recognize—and recognize myself in—that sort of "contract" imposed on me.[51] By contrast, according to the strictly Lacanian definition, the unconscious designates this same "discourse of the Other"—but here, it is "miscognized." Even more precisely, it is that part of the discourse of the Other in which I cannot recognize myself (or make myself recognized) because it cannot be integrated or can be integrated only poorly, in the symbolic: "The unconscious is that chapter of my history that is marked by a blank or occupied by a falsehood: it is the censored chapter" (1977a, 50/259).

Why Lacan feels the need to introduce this second definition of the unconscious, apparently more in agreement with the orthodox Freudian definition, is also fairly easy to understand. It is because the symbolic of Lévi-Strauss, a system of collective customs and institutions, characterizes quite precisely what is commonly called *normality* inside a given society. Psychoanalysis, for its part, deals with individuals—neurotics, psychotics, perverts—who are considered abnormal or deviant. In a word, it deals with "failures" of the symbolic (with "*suicidés de la société*," as Artaud said). Moreover, this is what Lévi-Strauss had already explained, in his *Introduction to the Work of Marcel Mauss*, with respect to those singular "mentally ill people" (in our Occidental eyes) the shamans and sorcerers. "No society," Lévi-Strauss recognizes, "is ever wholly and completely symbolic."[52] In reality, a given society always rest on *several* relatively heterogeneous symbolic systems, which occasionally entertain contradictory relations among themselves. It is therefore "inevitable," Lévi-Strauss continues, "that a percentage (itself variable) of individuals find themselves placed 'off system,' so to speak, or between two or more irreducible systems. The group seeks and even requires of those individuals that they figuratively represent certain forms of compromise which are not realizable on the collective plane; that they simulate imaginary transitions, embody incompatible syntheses,"[53] and all this in the form of a "sort of equivalent, twice diminished (by being individual and by being pathological), of forms of symbolism different from its own."[54] In short, shamans and other psychopaths symbolize, in their own way (which, more-over, is often prescribed by a "collective order which is not even neutral in relation to exceptions"[55]), what escapes from or has been skipped over by such a symbolic system.

Lacan, of course, would hardly have been able to resist the temptation of applying this schema to the analysis of the neuroses that he dealt with. These, he explains in turn, must be understood as "individual myths" (1978a)—that is, as symbolic subsystems provoked by a dysfunctioning of the symbolic defined by the *collective* myth (the psychoses, for their part, arise from a pure and simple a-symbolization, the famous "foreclosure of the Name-of-the-Father"). Thus, for example, could the contract of the symbolic speech presiding over my destiny be formulated in such an equivo-cal way that I cannot recognize myself (or make myself recognized) according to the admissible rules. Suppose that my real father was "discordant" (1978a, 305) in regard to his symbolic function, and that a "lapse in the truth of speech" occurred at the marriage of my parents (which was the case, Lacan recalls, for the Rat Man ana-lyzed by Freud; 1966, 354; see also 1977a, 88–89/302–303; 1978a, 294–300). What will happen then is that I will be unable to situate myself on the symbolic plane as the "son" that I nevertheless must be (that I am). Instead of fully recognizing myself (making my-self recognized) as the son of a dead father (Lacan's definition of the symbolic "*Name*-of-the-Father," since this "name" is independent of the real father; see 1981, 111; 1977a, 199/556), I will be reduced to recognizing myself in him through an Oedipal rivalry with an imaginary and unmurderable father (this is how the father of the Rat Man persisted, terribly, in the unconscious of his son). As for the speech to which I, like my father, am indebted with respect to the symbolic, it speaks itself "beyond the ego" in any case (hence the complex "ransom simulacra" fomented by the Rat Man; 1966, 354). Quite simply, just as I will not succeed in making this speech recognized under its imaginary travesties, so also will I be unable to recognize myself in it. This "individual myth of the neurotic," in which I desperately attempt to symbolize what has not been sym-bolized by the Other, will remain as closed and enigmatic as (ac-cording to Lacan) the "AZ" of the formula for trimethylamine that appeared in Freud's famous dream of "Irma's injection" (1988b,

147–171/178–204): a pure block of nonsense, a symbol lifted from the symbolic, a password to which I do not have the key because the Other has not given it to me.

In summary, then, we see that the Lacanian unconscious is not merely what is hidden from the individual's consciousness. For this Freudian alternative of the unconscious and consciousness, Lacan actually substitutes another alternative: the recognized and the unrecognized. That desire is "articulated" in the unconscious now means that it is spoken in the *language* (the marginal symbol) of the dream, the symptom, or the "individual myth," but without being recognized in that language in the form of full and authentic symbolic *speech*: "The symptom resolves itself entirely in an analysis of language, because the symptom is itself structured like a language, because it is from language that speech must be delivered" (1977a, 59/269). As for the analyst, a new Socrates, he limits himself, at the birth of that speech, to letting it speak itself to him and to giving it back to the subject "in inverted form," duly attested to and sealed by the symbolic whose representative he is: "In order to free the subject's speech, we introduce him into the language of his desire, that is to say, into the *primary language* in which, beyond what he tells us of himself, he is already talking to us unknown to himself, and, in the first place, in the symbols of the symptom" (1977a, 81/293). The analyst's action is therefore purely symbolic, not only because he rigorously restricts himself to what is said (the "symbol" of the symptom) but also and especially because, by accepting the discourse of the subject for what it is (a demand for recognition), he gives his word (*parole*) in return, the missing word that has blocked the subject's access to the symbolic proper, and thus the analyst "re-establish[es] the continuity of [the subject's] conscious discourse" (1977a, 49/258).

Let us make no mistake: Lacan, who certainly denounces any idea of "the adaptation of the individual to the social environment" (1977a, 38/245), has nevertheless not doubted for an instant that the aim of analysis is the reintegration of the subject into society. For Lacan, too, it is actually a question of reinscribing the patient into that "social life" that is the condition, according to Lévi-Strauss, of "the saneness of the individual mind . . . just as the refusal to enter into it . . . corresponds to the onset of mental disturbance."[56] The

difference between Lacan and the American psychoanalysts, denounced for "human engineering," lies elsewhere. The difference is
simply that the Americans conceive of society as a *reality* to which
the ego should conform, whereas Lacan, with Lévi-Strauss, conceives of society in its symbolic essence: what the subject must conform to is a pure and arbitrary *convention*, a pure linguistic *contract*,
which is to say that, for Lacan, the subject is to be introduced to the
very principle of sociality. And how is that done? Again, through a
convention: that of the analytic setup. Since one convention deserves
another, this setup is supposed to supplement a faulty symbolic system, whose deficiency was the origin of the subject's neurosis. Better
yet, it supplements *the* symbolic—the ideal symbolic that Lévi-
Strauss admits no society entirely realizes,[57] and which, Lacan is
close to believing, has ceased to exist in our "Oedipal," neurosis-
producing, paranoiac societies. In short, the analytic setup is a
utopia: it represents, within society as it *is*, society as it *should be*.
Precisely because it is entirely artificial and explicitly conventional,
it constitutes a sort of symbolic system in the pure state, where
henceforth a social contract—otherwise deficient and undiscover-
able—can be fictionalized (or refictionalized). To this subject (this
desire) who until now could symbolize himself only in the form
of an "individual myth," the analyst will grant civil rights in the
analytic office, that unreal enclave, a little substitutive *agora* where
everything can be said and where, by the same token, everything
can be recognized in its truth—that is, in its symbolic truth, its
fictive truth.

Once again, the important thing to recognize in analysis—the
subject of desire—is nothing real. On the contrary, this subject
is always already symbolized and is therefore equally well irreal-
ized, denatured, and fictionalized (the proof, Lacan says, being the
"family romances of the neurotic" discovered by Freud; 1988b,
41–42/57–58). Whether this symbolization is brought about correctly (in accord with the collective myth) or eccentrically (in the
form of the individual myth) changes nothing, from this point of
view; *for Lacan, the subject is always a myth*. The only difference is
that this myth is as such either recognized or unrecognized in its
fictive truth on the occasion of a no less fictive and conventional
pact. Analysis, where this recognition operates, therefore brings

about a true *fictionalizing* of the subject, as Lacan clearly explains (in his "Rome Discourse") with respect to the first hysterics cured by Freud.

Why, indeed, were the hysterics whom Breuer and Freud treated cured of their symptoms, often in such a spectacular manner? Breuer and Freud, as we know, attributed the cure to the bringing to consciousness of an actual "traumatic event"—or, more precisely, to its spoken recollection in a hypnotic trance induced by the doctor. But, as Freud quickly realized, these traumatic events were most often phantasies, with no basis in reality. Thus, real cures were effected through perfectly fictive "reminiscences." This explains Freud's constant embarrassment on this question, since in the absence of any "reality" in the memory, analysis seemed actually to be reduced once more to a technique of suggestion—indeed, it seemed to flirt dangerously with magic.[58] But, Lacan concludes, to say this is to completely mistake the power of speech and misunderstand its exclusively symbolic nature. What matters is not that hysterics become conscious of anything (since, as Lacan notes, they "vaticinate" under hypnosis; 1977a, 46/254), but only that they "recount" and "verbalize" the *epos* (1977a, 47/255; 1978a, 293) of their individual myths, getting these recognized by the collectivity incarnated in the doctor. Consequently, in this speech of the oracle or rhapsode there is nothing real but the magic efficacy of the pact of truth sealed in the shared fiction:

Hypnotic recollection is, no doubt, a reproduction of the past, but it is above all a spoken representation—and as such implies all sorts of presences. It stands in the same relation to the waking recollection of what is curiously called in analysis "the material," as the drama in which the original *myths* of the City State are produced before its assembled citizens stands in relation to a history that may well be made up of materials, but in which a nation today learns to read the *symbols* of a destiny on the march. . . . The ambiguity of the hysterical *revelation* of the past is due not so much to the vacillation of its content between the imaginary and the real, for it is situated in both. Nor is it because it is made up of lies. The reason is that it presents us with the birth of truth in speech, and thereby brings us up against the reality of what is neither true nor false. . . . For it is present speech that bears witness to the truth of this revelation in present reality, and which grounds it in the name of that reality. . . . I might as well be categorical: in psychoanalytic anamnesis, it is not a question of reality, but of truth, because the effect of full speech is to reorder past contingencies by conferring on them the sense of necessities to come [1977a, 47–48/255–256; my emphasis].

In other words, it scarcely matters whether speech adequately represents some past reality; what matters is only that it should performatively "found" the truth of the subject (and) of desire in the here and now of its enunciation, with all the consequences that this implies for the future (and for the past thus "constructed," "rewritten"). To say "I am a woman from the last century," as Emmy von N. did in a somnambulistic state, or to claim that one can no longer speak German, as Anna O. did, is certainly to lie with respect to reality (it is to "simulate," as was said of hysterics), but it is also to better institute oneself in the subject's pure and null truth (that of an Englishwoman, for example, or that of a "woman of the eighteenth century") by finally making oneself recognized on the analytic *scene*, that fabulous theater where the smallest lie is miraculously transformed into a "symbol of destiny." In short, the more one lies, the more one speaks the truth; the more one fictionalizes the past, the more one fashions (or predicts) the future.

As for the analyst, he has no reason to search for the truth beyond the speech addressed to him; he merely confers its "dialectical punctuation" by conferring "the sanction of our reply" (1977a, 95/310). Again, it scarcely matters whether the interpretation or construction proposed by the analyst is exact; what matters is only the "symbolic gift of speech" and the "secret pact" that it implies (1977a, 79/291). Lacan even goes so far as to suggest that Freud's cures were all the more effective for his interpretations' being erroneous—indeed, completely "indoctrinating" (1977a, 77–79/289–291). And, to tell the truth, why should that surprise us, since here it is no longer a question of restoring a subjective "reality" but rather of *producing* it, performatively, by "puttering around" with the patient to construct a communal myth where he can find himself again? Just like the American "narrativists," to whom we could compare Lacan in many respects, Lacan actually recommends a sort of pragmatic fictionalizing of the truth, which then passes from the status of "historical truth" to that of "narrative truth."[59] Oracle for oracle, the Lacanian analyst limits himself to "realizing" the prophetic "vaticination" of the subject, in sym-prophetizing it, so to speak: "You are my master," says the patient. "Yes," the analyst responds, "and you are the one who will follow me." As Daniel Bougnoux has so nicely observed, the Lacanian pragmatic functions in the manner of a "self-fulfilling prophecy,"[60] and this is what, in reality, makes it almost indistinguishable from the plain technique of suggestion.[61]

Again, we should make no mistake: Lacan, who certainly could not find enough disparaging things to say about suggestion, understood as an *imaginary* influence exercised with the aim of fitting the patient into a reality exterior to the analytic pact (1988a, 26–29/35–39; 1988b, 43/59), nevertheless advocated, underhandedly, what could very well be called *symbolic suggestion*. This formula is to shock many; but how else can we describe Lacanian "interpretation," that speech removed in principle from any guarantee in the Real, and which nevertheless transforms the subject into his ownmost being? And as for that abyssal opening of the subject to the discourse of the other, constantly described by Lacan, isn't it "suggestibility," in short? Indeed, it is difficult to see how the subject could resist the analyst's "interpretations," since the subject is nothing but what is said about him (since his desire *is* the interpretation given by the Other). By the same token, it is very easy to understand why an "erroneous" interpretation would be just as effective as any other, since, ultimately, the only criterion that allows for a definition of the "correct" interpretation is the singular agreement by which the analyst testifies to the patient's fiction and in return imposes it on him as *his* (?) truth.[62] In this strange analytic universe, where there is no real reality and everything is reduced to a contractual interaction, *all* speech by definition will be active and effective—all speech, and therefore *any* speech. As the poet Bruno Goetz has said about his Freudian analysis, Freud might just as well have said "Abracadabra"; the beneficial effects of his speech would have been none the less evident.

The Sorcerer and His Magic

This brings us back, by the same token, to that disquieting question of the "magic of words," which so preoccupied Freud.

After all, if the analyst's speech cures—as *pure* speech, stripped of meaning (as a pure "password")—what distinguishes it from the "abracadabra" of the magician, the *truc*[63] of the healer, the suggestion of the hypnotist? Isn't it a sort of trickery, like that of the shaman who claims to expel a malady by spitting a bloody object from his mouth? Isn't the analyst actually a modern sorcerer, all the more jealous of his tricks of the trade for being incapable of explaining their effectiveness, and thus equally incapable of transmitting them in any way other than the initiatory path? Lacan himself recognized this toward the end of his life, precisely with respect to the procedure called the "pass" (a sort of rite of passage instituted in the Lacanian School, to ensure replication of analysts and transmission of the doctrine):

Now that I think about it, psychoanalysis is untransmittable. What a nuisance that each analyst is forced—since it really is necessary that he be forced—to reinvent psychoanalysis. . . . I must say that in the "pass" nothing attests to the subject's [that is, the candidate-analyst's] knowing how to cure a neurosis. I am still waiting for someone to enlighten me on this. I would really love to know, from someone who would testify in the "pass," that a subject . . . is capable of doing more than what I would call plain old chattering. . . . How does it happen that, through the workings of the signifier, there are people who can cure? Despite everything I may have said on the topic, I know nothing about it. It's a question of trickery [*truquage*].[64]

This declaration left Lacan's audience flabbergasted and perplexed. Some chalked this impressive declaration of impotence up to the old man's fatigue; others saw it as an occasion for admiring once again the heroism without illusions of this Oedipus, thundering imprecations before throwing himself into the void he had so often celebrated. But we should not forget that this was really nothing new from Lacan, who had not hesitated to compare psychoanalysis to alchemy (1977b, 9/14), and who, since the time of the "Rome Discourse," had ridiculed

the analyst's guilty conscience about the miracle operated by his speech. He interprets the symbol and, lo and behold, the symptom, which inscribes the symbol in letters of suffering in the subject's flesh, disappears. This unseemly thaumaturgy is unbecoming to us, for after all we are scientists, and magic is not a practice we can defend. So we disclaim responsibility by attributing magical thinking to the patient. Before long we'll be preaching the Gospel according to Lévy-Bruhl to him [1977a, 92/306].

Does this mean that Lacan simply admitted to not being scientific by recognizing, in short, that psychoanalysis, too, is a practice that does not need to be elucidated in order to work (1990, 7) and that, as in magic, knowledge "is characterized here not only by its remaining veiled for the subject of science but also by the disguising itself as such, as much in the working tradition as in the act" (1966, 871)? Not at all: it is the Gospel according to Lévi-Strauss that Lacan is preaching. Indeed, we must understand that, in Lacan, the assertion of psychoanalysis's magical character does not contradict the assertion of its scientific character. On the contrary, *it is precisely its magical character* that reconciles analysis with the most advanced developments of modern science—and that, likewise, distinguishes the one from the other (1966, 870–877), since analysis is *both* magical *and* scientific. In fact, if the analyst is truly a shaman—and Lacan, as Catherine Clément notes,[65] was one, certainly more consciously and deliberately than anyone else—he is a shaman who has read and reflected on the structural anthropology of Lévi-Strauss and who knows, as a result, that nothing fundamentally distinguishes magic from mathematics. In a word, he is an authentic (and, what is more, multidisciplinary) man of knowledge who employs an *algebraic* alchemy of *linguistic* incantations and *topological* mumbo-jumbo.

This is what Lévi-Strauss had discussed at length in a series of articles from which Lacan obviously took much inspiration.[66] The "trickery" of the shaman, Lévi-Strauss essentially explains, is something quite different from ordinary trickery. It is actually a manipulation of symbols (or—what amounts to the same thing in this context—of "signifiers"), comparable in every respect to the manipulation of the mathematician playing with numbers and letters. Above all, it is a manipulation that is just as effective; as fantastic and arbitrary as they are, shamanic cures nevertheless have an indubitable "symbolic efficacy" in that they furnish the sick person and the social group with "a *language* by means of which unexpressed and otherwise inexpressible psychic states can be immediately expressed."[67] In other words, they are sociotherapies founded on a "collective consensus"—just like the symbolic writings of the mathematician.[68] The shaman, the sorcerer, and the magician (often themselves ex–"mentally ill persons") procure for both the sick person and the group a *myth*[69] in which both can integrate ineffable (that is, the unsymbolizable) psychic or physical pain into a communal language. Even more precisely, they procure a "zero symbol"[70] intended to bridge the gap between what can and cannot be said within a given symbolic system. The sorcerer (or, rather, the triangle formed by the sorcerer, the sick person, and the group) certainly believes in the *content* of the sacred symbol (in the omnipotence of the magician, in spirits, in the Devil, in "magnetic fluid," and whatnot). In fact, however, by muttering his magical formulas or invoking the mystery of *mana*, the medicine man, according to Lévi-Strauss, does only what we do every day when we call an adroit maneuver that surprises us a *truc*, or when we call something for which we have no name a *machin*:[71]

Those types of notions [*mana, hau, taboo*—in a word, the symbols of the sacred], somewhat like algebraic symbols, occur to represent an indeterminate value of signification, in itself devoid of meaning and thus susceptible of receiving any meaning at all; their sole function is to fill a gap between the signifier and the signified, or, more exactly, to signal the fact that in such a circumstance, on such an occasion, or in such a one of their manifestations, a relationship of non-equivalence (*inadéquation*) becomes established between signifier and signified, to the detriment of the prior complementary relationship. . . . Notions of the *mana* type . . . represent nothing more or less than that *floating signifier* which is the disability of all finite thought (but also the surety of all art, all poetry, every mythic and aesthetic invention), even though scientific knowledge is capable, if not of staunching it, at least of controlling it partially. . . . A simple form, or to be more accurate, a symbol in its pure state, therefore liable to take on any symbolic content whatever.[72]

In a word, the mysterious ritual formula of the shaman is to the "affliction" to be cured what the mathematician's x is to the unknown term of the equation: pure play of words or writing, all the more effective and performative for being perfectly void, conventional, and arbitrary. Therefore, it is useless to resonate with the harmonies of the sacred in order to understand it, as did Durkheim and Mauss and, even more gravely, those "sorcerer's apprentices"

Caillois and Bataille.[73] The magician is simply a mathematician who does not know it, just as, inversely, the mathematician is a sort of magician in the pure state (who nevertheless only "partially controls" the "floating signifier"). As for psychoanalysis, Lévi-Strauss, quite to the point, concludes that it is nothing other than a "modern version of shamanistic technique" and is thus indebted to the same theory.[74]

Now we certainly understand better how Lacan could subscribe to the somewhat insidious comparison of his anthropological friend and colleague: Lacan had, in the meantime, transformed the analyst into a *shaman conscious of being a shaman*—that is, as Lévi-Strauss would have it, into a distinguished mathematician-linguist-topologist.[75] Is analysis a sort of trickery? Of course, Lacan essentially answers—except that it exhibits the truth of trickery, which is precisely that the truth of the subject, being purely symbolic, has a "fictive structure." The speech that cures in analysis certainly arises from *mana*, from the play of words, from "trickery" (*truquage*), but this *truc*, precisely because it is perfectly void and *nonsensical* (1977b, 250/226), brings about the symbolization (the socialization, the recognition) of the subject—"what Lévi-Strauss calls a 'zero-symbol,' thus reducing the power of Speech to the form of an algebraic sign" (1977a, 68/279).[76] Henceforth, why not push Lévi-Strauss's reasoning to the limit and knowingly make magic? In his articles, Lévi-Strauss was content to propose a rationalist theory of magic and its effectiveness, a theory based on the supposed equivalence of the sacred symbol and the mathematical symbol. But Lacan, with his imperturbable sense of logic, immediately drew the inevitable conclusion (one, as we can imagine, that must have staggered Lévi-Strauss). If we say that the efficacy of magic, of mythic speech, is the same type of efficacy as that of mathematical symbols, doesn't this basically also mean that mathematical science, in its algorithmic advances (1977a, 149/497), is a supermagic? Doesn't this implicitly put magic and science on the same plane—that of an arbitrary manipulation of symbols, a pure "theoretical fiction" disconnected from reality? Well, *why in heaven's name shouldn't we make magic along with science?* Why not (re)create a myth with the "small letters of algebra" (1977b, 226/205), which after all are much more presentable, in our disenchanted societies, than the quaint epics of Oedipus or the Devil or God? To hell with the stodgy old mythemes; let's replace them with our modern mathemes; capital *A*, small *a*, *abracadabra*!

This, no doubt, was the source of the formalistic wandering—from "algorithms" to "graphs," from tori to Borromean knots—that progressively led Lacan to the project of wholly "mathemizing" the psychoanalytical field. His famous and amusing "mathemes," if they obviously have nothing to do with an authentic formalization, have everything to do with the Lévi-Straussian theory of magic. They are true magical formulas, supposed to be all the more effective for being devoid of meaning and, in the end, perfectly obscure: here, mathematical formulas replace, to great advantage, the degraded Latin of the alchemists. From the idea of formalization Lacan retains only the idea of *the arbitrary*, the very idea that allowed Lévi-Strauss to make the connection between magic symbolism and the algebraic symbol (or the linguistic symbol: hence Lacan's idea of a "logic" or "mathematics of the signifier"; 1966, 861). Nevertheless, whereas Lévi-Strauss clearly proposed to understand the arbitrariness of the magical symbol in terms of the *rational* (hence *necessary*, since binding) convention accepted among mathematicians,[77] Lacan proceeds in precisely the opposite direction, the better to demonstrate the *nonsensical* and *fictive* (fictionalized) character of the most scientific symbol (witness these peremptory assertions from the seminar on the psychoses: "To discover a natural law is to discover an insignificant formula. The less it signifies, the happier we are. . . . You would be wrong to believe that Einstein's little formulas, which relate inertial mass with a constant and several exponents, have the slightest significance. It is a pure signifier. And for that reason, thanks to him, we hold the world in the palm of our hand"; 1981, 208). In Lacan, the arbitrariness of the symbol once again becomes truly arbitrary—that is, turned over to the caprice and fiat of the scientist-magician. Symbols are all equally arbitrary, then? Very well, they are all equally valuable . . . a conclusion that, obviously, could spring up only in the mind of a psychoanalyst-magician; as for the mathematicians, they know only too well the constraints entailed by the most conventional logical symbols. Besides, this is why hoping to do anything with the Lacanian "mathemes" would be as silly as trying to make a surrealist "bachelor machine" work.[78] Like those anomalous machines, the Lacanian "formalizations" arise, quite frankly, from *anything at all*: a riddle turns out to be just as good as—and even much better than—anything else for producing a matheme, since Lacan is concerned simply with exhibiting the "senselessness" of his constructions.[79]

It scarcely matters that Lacan himself—toward the end of his life, and under pressure from his own disciples—seemed to believe in the scientific validity of his mathematical *Witz*; all we can say is that this circumstance arose from the "sorcerer's apprentice" psychology described so well by the Lévi-Strauss of "The Sorcerer and His Magic." The fact remains that, in the beginning, the stake in these pseudoformalizations was not at all to create a work of science, but rather to use science for magic's ends, relying on the supposed "omnipotence" of the "zero symbols." This is why it would finally prove rather futile to try to denounce the unscientific character of the Lacanian "mathemes" (do we denounce a joke for not being serious?). Lacan was the last to believe in his fictions, and his project was actually completely different, much more subtle in any case. It was the project—perfectly cynical, in one sense, because it was perfectly conscious—of a complete mystification of science, based on the complete demystification of magic: an extraordinary project, if we think about it, that seduced more than a few. Outlined behind the "little letters" that Lacan was tracing on the blackboard was nothing less than a new "scientific myth," more "up-to-date" than Freud's,[80] and a sort of modern religion of the Symbolic, intended to make up for religion's bankruptcy in our desacralized societies.

At this point, we must at least ask whether this new myth—the myth of science as myth—could lastingly replace traditional myths. There is every reason to doubt it, no matter how unarguable its success may have been on the banks of the Seine (and in several backwater trading posts). Even if we suppose that the Lévi-Straussian model does account for the efficacy of magical or shamanic cures (and this is very far from being obvious), it is hard to see how the model could be applied, as Lacan proposed, to the modern cure that is psychoanalysis. In fact, the efficacy of the magical symbol, if we follow Kojève, rests on a "*collective* consensus." Because the "zero symbol" furnished by the shaman or the sorcerer is recognized by the whole group, the sick person can in turn be recognized and thus "cured." Obviously, things are quite different in our planetary, demythologized societies, where such a symbolic consensus no longer exists. If it is true, as Lacan says, that "it is inasmuch as the subjective drama is integrated into a myth which has an extended, almost universal human value, that the subject brings himself into being" (1988a, 190–191/215), then this symbolic "bringing into being" simply will not take place. The Lacanian analyst may very well recognize the "individual myth of the neurotic" in its "fictive truth," but society as a whole will not recognize it (especially if this "myth" is reduced to a sequence of signifiers devoid of any communicable meaning, like the "magical formulas" of the Rat Man[81] or the *Poordjeli* of the obsessional analyzed by Serge Leclaire[82]; 1981, 250/226). Perhaps the analytic office is the place where the symbolic can be refictionalized (where, if you will, the shamanic cure described by Lévi-Strauss can be replayed), but it is still an *enclave* inside real society (too real, to our chagrin, since it does not conform to its symbolic essence).

This is as good as saying that the symbolic pact sealed between the patient and his analyst-shaman could easily give rise to a *sect* (and who would deny that the Lacanian School was just such a sect?), but not to a new religion or to a new collective myth, not even the myth of a "mathemic" mytho-science. Indeed, it is one thing to recognize through speech the "individual myth" of the neurotic in the unreal space of the office—or, more broadly, of the analytic society based on belief in the founding myth (the "new alliance" with the Word of the dead Father, and so on). It is another thing entirely to get this eccentric symbol accepted outside the analytic space. "You are my wife" is certainly well-formed, conventionally recognized speech, and as such it is "performative." But the copulative *Glejisamen* of the Rat Man? Nevertheless, this is exactly the type of "magic formula" that analysis must constantly deal with, and hardly anyone, except the analyst who believes in the "magic of words," can recognize such formulas in their truth, by integrating them into a magico-symbolic supersystem fictionalized to that sole end. As for the social entourage, it does not recognize them because, quite simply, it no longer believes in magic. The symbolic efficacy of analysis therefore remains confined, at best, to the analytic sect. Of course, this is not to deny its relative efficacy (for how many patients have found in their sessions, and in the movements of the small analytic world, enough balance to survive?), but at the least it puts the relative efficacy of analysis in its place—a very limited and precarious one. In this respect, what is it that fundamentally differentiates analysis from those other isolated islands of religiosity, lost in our disenchanted world—mystical sects, secret societies, extremist political organizations—all, indeed, united around a symbolic pact set in concrete? These little "hordes," as Freud had already noted, are by all accounts no less effective than analysis—to which we need only add, perhaps, that they are scarcely any better, assailed as they are by a social entourage that constantly tends to destabilize them:

Even those who do not regret the disappearance of religious illusions from the civilized world of today will admit that so long as they were in force they offered those who were bound by them the most powerful protection against the danger of neurosis. Nor is it hard to discern that all the ties that bind people to mystico-religious or philosophico-religious sects and communities are expressions of crooked cures of all kinds of neuroses.[83]

For the analyst, the only way to avoid this problem would be to agitate for the sect's extension to all of society, so that the breach between individual myth and collective myth would once again be reabsorbed, as in the traditional societies. In fact, this is precisely what Lacan, for whom the end of an analysis was strictly synonymous with the patient's becoming an analyst, was implicitly advocating. What does this mean, if not that the therapeutic aim was confounded, by the same token, with its didactic, proselytic, catholic, and universal aim? If Lacan could afford to scoff at the idea of the individual cure (1968, 17–18), it is because he put all his hope in a sort of collective cure: to cure is the same as to become a "healer" (an analyst) oneself, producing other "healers" (other analysts), who in turn. . . . Lacan, moreover, straightforwardly says as much in the preamble published in the first *Annuaire* of the *Ecole Freudienne*: "Psychoanalysis currently has nothing better for ensuring its activity than the production of psychoanalysts"[84]—a stupefying scheme, neither that of a science nor that of a therapy, but rather that of a religion (or a political version of religion). It was the project of exponential growth in the analytic group, the famous "mathemes" for their part ensuring both complete transmission of the myth (because they were considered purely symbolic) and flawless cohesion within the sect (because they were considered exempt from all imaginary impurities). Taken literally, it was, finally, the project of extension to society as a whole of that "scientific delirium" psychoanalysis[85]—an elegant solution to the problem of madness, since it amounted to dissolving that problem in the establishment of a society that was itself delirious (or, according to Freud, religious).

The project was a mad one, if you will, all the more so in its knowing itself to be mad. This is what differentiates it from another "madness," the totalitarian project, which was nevertheless also haunted by the possibility of reestablishing the unity of the social body through the imposition of a new "myth of the twentieth century." In Lacan, this project is somehow undermined from within by the simultaneous assertion of the symbolic—that is, "fictive," "fake" (*truqué*), or even "delirious"—character of the myth that Lacan was proposing to propagate. Freud, for example, could not help *believing* in his "scientific myth," and this is certainly one of the reasons why it was able to serve as the foundation of an analytic community and to become so widely diffused throughout culture. As for Lacan, he knew that the Oedipus was only a myth (1966, 818)—"less idiotic" (1966, 820) than others, of course, but a myth all the same, intended to defer confrontation with "the absolute Master, death." Exactly the same thing is true of his own symbolic myth (of the symbolic), since its only "truth" is to symbolize *nothing*—the void of desire, the nothing of the subject, the absence of the object. Henceforth, how would it be possible to believe (or make others believe) in a "truth" simultaneously asserted as a "fiction"—an absolutely inevitable fiction, certainly, but none the less *absolutely fictive*, infinitely veiling in its very unveiling? How to believe (or make others believe) in a myth known to be a myth, a pure "zero symbol" intended to symbolize the "lack of that zero symbol" (1966, 821)—that is, the (impossible, unlivable) absence of all symbols: death, period?

We could pretend to believe in it, but then we would once more be propagating the mythico-religious "idiocy" and "the imaginary obscenity" of "the group effect" (and who, again, would deny that this was one of the most *effective* effects of Lacan's teaching?); or we could cynically expose the sham (the fictionalizing), but then we would leave both the myth and the group without hope (and who would deny, as delicate as this question may be, that despair and sometimes suicide were also effects of the *truth* of Lacan's teaching?). Lacan himself put it very well, finally establishing his whole enterprise on an explicit impossibility—"the impossibility of the analytical group" (1968, 31):

We have no final truth to respond to, especially not for or against any religion. It is already a great deal that, here in the Freudian myth, we had to place the dead Father. But, without supporting some rite, a myth is not enough, and psychoanalysis is not the rite of Oedipus, an observation to be developed later. No doubt the corpse really is a signifier, but Moses's tomb is as empty for Freud as Christ's is for Hegel. To neither one did Abraham hand over his mystery [1966, 818].

6

Linguisteries

> When, thanks to the absolute power of Understanding, essence becomes meaning (*sens*) and incarnates itself in a *word*, there is no longer any "natural" relationship between essence and its prop; otherwise, words that have nothing in common in terms of their spatiotemporal, phonetic, or graphic reality (*chien*, dog, *Hund*, etc.), could not serve as a prop to the same unique essence, all of these words having a single, unique meaning. Thus, there has been a *negation* here of the given such as it is given (with its "natural" relationships between essence and existence)—that is, a *creation* (of concepts or words-having-a-meaning, which, as words, have by themselves nothing to do with the meaning that they incarnate).
>
> —Alexandre Kojève

> The psychoanalytic interpretation conceives of the phenomenon of consciousness as the symbolic realization of a desire repressed by censorship. Let us note that for consciousness this desire *is not implicated in its symbolic realization*. . . . It follows that the signification of our conscious behavior is entirely external to the behavior itself, or, if one prefers, the *signified* is entirely cut off from the *signifier*.
>
> —Jean-Paul Sartre [1]

We could begin this way: What do you call a cat? A cat, obviously.[2] Yes; but what do you *call* "a cat"? Is the named cat the same as the unnamed cat, the cat *before* it was named? This is what ordinary language believes (or makes us believe), as Maurice Blanchot recalls in an article where, in his own way, he hails the publication of Kojève's *Introduction to the Read-*

ing of Hegel: "Everyday language calls a cat a cat, as if the living cat and its name were identical."[3] But everyday language is wrong, as the (Hegelian) philosopher and the writer know very well. The named cat is a dead cat, an absent, negated cat: "The word gives me what it signifies, but first it suppresses it. . . . It is the absence of that being, its nothingness. . . . Language begins only with a void. . . . In the beginning, I don't speak in order to say something; rather, it is a nothing that asks to speak, nothing speaks, nothing finds its being in speech, and the being of speech is nothing."[4] The upright, prosaic person who proposes to call a cat a cat—and not, as a writer does, "a dog"[5]—is therefore "more mystifying than ever, for the cat is not a cat."[6] In fact, how can we name the cat that has *disappeared* into speech? The real integrity of language is the paradoxical and impossible integrity of the writer, who creates *from nothing*[7] by constantly struggling to name the death that he resuscitates as he goes along, and which escapes from him as well, since his "speech is the *life* of that death."[8] Thus, literary creation is a perpetual idleness (or "unworking") (*désoeuvrement*)[9] that tries to climb back beyond the work, toward Creation itself, and which can accomplish this only through an aborted creation (or, what amounts to the same thing, through an interminable apocalypse):

Hegel, . . . in a text preceding the *Phenomenology*, wrote: "The first act by which Adam made himself master of the animals was to give them a name; that is, he annihilated them in their existence (as 'existants')." Hegel meant that, from that moment, the cat ceased to be simply a real cat and became an idea as well. Therefore, the meaning of speech demands, as preface to all speech, a sort of immense hecatomb, a preliminary deluge, plunging all of creation into a total sea. God created beings, but man had to annihilate them. In this way, they became meaningful for him, and he in turn created them out of that death into which they had disappeared.[10]

In the Beginning Was Language

Let us recall that Lacan, in his "Rome Discourse," was rectifying Goethe's formula: in the beginning was not the Action, but the Word (1977a, 61/271)—by which he meant creative *speech*, the performative *speech act*. But two years later, in the second seminar, he modifies the accepted translation of St. John's *logos*: in the beginning was not the word (*parole*), he maintained before his astonished listeners, but *language* (1988b, 309–314/355–361).¹¹ This comment, apparently purely philological (and, as such, rather fanciful), actually introduces an important reversal, one whose importance will only increase. Creative speech is far from being what is opposed to representative language (revealing the nothing hidden by the latter); on the contrary, language "gives [speech] its radical condition" (1988b, 313/360):

We can turn it [the inflection of *logos* in *verbum*] into something completely different from the reason for things, namely, this play of absence and presence which already provides the frame for *fiat*. For, in the end, *fiat* is made (*se fait*) on a backdrop of the un-made (*non-fait*) which is prior to it. In other words, I think that it isn't inconceivable that even the *fiat*, the most primary of creative speeches, is secondary. . . . What's at issue [in language] is a succession of absences and presences, or rather of presence on a background of absence, of absence constituted by the fact that a presence can exist. . . . It is the original contradiction of 0 and 1 [1988b, 312–313/359].

Therefore, language *in general*, and not just speech, is invested with the power of bringing non-being (the zero) into being. More precisely, speech does not create ex nihilo except against the backdrop of the simultaneity of presence and absence in language. This is another way of saying that, for Lacan, language is heir to all the characteristics previously attributed only to full/performative speech: no matter what he says, no matter what his utterance, the subject of the enunciation presents himself in it (only) as absence. This is a sign (if we need one) that Lacan no longer believes in the possibility that one speech would be more "true" than another, and that this opposition within language is henceforth displaced onto the "original" opposition between language as a whole and nothing (between 1 and 0).

At any rate, what is this "language," heir to the defunct "full speech" (a "language" where, inversely, full speech revives or survives clandestinely)? Obviously, it cannot be the same "language" that Lacan had previously denounced as the "wall of language" and the "mistaken notion of 'language as a sign.'" How could the latter reveal the nothing, since it stubbornly asserts that a cat is a cat and that the word "cat" *represents* the cat? It must be some other "language" (or another acceptation of the word "language")—and Lacan's allusion to the binary alternation of cybernetic "bits" immediately puts us on the right track. Anyway, there is no reason to be so mysterious about it, since it is something we all know (or think we know): this "language," which the unconscious is structured like (or which is its "condition"; 1970, 58), is actually the language of structural linguistics. Whatever distance Lacan may have tried to put, later on, between himself and linguistics (to which he opposed his own "linguistery"; 1975c, 20), it is clear that the major model of reference for his theory of language, from the mid-1950's on,[12] was indeed linguistics in its Saussurian version: *langue* as a closed system of regulated oppositions, ordering a homogeneous multiplicity of signifying unities independent of the reality that it designates.

As we know, this *langue*, the specific object of linguistic *science*, is not spoken by anyone. It is a language that, in principle, should be called dead,[13] separated as it is, by the Saussurian scalpel, from its individual and discursive actualization, speech: "Within the total phenomenon represented by language (*langage*), we first singled out two parts: *langue* and speech (*parole*). *Langue* is language, less speech."[14] How, then, did this *langue* come to inherit (under its Lacanian name, "language") the essential traits of *speech*? That is what remains to be understood. In what respect (or at what price) can Saussure's *langue* manifest the subject of desire, since *langue* is constructed through the methodical exclusion of all subjectivity and every consideration of the individual utterance? We may very well suspect that this cannot happen without several "linguisteries," and this is already indicated by the speed with which Lacan strides across the Saussurian distinction between *langue* and speech: Lacan's "language" is never anything but *langue*, *plus* speech, a sort of strange "speech-*langue*" ("*parlangue*")[15] in which speech becomes a dead *langue* and *langue* becomes nobody's speech.

But before we deal with this rash extension to discourse of the mechanisms that regulate *langue*, we must examine the other important modification that Lacan brings to Saussure's theory: the one that touches on the dissociation of signifier and signified, the two elements of the linguistic sign (which, according to Saussure, are inseparable). Indeed, this first modification, being a direct outgrowth of the critique of the "language-sign" launched in the "Rome Discourse," will allow for a better understanding of the conditions that "language" must fulfill in order to take the place previously occupied by "speech." In short, just as "full speech" was performative and non-constative, so Saussure's *langue* does not gain entry into Lacan's doctrine before having been emptied of all representative functions and invested with a "signifiance" (*signifiance*) that *creates* meaning.

Does this mean that Lacan was unfaithful to Saussure's teaching, or that he simply did not understand it (as some professional linguists—Mounin, for example—have protested)? First of all, Lacan's distortion of the Saussurian "sign" really does nothing but determine the ambiguity of that concept, in agreement with the strictest post-Saussurian orthodoxy. For Saussure himself, the theory of the sign is anything but univocal. On the contrary, in the *Course in General Linguistics*, it is already more or less torn between two rival hypotheses. The first, which Saussure inherited from a long philosophical tradition, is the "arbitrariness" (or "unmotivatedness") of the sign. It consists in admitting, first, that the word "cat" does not at all signify the real cat (even if it does designate or refer to it, which does not concern the Saussurian linguist): "The linguistic sign unites, not a thing and a name, but a concept and a sound-image" [16]—that is, once again, a "signified" and a "signifier." In turn, this union (which, properly speaking, is the relation of signification) is by rights just as arbitrary as it is necessary (and, in fact, indissoluble) for every user of a given *langue*: the signifier "has no natural connection *with the signified*," [17] since what is pronounced "*b-ö-f* ["beef" in French] on one side of the border" is pronounced "*o-k-s* on the other." [18] As for Saussure's second hypothesis, undoubtedly the more fruitful one, it pertains to the "value" of the linguistic sign: the sign /biːf/ (or /kæt/, or /hɔːrs/, since animals apparently must always carry the weight of these linguistic examples) is this sign in opposition to all the other signs that it is *not* (/biː/, /biːt/, /bɪf/, and so on). In other words, the signification of a term is only the "summary" of its value [19]—that is, of the paradigmatic and syntagmatic relationships between it and its surrounding terms (think of the dictionary, which enumerates words vertically according to their similarity and combines them horizontally with other words to specify their uses). Hence this conclusion: "In language, there are only differences *without positive terms*."[20]

It is easy to see that these two hypotheses are ultimately incompatible. Indeed, even when we admit that the theory of arbitrariness is not simply a new form of conventionalism,[21] the fact remains that to speak of an "arbitrary" relation between the signifier and the signified is the same as to admit, if only negatively, that the first *represents* the second. By the same token, this inevitably means reviving the idea that there is a signified *independent* of the signifier that represents it, just when we are asserting that they form a unity as inseparable as the two sides of a sheet of paper.[22] It is precisely this mirage—of a signified independent of the signifier—that the hypothesis of value dispels. Indeed, it is through pure abstraction that Saussure can say that *the* signified "beef" is here pronounced /biːf/, there /bœf/ or /ɔks/, as if this "concept" had existed *before* Babel, independently of the dispersion of national/maternal *langues*. In reality, for the speakers of a given *langue*, as Benveniste had already noted in 1939, there is no difference between the signifier /biːf/ and the signified "beef": "Between the signifier and the signified, the connection is not arbitrary; on the contrary, it is *necessary*. The concept (the 'signified') *bœuf* [beef] is perforce identical in my [French] consciousness with the sound sequence (the 'signifier') *böf*. . . . There is such a close symbiosis between them that the concept of *bœuf* is like the soul of the sound image *böf*."[23] In other words, there is strict adherence between the signifier and the signified, and if this is so, it is because, in accord with the theory of value, they vary in concert within a linguistic system with which they are in solidarity (hence the despair of translators, who know only too well that /bœf/ will never have exactly the same *meaning* as /biːf/, even if they both refer to the same *thing*).

Signification, therefore, does not reside in the representation of a signified by a signifier, even an "arbitrary" one. If we follow the hypothesis of value, the meaning of a sign is always (to use Peirce's vocabulary, quoted by Jakobson) in another sign that "interprets" the first: "The function of such an interpretant is performed by another sign or set of signs that occur together with a given sign, or might occur instead of it."[24] Even more precisely, the signified is inseparable from the signifier, whose differential destiny it shares. As Lacan says, there is no signified "day" before the signifying opposition that places day against the background of night's absence, and vice versa (1981, 169–170), no signified "man" without the signifying polarity that differentiates him from "woman" (1981, 223–224, 282–283). And so it turns out that we can never lay our hands on *the* signified of a signifier except in another signifier, and so on. This is illustrated, in "The Agency of the Letter," by the incongruous rewriting (1977a, 151/499) of the Saussurian schema of the sign:

LADIES   GENTLEMEN

The two doors, indistinguishable *in reality*, receive their imponderable "meaning"—"the imperative . . . of urinary segregation" (1977a, 151/500)—from the pure difference in places between the *two* signifiers "Ladies" and "Gentlemen."

By the same token, if the signified of a signifier is itself a signifier, *what can the distinction between signifier and signified* (advanced by the Saussurian doctrine of arbitrariness) *correspond to?* As Benveniste noted in 1939, this distinction is actually only the relic, within a theory allergic to it, of a representationalist problematic of the sign. Therefore, Benveniste amends, arbitrariness concerns only the relation of the sign to the thing designated, and not the relation of the signifier to the signified, which itself is necessary and indissoluble. The signifier is not the "arbitrary" representative of the signified, for the latter *is nothing* without the former, except through mirage or illusion. "Meaning" is "an internal component of linguistic form," [25] and therefore the signified is not to be sought anywhere but in the relations among signifiers.

We can see what Benveniste's rectification implies: it methodically reduces the theory of signification to a theory of value, and by the same token, as Jean-Claude Milner opportunely remarks, it justifies the notion "that in order to designate any system structured like a language [let us correct this Lacanian slippage: like a *langue*], one adopts a single term—for example, 'the signifier.'" [26] Now, as we know, this is the side taken by Lacan, who on this point merely draws the strict conclusions of the theory of value. Indeed, if the sign represents nothing—neither the referent nor even the signified—then there is nothing to sink one's teeth into but the signifier. Only the signifier survives the deluge (as Blanchot says) that swallows up every "signifiable" (1977, 288/692). As for the concept of the "sign," it is totally abandoned; witness the double and significant destiny that it meets in Lacan. Either it is criticized as what the signifier is *not*—that is, "what represents something for someone" (1970, 65), a definition borrowed from Peirce but implicitly entailing that of the Saussurian sign—or it is simply *identified* with the concept of the signifier ("The signifier is a sign that refers to another sign"; 1981, 188).

Therefore, the stakes are clear enough in this methodical reduction of sign to the signifier alone. For Lacan, it is a question of emptying the linguistic sign of every representative function, in order to invest it with the role previously imparted to speech: the role of producing (presenting) *nothing*, from *nothing*. There is, Lacan repeats after Lévi-Strauss,[27] an "autonomy" of the signifier relative to the signified (1981, 223; 1970, 55), in the sense that the signifier "does not depend on the signification . . . but is its source" (1981, 282). This formula summarizes very well the double demonstration to which Lacan yields whenever he presents his doctrine of the signifier (see, for example, the first section of "The Agency of the Letter," which is entirely constructed on the following pattern):

  1. The signifier does not *depend* on the signified. Indeed, not only does "the signifier [not] answer to the function of representing the signified," it cannot answer to "any signification whatever" (1977a, 150/498; see also 1975c, 31–32). Taken in itself (that is, separated, as if that were possible, from other signifiers), the signifier "signifies nothing" (1981, 210), and this is what Lacan tries to express by speaking of its "materiality" (1988b, 82/104–105; 1966, 24), its "localized" (1977a, 153/501) and "literal" structure: "By 'letter' I designate that material support that concrete discourse borrows from language" (1977a, 147/495). Admittedly, these are ambiguous formulations, but they do signify, at any rate, that the signifier does not *incarnate* a prior ideality.[28] If, as Benveniste pro-

poses in his rectification of Saussure,[29] "the concept *boeuf* is like the soul of the sound-image *böf*," then, according to Lacan, we must add that the literal body of the signifier contains no soul (no meaning) before the spirit comes to it from its coupling with other bodies just as stupid as itself. The signifier is truly senseless (*in-sensé*), "stupid" (*bête*; 1975c, 24), and, just like a character on a typewriter keyboard, it makes sense only by effacing another signifier, taking its *place* on the written page, *next to* other signifiers (with all the other, no less stupid, "typos" that this may imply—slips of the tongue and the pen, *Witz*, and so on).

2. The signifier is the *source* of the signified. The latter is never anything but an "effect" of these couplings and encroachments of signifiers, a "signified effect" (*effet de signifié*; 1975c, 22–23) in the sense in which we speak, for example, of a "Larsen effect" or an "optical illusion" (*effet d'optique*). This signified is truly nothing— nothing that would *in effect* be caused or produced by the signifier. In accord with the theory of value, meaning is never anything but an illusion, produced "between" signifiers, which themselves have no meaning—a sort of rainbow that eludes our grasp as soon as we try to approach it. "Sense," Lacan maintains, "emerges from nonsense" (1977a, 158/508), and here is the whole "sense" (if we may call it that) of Lacan's rewriting of the Saussurian schema of the sign, in which

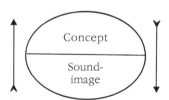

is transformed into the "algorithm"

$$\frac{S}{s}$$

"which is read as: the signifier over the signified, 'over' corresponding to the bar separating the two stages" (1977a, 149/497). S, the creative and capital signifier, hereafter precedes, in all its supremacy, its passive and secondary effect: the *s* of the signified.[30]

From the Floating Signifier
to the Flowing Signified

The reader will have noted already that Lacan, while suppressing the ellipse and the inverted arrows that indicate the unity of the sign in Saussure's diagram, nevertheless maintains and even accentuates the bar separating signifier from signified. The bar, he says enigmatically, "resists signification" (1977a, 149/497) and "creates a real border . . . between the floating signifier and the flowing signified" (1970, 68; see also 1970, 55; 1975c, 22, 35). In this way, every signifier becomes a "floating" one (that is, as Lévi-Strauss said of the singular "zero symbol," "empty of meaning"), and, like Noah's ark, it sails the floodwaters of the signified, *without clinging to them*. This seems to contradict not only the Saussurian formula but also its reformulation by Benveniste. Benveniste's formula, we recall, reabsorbed the signified into the signifier only because of their *union*, which is also to say because of the perfect *transparency* that linguistic signs have for their users. Lacan, conversely, accentuates linguistic signs' *duality* (he even calls it "duplicity"; 1981, 136, 187) and, by the same token, their *opacity*, since a suitably repressive bar henceforth separates signifiers from their signified.[31] Indeed, it is clear that Lacan is thinking here primarily of the incongruous products of the "dream work" or the *Witz* (such as "*Autodidasker*," "famillionnair," and so on), in which the one-to-one correspondence between signifier and signified is upset in favor of overdetermined and multivalent neologisms. The "duplicity" of the signifier, Lacan tells us, is such that it can always still signify the most diverse things: "If the unconscious is the way that Freud describes it, a pun in itself can be the mainspring that sustains a symptom. . . . Without the fundamental duplicity of signifier and signified, no psychoanalytic determinism is conceivable" (1981, 135–136).

Already this means that the "signifier," separated from the signified, is no longer the Saussurian linguists' signifier; the latter, we should emphasize, cannot be equivocal. To concede that it could be equivocal would be to annul the very principle of the sign's diacritical "value," as Benveniste firmly points out with respect to the hypothesis of Abel and Freud on the "antithetical meaning of primal words": "It is thus a priori improbable . . . that . . . languages (*langues*) . . . escape the 'principle of contradiction.'"[32] If polysemia exists, it can only be a polysemia *regulated* within the lexical order of the *langue*. From this perspective, the *langue* of the linguists—which, as we too often forget, is an object *constructed* in theory—is farther from natural languages than from those artificial languages that Lacan regularly criticizes for their wish to get rid of signifying equivocation ("If artificial languages are stupid, it is because they are constructed on the basis of signification"; 1981, 65; see also 1975c, 22–23, and 1973a, 4, 47–48). There is no linguistics of the pun (or there is only a "linguistery"), for puns, like oneiric "portmanteau" words, the neologisms of delirium, and poetic metaphors, *transgress* the differences coded into *langue* (Lacan was later to express this by creating the conceptual pun *lalangue*, which concept, he said, cannot be reduced to what linguistic science can know; 1975c, 126–127).[33] In the eyes of linguists, all the phenomena of equivocality which Lacan alleges as support for his theory of the "duplicity" of signifier and signified, have nothing to do with linguistics but rather with (as Benveniste once more observes) a stylistics (or a rhetoric) of discourse.[34] Indeed, only at this level, that of *spoken* language,[35] can the "signifier" (if it still is one) "float" freely enough to create a new meaning.

As for Lacan's citing the fact that "under the same signifier there are, down the ages, slippages of signification, proving that we cannot establish a one-to-one correspondence between the two systems" (1981, 135), this does not at all "prove" that the signified slides under the signifier *in the order of synchrony*. That the adjective *atterré* first meant "set upon the earth" (*mis à terre*) and then, through progressive homophonic contamination, came to mean "struck with terror" ("*frappé de terreur*") (SV, 13 November 1957) may afford a glimpse into how *langue* evolves diachronically. Nevertheless, the linguists would say, only through a retrospective illusion can we conclude, as Lacan does, that the signifier is separated from the signified by "a bar that resists signification." According to the era considered, *atterré* signifies *either* "set upon the earth" *or* "struck with terror," and this is all that structural linguistics can and wants to know. Again, for linguists, the fact that the signified is an effect of the signifier does not at all mean that the signifier could signify any old thing (or, what amounts to the same thing, nothing at all); on the contrary, it means that they adhere so closely that they can be separated only through an abstraction.

Must we conclude, then (as Jean-François Lyotard does in *Discours, figure*), that Lacan's emphasis on the bar between signifier and signified surreptitiously reintroduces the problem of meaning, in its classical "thickness" or "depth," within a theory of signification and value that specifically suspends it?[36] In a way, we must, since Lacan actually does revive the mirage of a signified independent of the signifier (and we will see why in a moment). But he does this, it seems to me, the better to present the evanescence of this mirage. On this point, Lacan does not challenge the principle of structural linguistics, even if he does apply it unduly, as Lyotard justly notes, to the realm of discursive speech. In Lacan, meaning is certainly maintained apart from the signifier, but only as a void, a vanishing point, or, as Merleau-Ponty also says with respect to Saussure, as "the idea in the Kantian sense."[37] Indeed, that there is a "bar that resists signification" does not at all mean that there is some opaque signified hidden "behind" or "under" signifiers. On the contrary, it means that the signified, *precisely because it is an effect of the signifier*, perpetually "slips" and "flows" under the signifier (1977a, 153–154/502; 1981, 135, 296–297), like ungraspable water.

Hence, Lacan explains, the impossibility of establishing a one-to-one correspondence between the "tide" of signifiers and the "tide" of signifieds, as the Saussurian schema of the two "floating realms"[38] had suggested (1981, 135, 295–303; 1977a, 154/502–503):

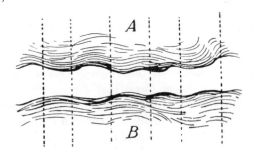

It is well known that this schema's purpose, in Saussure, was to illustrate the simultaneous segmentation of otherwise "amorphous"
masses of "sounds" and "thoughts." Thus it involves a sort of *synchronic* "cross section" intended to illustrate, in quasi-mythical
form, the strictly nontemporal principle of any *langue*: either there
is discontinuity (there are "discrete" unities) or there is only an undifferentiated continuity where nothing makes sense. Lacan, very
significantly, sees in this the figuration of an uninterrupted sentence. More precisely, he connects the Saussurian schema to the
linear combination of signifiers on the syntagmatic axis, which
is itself surreptitiously applied to the "*diachrony* [of] discourse"
(1981, 66; my emphasis) [39]—a way of putting the aforesaid "amorphous" masses into movement and introducing the idea of "an in-
cessant sliding of the signified under the signifier" (1977a, 154/
502). Indeed, what happens if I add one signifier *after* another, to
form a sentence (a "signifying chain," in Lacan's vocabulary, inspired here by Hjelmslev)? According to Lacan, no signifier will
have any definite signified *before* being combined with other signifiers, until the point where a period retroactively and provisionally seals the meaning of the sentence (1981, 303, 338; 1977a,
153–154/502–503, 304/806)—as we see if we successively consider the signifying unities that compose the present sentence ("Ac-
cording/to/Lacan/. . . /./"/). Whence Lacan's conclusion: "We can
say . . . that none of [the elements of the chain of the signifier] '*consists*' in the signification of which it is at the moment capable"
(1977a, 153/502). The operative phrase here, certainly, is "at the
moment." Lacan means to say that there is no synchronic correspondence between signifier and signified because the meaning of a
signifier is always yet *to come* in another punctuating signifier (baptized S_2 in Lacanian "algebra"), which in turn, and so on: "The signifier, by its very nature, always *anticipates* meaning by unfolding
its dimension *before* it" (1977a, 153/502; my emphasis). We can
understand this only if we concede a sort of intentionality of the signifier (or of the subject?), akin to the "signifying intention" spoken
of by Merleau-Ponty: "The reason why a language finally intends to
say and does say (*veut dire et dit*) something is not that each sign is
the vehicle for a signification that allegedly belongs to it, but that

all the signs together allude to a signification which is always in abeyance when they are considered singly, and which I go beyond them toward, without their ever containing it." [40]

This empty intentionality, never filled, is what Lacan calls "metonymy" (inspired by Jakobson's article on aphasia [41]), successively (and dangerously) identifying it with (1) the "word-to-word" of syntagmatic combination (1977a, 156/506); (2) metonymy in the rhetorical sense (1977a, 156/505); (3) the Freudian mechanism of "displacement" (1977a, 160/511), which, however, refers in Freud only to affective "emphasis"; and (4) desire as a perpetual "desire for something else" (1977a, 166/518). Hence this "formula" for metonymy: $f(S \ldots S')S \cong S(-)s$, which is read in the following way: The function of the metonymic connection of the signifier is congruent (more or less: $\cong$) with the maintenance of the bar that prevents the signifier from ever corresponding to its elusive signified except "at infinity." In short, the more you speak, the less you know what you mean to say (or desire), for the signification retroactively produced by the "punctuation" that pins one signifier to another always runs behind the signifying production itself. In a word, the signified fluctuates and "slips" indefinitely *as a function* of the signifiers, insofar as none of them manages to furnish the "last word" of meaning (and when that happens, Lacan says, we are in the realm of psychosis; cf. 1981, 30–31, 219–220). We can illustrate this point with the following (algorithmic?) diagram:

$$\underset{\text{\large \leadsto}\; s}{S_1, S_2, S_3 \ldots S_n}$$

Better yet, we can use a sort of eternal cascade as illustration (since Lacan also speaks of "stages" with respect to the two elements of the "algorithm," presupposing that the signifier *falls* regularly to the level of the signified, in order to "toss a cobblestone into the pond of the signified"; 1970, 68): [42]

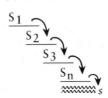

Indeed, according to Lacan, the result is the same if we turn to the other operation of speech noted by Jakobson: that of the "vertical" selection of terms from among those capable of being substituted for the signifier on the paradigmatic axis. This substitution certainly produces meaning and, Lacan writes, therefore a "crossing" (1977a, 154/503, 164/515) of the bar separating the signifier from the signified. This is what Lacan calls "metaphor," which he successively (and just as dangerously) identifies with (1) the "one word for another" of paradigmatic selection (1977a, 157/507); (2) metaphor in the rhetorical sense (1977a, 156–157/507); (3) the Freudian mechanism of condensation (1977a, 160/511), which, however, designates in Freud less a substitution than a *compression* of several terms; and (4) the psychoanalytic symptom (1977a, 166/518). He notates it thus:

$$f\left(\frac{S'}{S}\right)S \cong S(+)s$$

The + manifests "the crossing of the bar—and the constitutive value of this crossing for the emergence of signification" (1977a, 164/515). But this crossing, we should add, is never anything but a transgression that maintains the prohibition implacably separating signifier from signified. That repressive bar is not suppressed, for its "crossing" only adds (+) something extra—namely, an "effect of signification . . . that is creative or poetic" (1977a, 164/515): the signified is only a "poetic spark" (1977a, 156–158/507–508) produced between signifiers on the occasion of their substitution.

What is inspiring Lacan here is obviously Jakobson's linguistic model: if I say "house," this term makes sense only because it is substituted in the sentence for, say, "louse." Neither /haʊs/ nor /laʊs/ makes any sense outside their commutativity. Lacan extends this strictly linguistic thesis (granted, he was encouraged in this by Jakobson himself)[43] to the rhetorical and, more broadly, the psychoanalytic realms, concluding that *any* substitution of signifier for signifier produces meaning—for example, the phrase "his sheaf" that is substituted for the proper noun "Boaz" in this line by Victor Hugo: "His sheaf was neither miserly nor spiteful" (cf. 1981, 247–248; 1977a, 156–158/506–508). Lacan emphasizes that nothing predestines "sheaf" to replace "Boaz"—which is another way of saying that this substitution, from the perspective of code, is pure non-sense. And yet, Lacan adds, this substitution *makes sense* (it produces a poetic effect). Why is this? Not because the sheaf would represent Boaz (as we have seen, they have no relationship, especially none of similarity; normally, a sheaf is neither generous nor helpful). "Boaz," therefore, is not (as classical rhetoric maintained) the hidden meaning of the signifier "sheaf," in whose place we expected "Boaz." On the contrary, "Boaz" arises from it. Here, Lacan proposes, there is an unexpected signification, *produced* by "the substitution of one signifier for another in a chain, without anything natural predestining it for this function . . . except the matter of two signifiers, reducible as such to a phonemic opposition" (1966, 890).

In short, put one signifier in place of another, and something will always emerge: meaning. A linguist would certainly call this theory completely surrealistic (even if Lacan, incidentally, criticizes André Breton's theory of the metaphor; 1977a, 157/507), for where has anyone ever seen that the improbable "phonemic opposition" of "Boaz" and "sheaf" makes sense in *langue*? Obviously, the "signifiers" that Lacan has in mind are not those of the linguistic code, which constitutes a "filing cabinet of *prefabricated* representations,"[44] but rather those unpredictable, uncodable signifiers of the dream and the symptom, where anything can refer to anything else. Why, then, continue to speak about "signifiers" at all, if we are no longer in the realm of *langue* (and probably, if we consider the dream and the symptom, not even in the realm of language)? All that these two types of "signifiers" have in common is that they have no meaning *in themselves*—and this, in fact, is exactly what Lacan is driving at: that point where sense arises from non-sense. In this limitless expansion of the concept of the "signifier," what matters to him is to prove yet again that language (a term vague enough to crush out all difference among *langue*, speech, and the productions of the unconscious) represents *nothing*. The reason why the "signifier" does not represent the signified is that it creates the signified metaphorically: the "metaphor occurs at the precise point at which sense emerges from non-sense" (1977a, 158/508). And it can create this signified only on condition of abolishing it, volatilizing it in its creation: a metonymy of nothing, a nihilistic metonymy that "permits the elision in which the signifier installs the lack-of-being in the object relation, using the value of 'reference back' possessed by signification in order to invest it with the desire aimed at the very lack it supports" (1977a, 164/515).

We see, then, that the signified *s*, which figures under the resistant bar of the Lacanian "algorithm," is nothing that would be independent of the signifier. On the contrary, Lacan separates signified from signifier, apparently a highly classical gesture, but only the better to underline its evanescent character, its radical nonexistence outside the references among signifiers. Since this is precisely what Benveniste, Jakobson, and all of structural linguistics in general assert of their own object of study, Lacan does not diverge from the principle governing structural linguistics, even if he retains *only* that principle (or that philosophy) and applies it to realms where it really has no business being. Like it or not, Lacan's thesis of the sign's "duplicity," so controversial, finally implies nothing more than what linguists call its "unity," and so Lacan's thesis is in perfect agreement, if not with the letter, at least with the spirit of Saussurianism.

What Is Called a Subject?

It is an entirely different story if we examine the other thesis that, for Lacan, completes the thesis of the signifier's autonomy: "The signifier represents a subject . . . (not a signified)—and for another signifier (which means: not for another subject)" (1970, 65). Indeed, it is one thing to say that the sign does not represent reality and that the signifier in turn does not represent but produces the signified; it is quite another to say that the signifier represents the *subject* for another signifier. As for structural linguistics, it never says anything of the kind, methodically excluding the subject in order to constitute itself as a science,[45] and only reintroducing it as one of the purely formal markers of subjectivity (personal pronouns, tenses, and so on) that "shift" the statement (*énoncé*) onto the subjective point of enunciation (*énonciation*) that supports it. As Benveniste bluntly puts it, " 'Ego' is he who *says* 'ego,' "[46] and that is as far as linguists permit themselves to go. Again, the ideal *langue* constructed by linguists is spoken by no one. It cannot, a fortiori, "represent" any given subject.

This, however, is precisely what Lacan maintains, just when he is insisting on language's "preexistence" for the subject and the subject's preinscription in discourse (1977a, 148/495). Admittedly, the Lacanian subject is the subject subjected to the signifier, the subject dispossessed of any meaning (*vouloir-dire*) or mastery of language, which speaks him more than he speaks it; but, inversely, the signifier represents nothing but the subject, by means of which it is reinvested with that function of *representation* that Lacan so stringently denies elsewhere—which, by the same token, helps us understand why Lacan felt the need to separate signifier and signified by a "bar that resists signification." On one side of the question (the side we have just investigated), this thesis says the same thing as linguistics: the signifier represents nothing but another signifier. But on the other side (the one that really interests Lacan), this thesis can also be read as saying that the signifier *represents* nothing, and that the signifier (re)presents the *nothing* that the subject of desire "is." Signifiers do not mean to say anything (*ne veulent rien dire*), by which Lacan understands that they all say the *same* thing—that is, the subject as nothing—and this is why they are perfectly equivalent in their very difference. Since they say *anything at all* (*n'importe quoi*), they all say not what is identical but what is the same—the same "eclipse" of the subject as a "being of non-being" (*être de non-étant*; 1977a, 300/802), the same "disappearing appearance" (1973b, 33) of that μὴ ὄν . . . that brings to being an existent in spite of its non-advent" (1977b, 128–129/117).

In this way, we finally see that the "signifier" inherits the function previously assigned to "full speech" (that of saying nothing), and that the subject, for his part, inherits the disappearing "place" of the signified. Just as the linguists' signified arises only from the reference of one signifier to another, so the Lacanian subject appears/disappears only by making himself represented, through a signifier, to another signifier. Lacan himself is very clear about it: "This whole signifier can only operate, it may be said, if it is present in the subject. It is this objection that I answer by supposing that it has passed over to the level of the signified" (1977a, 155/504). And a bit later, with respect to the "crossing" of the S/s bar, he says, "This crossing expresses the condition of passage of the signifier into the signified that I [have already] pointed out, although provisionally confusing it with the place of the subject" (1977a, 164/516). Why does Lacan say "provisionally"? Because the signified is only a momentary and provisional "effect." If the signifier, as Lacan says, "represents a subject," and "not a signified," it is not because the subject has nothing to do with the signified but only because the subject is distinguished from the traditional "fixed" signified: the subject is now the *elusive* signified of all signifiers, what they all represent in his absence; but he is none the less their signified, to which their references refer. As Lyotard aptly remarks, "When he says 'signified' Lacan thinks 'subject.' Lacan's whole theory of the metaphor is a theory of the metaphor of the *subject* [indeed, this is the title of a text reproduced in the appendix to *Ecrits*; 1966, 889–892]: this subject can grasp himself only through metaphor—that is to say, by missing himself—precisely because he is signified by a signifier." [47] As for the metonymy that is forever putting the signified off till doomsday, it too is a metonymy of *desire*—that is, once again, a metonymy of the subject.

And so we must ask what this abrupt reintroduction of the subject—and its inevitable correlative, representation—can mean in a discourse that, in principle, should be absolutely inhospitable to it. The hypothesis here (and it will certainly come as no surprise to any reader with the laudable courage to have persevered this far) is that the subject's reintroduction corresponds to the linguistic model's massive overdetermination by the philosophical problematic of the subject of representation, a problematic Cartesian in origin, of which Lacan provides an ultramodern version inspired by Kojève's commentary on Hegel.

In this respect, we recall that Lacan, almost from the beginning, links the problem of language to the problem of the subject. For example, let us reread what he has to say in "Beyond the Reality Principle":

Language, before signifying something, signifies for someone. By the single fact that he [the analyst] is present and is listening, the man who speaks [the patient] addresses himself to him, and since he imposes upon his discourse a not wanting to say anything (*de ne rien vouloir dire*), what remains is that he *wants to speak to him* (*veut lui dire*). What he says may indeed make no sense; what he says *to him* receives a meaning [1966, 82–83].

"Meaning," in other words, is not to be sought in *what* language says (in the statement) but in the *fact of its being said* (in the enunciation, in speech). And this meaning, constituted in interlocutive speech and nowhere else, this "signified = *x*," is the subject insofar as he "wants to speak" (*veut dire*), insofar as he *ex*-presses himself to the intention of another. Language is first of all speech, and thus it says nothing—nothing but the subject, to the extent that he wants to speak (himself) (*veut* [*se*] *dire*).

We see what these (still very phenomenological[48]) early formulations of Lacan already presuppose: the whole critique of the "language-sign" that will be carried out under the auspices of "full speech" and, later, of the "signifier." In this passage, we are witnessing an actual bracketing off (or "reduction") of every realist reference, for the sake of an entirely autoenunciative and self-referential (because "subjective") model of language. This language is essentially speech that speaks itself, in the very precise sense of a subject's intentionally *ex*pressing himself within it, manifesting himself in exteriority by passing through the mediation of the other—in short, in the sense of the subject's speaking *himself*, performing an autorepresentation.

This is why speech, for Lacan, is not a question of reality but, as we have been confirming, of truth. We must understand by this that the subject grasps himself through a subjective *certitude*, which is what Lacan says again in this passage from the first seminar, which we have already cited: "What is at stake [in psychoanalysis] is the realization of the truth of the subject, like a dimension peculiar to it which must be detached in its distinctiveness [*originalité*] in relation to the very notion of reality" (1988a, 21/29). And we certainly recognize this "peculiar dimension": it is that of the Cartesian cogito, here reformulated by Lacan in terms of "speech." The subject of speech, like the subject of the cogito, grasps himself in his truth by negating ("reducing," questioning) objective reality, for the sake of an autorepresentation by which he poses himself "before" himself through a *Vor-stellung*:[49] his objects (or, what amount to the same thing in this context, his representations) are henceforth his own. In this sense, the progress of an analysis follows the course of the first two Cartesian meditations. It proceeds from language, which says "something" or represents objects, to speech, in which the subject (of the enunciation) speaks himself in everything that he says (in all his statements): *dico, sum.* Lacan later makes this very clear: "Let us say that it is by taking its place at the level of the enunciation that the cogito acquires its certainty" (1977b, 140/129). In other words, it would be impossible that, saying something (no matter how nonsensical), I would not "be" at the very moment when I spoke (made the statement). This reformulation of the cogito presupposes, of course, the assimilation of the "I think" to an "I speak (myself)"[50] and, therefore, in accord with Heidegger's interpretation, to an "I represent (myself)," which already implies all the *distance* between the subject of the enunciation and the statement that represents him: this subject, in the act of enunciation, is related to himself only on condition of projecting himself "outside" himself in the utterance of the statement where he (re)presents himself. Let us pause here a moment, for this point is extremely important: if the subject of speech and/or of the signifier is none other than the Cartesian subject, as Lacan asserts later (1977b, 36/36; 1966, 856, 858), it is only as a subject of *representation* (and not of an immediate certitude—that of affect, for example).

Confirmation, if any were needed, could be found in the Hegelianism of Lacan's first formulations on language and speech. Whereas one could say that the cogito is a monologue, Lacan describes a dialogue, but only because he was reformulating, in the 1940's and 1950's, the cogito in Hegelian terms: only by speaking to the other, by alienating/exteriorizing himself in a communal language, can the subject represent himself "in front of" himself and thus arrive at self-consciousness. In other words, he can manifest himself in his truth only by passing through the mediation of the other, by making himself recognized by the other. Thus the Lacanian cogito is from the very start a linguistic, social, and intersubjective cogito, a cogito in the first person plural (1977a, 86/299). But this changes nothing of its structure as cogito, understood as the structure of the subject of representation. The subject of speech, for the Hegelian who was the young Lacan, continues to speak *himself* in the other to whom he speaks, for the good reason that the subject makes himself recognized by the other only by recognizing himself simultaneously *in* that alter ego. Thus, as we have seen, unfolds the efficacy of the analytic cure, as Lacan conceived of it until the end of the 1940's: here, the subject speaks to an alienated image of himself until the analyst, that image's specular prop, returns it to the subject, who finally recognizes himself in it. This accords, obviously, with the structure of the cogito, since now there is an identity (a dialectical one this time) between the subject of the enunciation and the subject of the statement: the "subject" who speaks is the *same* as the "ego" of whom, with whom, he speaks.

Will this reminder help us solve the problem of the relationship between subject and signifier? It will to a certain extent, since all of this explains very well why Lacan would later come to claim that "the signifier represents the subject," although it does not explain why he added "for another signifier." The precise meaning of this thesis is that the subject cannot speak himself except by dividing himself and endlessly escaping from himself into the signifier. He is undoubtedly the "signified" of all signifiers, but "the S and the *s* of the Saussurian algorithm are not on the same level, and man only deludes himself when he believes his true place is at their axis, which is nowhere" (1977a, 166/518). Therefore, the subject of the enunciation cannot be the same as the subject of the statement (1977b, 138−139/127): this "man" will always be *other* than (what) he says, which is also the reason for Lacan's explicit rewriting of the cogito: "I think where I am not, therefore I am where I do not think" (1977b, 166/517). The one who says, "*I think, I am*" (or "I/represent/myself") is not identical to the one who *says*, "I think, I am" (or "I/represent/myself"): "Of course, every representation requires a subject, but this subject is never a pure subject. . . . There is no subject without, somewhere, *aphanisis* of the subject" (1977b, 221/201). In other words, the subject of the enunciation is *not* the subject of the statement—or, to reprise Sartre's famous para-Hegelian formula, the two are the same only "in the mode of not being so." Like the ungraspable Sartrean "for-itself"—with which, in many ways, this subject is comparable [51]—he is not what he *is* (the "signifier," or the statement that claims to fix him in his being "in-himself"), and he is what he is *not* (a perpetual nihilation, a perpetual overtaking of the signifiers/statements that objectify him). In a word, he "is" a permanent *self-negation.*

No doubt the reader has already seen what we are driving at with these insidious comparisons: if the subject, in the signifier, cannot speak himself as he is, it is because he speaks himself in it as he is not—in short, because (in accord with the Kojèvian lesson reprised by Sartre) he is the radical negativity of a subject who can pose himself "for-himself" only by ceaselessly negating himself as he is "in-himself"; he is pure Desire, pure difference from himself as the condition of relationship with himself, pure transcendence, through which he can rejoin himself only at infinity, since when he rejoins himself as he is in-himself, he is no longer for-himself (he is a corpse, an inert thing). This subject is the subject of Kojèvian "error-truth" or (what amounts to the same thing) Sartrean "bad faith," a subject who cannot speak himself (as "for-himself") except by negating himself (as "in-himself"), without ever being identical to himself.[52] Under these conditions, we understand why the subject of the enunciation can no longer speak himself as he is in his statements—not because he is no longer the subject of the cogito, the subject of representation, but, on the contrary, because he has become this subject so well that he is now reduced to the cogito's pure *relationship* with self as structure of representation (that is, as structure of the transcendence by which he leaves himself in order to be able to pose himself "facing" himself). At present, this subject can no longer speak *himself* except on condition of *speaking* himself, and the "spoken" (*dit*) is able to manifest the "speaking" (*dire*), through which he relates himself to himself, only by absenting the self: "The fact that one is speaking is forgotten behind what is spoken within what is given to be understood. . . . Thus the spoken does not go without saying (*le dit ne va pas sans dire*). But if the spoken is always posited in truth, . . . the speaking is joined to it only through ek-sisting to it—that is, by not belonging to the spoken dimension (*dit-mension*)[53] of truth" (1973a, 5, 8). The subject "ek-sists to language," Lacan says again and again, because he has no other essence than his ek-sistence, than his perpetual ek-stasis beyond what he is: Lacanism is an existentialism.

Now let us take things a bit more slowly. We have already seen that language, for Lacan, does not represent reality but rather the subject. We must now take the matter farther and explain why: because the subject is negativity (separation from himself, separation from what is), and he manifests himself in language only by negating reality, reducing it to nothing. This, precisely, was Kojève's

lesson as he commented in his own way on Hegel. "Discourse"—
identified with the "Subject" ("Discourse = Subject"[54])—reveals
the "Real,"[55] but only on condition of "nihilating" it, causing to be
what is not by negating what is: the man who "through his discourse . . . succeeds in *preserving* error in the very heart of reality . . .
is a Nothingness that nihilates in Being, or an 'ideal' that is present
in the Real."[56] Indeed, the Real is "being" as it is, being without
alterity, "given," "identical to itself," "omnipresent and dense,"[57]
mired in its "*hic et nunc*"[58]—and both Sartre[59] and Lacan faithfully repeat this lesson: the real, Lacan says, is "pure and simple,"
"undifferentiated," "non-human" (1988a, 68−69/81−83), "without fissure" (1988b, 97/122), "always in the same place" (1988b,
238/278, 297/342; 1977b, 49/49). Discourse (or the Subject), on
the contrary, is "being" as it is not, being that differs from itself because it relates to itself. More precisely, it is "being" separating
from itself in order to promote itself to the status of an ideality—
that is, to the status of a subjective representation: "Thus the concept 'this dog' does not differ at all from the real, concrete dog to
which it 'refers' except that the dog is here and now, whereas its
concept is everywhere and nowhere, always and never"[60]—an idealizing abstraction, which obviously entails a radical negation of the
empirical Real. Just as the Cartesian subject reaches the certitude of
subjective representation only at the price of a radical suspension of
all reality (his own included), so Discourse and/or the Subject can
only emerge at the price of what Kojève and Lacan call a "murder of
the thing" (1977a, 104/319; 1988a, 174/196): "When the Meaning (Essence) 'dog' passes into the *word* 'dog'—that is, becomes an
abstract Concept which is *different* from the sensible reality that it
reveals by its Meaning—the Meaning (Essence) *dies*: the *word*
'dog' does not run, drink, and eat. . . . the *conceptual* understanding of empirical reality is equivalent to a *murder*."[61] Lacan translates this as follows: "Through that which becomes embodied only
by being the trace of a nothingness and whose support cannot there-
after be impaired [since it is an ideality], the concept, saving the du-
ration of what passes by, engenders the thing" (1977a, 65/276).

Indeed, this is what Hegel also said, Hegel for whom the sign's
"arbitrariness" (*Willkür*) was a manifestation of the free negativity
of intelligence disengaging itself from the immediacy of intuition.

Say the word "lion," he writes, and you create the lion ex nihilo, by abolishing it as a tangible thing.[62] Say the word "dog," Kojève comments, and you kill the real dog that barks and wags its tail.[63] Pronounce the word "cat," Blanchot continues, and "death speaks."[64] Say the word "elephants," Lacan concludes, and here comes a herd of elephants, present in its absence and filling up the room (1975b, 201, 244, 267). What is left at the end of this interesting hecatomb? Nothing but words, words, words—*that is, a subject*. Thus language, the manifestation of the negativity of the subject who posits himself by negating (himself as) the Real, works the miracle of manifesting what is not: the tearing apart, the ek-sistence, and the perpetual self-overtaking that "is" the subject, the subject who speaks himself in everything by negating everything. Language, as Kojève says of Desire, presents "the absence of a reality,"[65] and thus, Lacan continues, it manifests the disappearing "nothing" that is the subject.

It is probably easier to see now the way in which structural linguistics, at a certain point, came to be grafted onto the Lacanian theory of language, progressively supplanting the problematic of "full speech." After all, the distance from the Hegelian-Kojèvian thesis concerning the "murder of the thing" to the thesis of the sign's "arbitrariness" was only a small step, which Lacan was quick to take; on this point, see the end of the first seminar, where Lacan abruptly passes from the theme of "creative speech," formulated in Hegelian terms (1988a, 242–243/267), to that of the "arbitrariness" of the Saussurian sign (1988a, 248/272). From there, it was also easy and tempting to glide imperceptibly from the conception of discourse as "the presence of the absence of a reality" to the linguistic theory of value, where each signifying unity is defined by opposition to all the other unities which it is *not*, and which it thus presents in their absence (on this point, see the passage in the third seminar where the opposition of the "signifiers" "night/day" is described as a "symbolic nihilation" of reality; 1981, 168). But we see also that these borrowings from structural linguistics take place in the shadow of a philosophy of the subject and of language, which predates them, and to which they bring nothing more than a sort of compelling scientific "guarantee."

If it is so important to Lacan to stress, by way of Saussure, that the signifier represents nothing—neither reality nor even the signified—it is precisely because above all it is important to him to show that it represents (that is, manifests) the "nothing" that is the subject. The subject truly continues to speak "*himself*" in everything that he says, even when he is *nothing other* than the language that represents him, in his absence, to another signifier. Once again, it is by saying nothing (by negating everything) that the Kojèvian-Lacanian subject speaks himself (in everything). Indeed, the fact that the subject speaks himself in language, by negating every real referent, also signifies that he speaks himself in language and simultaneously abolishes *himself* in it (just as he abolishes the dog or the elephants whose vanishing "being" he is). This is what Blanchot understood so well:

> It is clear that in me the power of speech is also tied to my absence of being. I name myself; it is as if I were pronouncing my funeral chant: I separate myself from myself; I am no longer my presence or my reality, but rather an objective, impersonal presence, that of my name, which overtakes me and whose petrified immobility performs exactly the function of a tombstone weighing on the void. When I speak, I negate the existence of what I say, but I also negate the existence of him who says it: my speech, if it reveals "being" in its nonexistence, affirms that this revelation is made on the basis of the nonexistence of the speaker, his ability to separate himself from himself, to be other than his being.[66]

And this is why, Blanchot adds, I cannot speak myself except in the form of an interminable "dying" that manifests the "impossibility of dying."[67]

What, then, is called a subject? A call from the void, through which the subject calls himself to being by tearing himself away from himself, by nihilating himself. In the end, to say "I" is always the same as saying (as did Poe's character quoted by Lacan; 1988b, 231/270), "I am dead"[68] "I am nothing," "I am non-being, pure non-existent negativity." In other words, the subject of the enunciation disappears by appearing in the subject of the statement, where he represents himself and "separates himself from himself." Inversely, the subject of the statement presents the subject in his absence, by representing him. Thus, this subject is no longer the one spoken of by Lacan in his early writings, that "signified = x" who manifested himself in and through the *mediation* of speech addressed to the other. At present he "is" that mediation itself—that is, the pure *relationship* to self as such; he *is* the "discourse of the Other," in the very precise sense of this discourse's manifesting him as nothing, of his appearing/disappearing in(to) it, like the "signified = *x*" of an "enunciation that denounces itself" and a "statement (*énoncé*) that renounces itself" (1977a, 300/801).

This complete reabsorption of the subject into the "discourse of the Other" that represents him is what has made inattentive readers think that Lacan had finished once and for all with the subject of the cogito. But that is simply not true, as Lacan himself very well knew. To say that the subject *is* language is also to say that language *is* the subject "himself"—or, if you will, that the two are the *same*, the vanishing sameness that relates the subject of the enunciation to the subject of the statement, and vice versa. In reality, language in Lacan speaks only of the subject (and this is what finally distinguishes it, as we have already noted, from the Heideggerian *Logos* with which one could be tempted to compare it): it is the *alētheia* of a subject who speaks himself in his disappearing. Thus this language remains autoenunciative through and through, even when its *autos* is reduced to nothing—which, moreover, if we think about it, was what had happened already at the extremity of the Cartesian cogito.[69] For Lacan, this nothing that signifiers represent for one another remains the *subject* of representation—that is, what *relates* or *rejoins* the signifiers to one another and makes them what they are, by Lacan's own admission: representations, "representatives," *Vorstellungsrepräsentanten* (1966, 714).

This "nothing" is therefore anything but an indifferent "nothing," henceforth to be ignored; on the contrary, it is precisely what makes the otherwise sense-less machine of the signifier run, what makes the *langue* of the linguists *speak*—or, if you will, it is that "prodigious energy"—the negative—which makes *langue* signify, makes it "produce" meaning. And this meaning is once again, now and forever, the "subject = o" who speaks himself in everything.

And so Lacan has actually said nothing different from what Hegel had already said in this very Lacanian passage from the *Philosophy of Spirit*:

The name is solitary, without relation or tie. [Names comprise] a series which is not self-supporting, since the name has no determinacy in it, no intrinsic relation to something else. The *I* [which, as a variant states, "is the form of pure unrest, movement, the Night in which all disappears"] is all alone the bearer, the space and substance of these names. It is their *order*, their interrelation of complete mutual indifference. In themselves they have no rank or relation. Thus the *I* must now look at itself as ordering this, or look at them as ordered and maintaining this order, so that it is permanent.[70]

Desire Caught by the Tail

> We say that Φ, the phallus, is the signifier that intro-
> duces the relationship with the other (*small*) o into
> O[ther], as the locus of speech, . . . insofar as the sig-
> nifier has something to do with this relationship. And
> it looks as if it's biting its tail—but it has to bite
> its tail.
> —Jacques Lacan [1]

Diana, invisible, observes Actaeon in the thicket
from which he imagines he can spy on her. Actaeon lies in wait for
Diana, the Huntress hunted, to see her finally dripping wet at her
bath, *resting* from the hunt. Diana enjoins her worshiper to spy on,
track, fall upon his prey. How, in the end, could Actaeon not wish
to seize the essence of his hunt, the calm principle of that desire to
which he himself is prey? But how, too, could he seize anything but
the shadow of that prey? Possessed, Diana will no longer be the unpossessed virgin who drives both gods and mortals mad. Observed
in her woman's body, she will no longer be the luminous adolescent
girl who displays that boyish body so envied by Aphrodite. Aroused
by Actaeon's desire, would she remain the impassive, asexual Goddess against whom our most heated imaginings shatter? By what
ruse, what unsuspected good luck, could Actaeon manage from
that point to penetrate the "cruel principle of her virginity"? [2] In what
space will he ever cross Diana's *inviolate* gaze? This is what we
burn to know. Where, then, will the theophany of Diana's Bath—
our quarry, sole object of our quest—take place?

"Diana, invisible, considers Actaeon imagining the nude goddess," [3] and from this desire, inflaming the mind of a mortal, "the

desire to see her own body"[4] comes to her. Diana wants to manifest herself! She loves us! But where will the impassive Goddess borrow this visible body, already aroused by the gaze that profanes it, if not from her idolator's lustful imaginings, from our guilty desire to see? She, *the* Woman, exists nowhere but in the gaze of the man who imagines her, and only in our mythic pool does she bathe. Between Diana invisible and Diana unveiled, between Diana and the Diana who separates from herself to see herself in Actaeon's haggard eyes, creeps the "mediating demon," a being without body or sex, who *simulates* the Goddess's haughtily scattered bait: "He becomes the fantasy of Actaeon and the mirror of Diana."[5] Thus can Diana reveal herself to Actaeon and enjoy the roguery of that revelation, opening herself to her chastity's shame. In the gaze that gives her substance, the reflected Diana now knows herself to be a virgin, having already ceased to be one. And the more she tries to conceal from Actaeon the nipple, the vulva darting between her fingers, the more she intimates her unfathomable shamelessness, the more "she savors the vile breach opened in the closed being of her body"[6]: unpossessed as soon as possessed, possessed as one unpossessed, "ruse of the demon who lends her these visible charms as the most opaque veil of her divinity."[7]

Actaeon, uncontrollably excited, can take no more of this abomination that flouts his desire. "Shameless bitch!" he cries. Diana's breasts, Diana's buttocks, Diana veiling herself in her nudity, Diana lewdly inviolate under his gaze—these are all just so many simulacra of the unsoiled Diana, of Diana sexless before he saw her. Actaeon the idolator now becomes an iconoclast, and with a vengeance. The *moon* ornamenting Diana's hair, false emblem of a rite "reserved for the tongues of her dogs"[8]—he no longer wants it in effigy, lunated, in a *crescent*. Now he wants the real moon, the whole crescent, "in that very place within Artemis where the most initiated of her dogs will make it grow again."[9] Actaeon pounces on Diana,

at last he bares her ass, and delivers a blow . . . to Diana's buttocks; and, indeed, from their shadow emerges the horn of the luminous crescent whose brilliance she still hides with her long, shadowy hands; but the more the spanking intensifies, the more fully the crescent blooms; and as the idol's posterior begins to open, Actaeon flings himself upon it, head lowered—

here he is, at the limit of his vocation: crouching, mouth gaping, jaws lined with fangs: himself a dog at last! . . . The crescent slips and slides between his teeth, it gets away and scales the heights, . . . foam drowns his last insults . . . , a dog for nothing? . . . He howls—O glorious death of the Stag! . . . when *the bright crescent rises above the crest of the mountains and takes its place in the emerald vault of dusk.*[10]

The Sterile Crescent

"The truth," Lacan declared in 1964, "is that which runs after truth—and that is where I am running, where I am taking you, like Actaeon's hounds, after me. When I find the goddess's hiding place, I will no doubt be changed into a stag, and you can devour me, but we still have a little way to go yet" (1977b, 188/172). Running, hunting, tracking—this is how truth, "stubborn to the choice of sex, akin to death and, all in all, rather inhuman, Diana perhaps . . . will recognize the hounds" (1977a, 145/436).[11] Truth takes her lovers for a ride, and that is how she loves them: thrown off the trail, frustrated, grasping only her tracks. And how could it be otherwise, since this truth is the truth of desire, the indefatigable huntsman never satisfied with any prey, always turning it loose for the nothing he pursues?

But we must ask this: Would Actaeon continue this pursuit, persist in this dog's life, if he did not imagine someday stumbling onto the Goddess? Isn't it *Diana's bath*, and nothing else, that haunts his desire? In short, and in spite of everything, doesn't desire have an *object*? The Goddess certainly cannot appear to the man who is dying to see her, and yet he would not desire her if she were not appearing to him in some way. This is the hard lesson of Klossowski's "demon": desire cannot be pure, for, strictly speaking, desire of nothing is nothing but an absence of desire.

How will our hero, Actaeon/Lacan, solve this problem? In the Lacanian doctrine, it is clear, desire cannot really have any object at all, if desire is to remain what it is: the pure negativity of a *subject* who desires himself in his objects (Hegel), and who can do so only by perpetually negating himself in them, by negating them as what he is not—a "given object" (Kojève), a thing "in-itself" (Sartre). Thus we must exclude the possibility that this subject/desire has even the slightest relation to an object (the famous "object relation" of the post-Freudians; cf. SIV, 21 and 28 November 1956), since this object, far from being something with which he would maintain a complementary or harmonious relationship, is instead what he himself is, by not being it. In this sense, the object is always a "failed" object (1975c, 55)—that is, as Sartre explains in *Being and Nothingness*, what desire "lacks"; for example, it is not the full moon that the crescent lacks in order to become finally what it is (in-itself), but rather the "lack of being" (*manque d'être*) that defines the crescent from the inside *as* crescent (for-itself).[12] (And, Sartre continues, "The existence of desire as a human fact is sufficient to prove that human reality is a lack. . . . If desire is to be able to be desire to itself . . . it must be a lack—but not an object-lack, a lack undergone . . . it must be its own lack of —. Desire is a lack of being. It is haunted in its inmost being by the being of which it is desire. Thus it bears witness to the existence of lack in the being of human reality."[13]) Under these conditions, it is not surprising that Actaeon never captures Diana's "moon": he seeks it only as a crescent, a taut bow that strikes its target only by missing it.

From this entirely negative definition of desire there follows a series of no less negative definitions of the "object" of desire:

1. It is not the *object of knowledge*—that is, the ob-ject in which a subject would pose himself before himself in order to retrieve himself in it (SX, 9 January 1963), nor is it the noema correlative to a noesis (SX, 16 January 1963). Not that Lacan really rejects the possibility of the "object" of desire's being the subject himself (or, if you will, of the subject's being transcendence, exit-from-himself); on the contrary, the subject actually continues to desire *himself* (to transcend *himself*) in his "object" (and we will fully confirm this). But so completely is this subject transcendence that he can no longer find or recognize himself in any object except by abolishing it as what he lacks—as what he is in terms of "lack-of-being" (1977a, 164/515), "want-to-be" (1977a, 170/522—523), and ek-sistence without essence. The "object" of desire therefore is not symmetrical with the subject, not the specular and imaginary object of ("paranoiac") knowledge. It is the "lack of object" (SIV,

28 November 1956) insofar as the subject finds himself in it as the object he is *not*—that is, as desire.

2. The "object" of desire is no more *real* than imaginary (SIV, 28 November 1956). Or, if it is real (as Lacan occasionally says of the "*objet a*"; cf. SX, 6 March 1963), it is so only as irremediably lost. This follows from the very definition of desire, as Lacan takes it from Kojève. Whereas the real (nature) is content to be what it is, desire (man) is not content—he wants *not to be* what he is. It follows that desire is not strictly desire (that is, strictly human) except at the moment when it radically negates (itself as) real being and begins to desire that most unreal and most impossible of all "objects," death.

3. Not being real, the "object" of desire is not *natural*, either. Here again, Lacan is in rigorous accord with Kojève's "dualist ontology": whereas animal (natural) desire aims at the maintenance of the identical (preservation in being, the instinct of conservation or reproduction), human (historic) desire constantly differs from itself and is directed toward a "non-natural object," "perfectly useless from the biological point of view."[14] The "object" of human desire is neither the object that saturates a need (which, as Sartre also says, is never anything but a "state" closed in itself)[15] nor the fixed and preestablished object of instinct; it is, properly speaking, their negation. It is the "unnatural" object (*contre-nature*) of a subject/desire who meta-physically transcends, transgresses, and exceeds every corporeal or vital "given"; or, what amounts to the same thing, it is the vanishing "object" of the symbol, an infinitely variable and vicariable object, because it is always already deferred and "metonymized" in the ideal signifier that annuls it. The analyst, inasmuch as he is interested in desire, never deals with anything but a nature that is lost, abolished, and *worked* by the signifier:

The analyst finds himself in somewhat the same position as the engineer in a hydroelectric plant who is interested in what goes on in the machine where the energy accumulates and is transformed, but who does not concern himself with the landscape that *predated* the construction. . . . In other words, linguistic ones this time, let us say that there is nothing in the *signified*—fluxes, needs, drives—that does not appear to be marked with the imprint of the *signifier*, with all the resulting slippages of meanings that constitute symbolism.[16]

   4. Not being natural, the "object" of desire is not *sexual*, either, at least if what we mean by that is the object of a "sexual instinct": "The libido is not the sexual instinct. Its reduction . . . to male desire (a reduction found in Freud) should be enough to warn us. . . . Its sexual coloring, so formally maintained by Freud . . . , is the color-of-void: suspended in the light of a gaping hole" (1966, 851). Sexuality may very well make the void of desire iridescent, may "color" it, but this in no way prevents the void from being sexually neuter, indifferent to the anatomical difference between the sexes. And how could it be otherwise, since it is a question of the perfectly ideal desire of a subject who desires *himself* beyond any object? The penis is no more the object of woman's desire than the vagina is the object of man's, for "it is not true that God made them male and female" (1966, 850). The *subject* of desire, as we may have expected, is not sexed—nor is his "object," being nothing but this same subject insofar as he differs from himself and desires himself as he is not (self-identical). Hardly has he stumbled upon Diana's bath than Actaeon realizes that the "object" of his desire is *not* that woman who awaits him, but rather the androgynous, impossible Diana whom he can attain only by desiring her/him beyond any seizing, as he/she would be if Actaeon had not already soiled him/her with his masculine gaze. If truth is woman, "at least for man" (1975c, 108), it is not at all because desire is "male"; on the contrary, it is because desire is neither masculine nor feminine, and its object can only be deceitful (as are all women, in male memory) from the moment it is embodied in the "female" pole of a "male" desire. "*There is no sexual intercourse* [or rapport: *rapport sexuel*]" between man and woman (1975c, 35), only a "male way" and a "female way" of messing it all up: "The essence of the object is failure" (1975c, 53—55).

   Unknowable, unreal, denatured, sexually neuter, the "object" of desire is therefore a non-object, a negated object. We could object that Lacan nevertheless does give a positive definition, since, with Kojève, he characterizes it as desire: the "object" of desire is to *be* desired, and "desire is desire of desire, desire of the Other" (1966, 852). But this only confirms the non-objective nature of that "object," since this is once again to say that desire desires "itself," beyond any object. Since the subject of desire defines himself through negation of the object that he wants *not to be*, it goes without saying that he can desire himself (that is, "objectivize" himself) only in and as a non-object: in and as the pure negativity of another subject, in and as his *desire*. We must be careful to note that, for Lacan, "desiring to be desired" does not at all mean desiring to be the *object* of the other's desire. This is the principle "of the deception and baseness of love (to love is to want to be loved)" (1966, 853), whereas "desiring to be desired" is desiring to be the *non-object* of the other subject's desire, wherein he too desires himself as what he is not: "Desire . . . is not desire of an object but desire of that lack which designates, in the other, another desire." [17] Therefore, to say that desire desires to be desired means that desire (the subject) desires itself as desire (as subject): it wants "not to be" an object—or, more simply, it wants not to *be*. Desire is desire of nothing, desire of the impossible, desire of death. [18]

And so the following question arises: How to explain that, in spite of everything, this desire takes on a body (that is, *life*) and gives itself an object? Again, to desire nothing would be, strictly speaking, not to desire at all: we would be angels, flying off into the clouds. But the fact is that we are not angels, and the *rapport sexuel*, messed up or not, is all we ever think about. It even so happens that we fornicate, or so they say. How to explain this oddity? How to explain that, against all expectations, a man desires the body of a woman, and vice versa? How to explain, more generally, that we make (in Freud's terms) sexual "object-choices"? Granted, the object of desire may be non-natural (perverse), non-real (symbolic), and the subject may even desire himself in it (Freud's "narcissistic object-choice"); the fact still remains that this object is erotic and, what is more, particularly fixed and unsubstitutable: any given man will seek just *this* curve of the hips, just *this* beauty mark, in all his mistresses; the male homosexual will desire (himself) *only* (in) phallus-bearing individuals; the fetishist will reach orgasm only with *this* boot; the masochist will request *this* whip, and so forth. In other words, desire organizes itself into imaginary scenarios, where it imagines (itself in) an object.

Can we be content, from that point on, with seeing this phantasmatic object as pure illusion, a "perverse 'fixation'" of desire "at the very suspension-point of the signifying chain where the memory-screen is immobilized and the fascinating image of the fetish is statufied" (1977a, 167/518; translation modified)? Isn't it rather that the other, from the Lacanian perspective, must *manifest* his desire to me in one way or another, so that I in turn can manifest myself (that is, desire myself) in the object that I am not? Since the subject of desire is defined as "ek-sistence," ek-stasy outside himself, he will need an object in which he can manifest himself outside, as he is *not*, as the pure transcendence that he "is." Once more, we see that the question of desire's "object" *is the same as the question of the manifestation of desire's subject*, and we know how Lacan has resolved this question until now: through "full speech" and/or the "signifier," understood as the presence of the absence of the subject. The problem, however, is that now this signifier must be "sexualized," made into an erotic "object," so that the doctrine of desire can be reconciled with analytic experience.

But where will we find such a non-objective "object," one that is neuter enough, unreal enough, to embody the subject by not being the subject? What will be *the* signifier of the "object" of desire, a signifier fixed enough to take account of the monotony of *eros* but evanescent enough to function as the signifier of desire's unobjective transcendence, to serve as the transcendental signifier of "signifiance" (that is, to serve as the signifier of the absence of *one* signifier of the desire/subject/signified)?[19] How can the other (sex) *signify to me* his/her (asexual) desire, so that I can desire myself in him (her) as what is *lacking* in her (him)? We already know Lacan's answer, and it is not surprising that it took on such importance after 1956, the year when Klossowski's *Le Bain de Diane* was published:[20] Lacan's answer is the *phallus*—not the organ of sexual pleasure, whether penis or clitoris, but the transsexual "simulacrum" (1977a, 285/690) of its common absence; not the man's erect penis or the woman's fertile womb, but the sterile crescent of desire, the symbol of their impossible conjunction.

Deduction of the Phallus

Let us trace the deduction of this peculiar "object," as Lacan presents it in his lecture on the signification of the phallus. And let us pretend with him, at first, that this is not an a priori deduction but a sort of empirical genesis.[21] Let us put ourselves in the place of the *infans*, the little human animal who as yet knows only objects of need: the mother's milk that satisfies his thirst, the air that oxygenates his blood, the warmth that maintains his temperature at a constant level, and so on. These objects are simultaneously real (the child's thirst cannot be satisfied with the image of a bottle or with the word "milk"), particular (it is *this* milk, here and now, that will relieve the baby's thirst, and not milk in general), and unsubstitutable (an offer of whiskey, or even of water, will not replace an offer of milk). Moreover, strictly speaking, they are not objects at all: they are so complementary to the organism that the organism makes them its own by assimilating them in order to stay identical with itself. Here, as Kojève says, we are at the level of a "merely living I," who "can be revealed to itself and to others only as Sentiment of self."[22]

How will this needy "I" take leave of itself, how will it become the subject desiring an object that it is not? Is it enough to cite here, as Freud did, the "biological factor" of this little human animal's total dependence on the (m)other?

The biological factor is the long period of time during which the young of the species is in a condition of helplessness and dependence. Its intrauterine existence seems to be short in comparison with that of most animals, and it is sent into the world in a less finished state. As a result, the influence of the real external world upon it is intensified and an early differentiation between the ego and the id is promoted. Moreover, the dangers of the external world have a greater importance for it, so that the value of the object which can alone protect it against them and take the place of its former intra-uterine life is enormously enhanced. The biological fact, then, establishes the earliest situations of danger and creates the need to be loved which will accompany the child through the rest of its life.[23]

In other words, is it because man's needs are initially satisfied by the mediation of another that they "return to him alienated" (1977a,

286/690)—that is, both altered (denatured) and differed (separated from him)? Lacan's response is trenchant: "This is not the effect of his real dependence (one should not expect to find here the parasitic conception represented by the notion of dependence in the theory of neurosis), but rather the turning into signifying form as such, from the fact that it is from the locus of the Other that its message is emitted" (1977a, 286/690).

Thus, as might have been expected, the object of desire does not stem from the object of need ("anaclitically," as Freud says); on the contrary, it emerges from its negation in language. In accord with Kojève's "dualist ontology," Lacan a priori separates this linguistic negativity from the Real that it negates (and necessarily so, since this negativity is the a priori of transcendence as such). Thus his point of departure, appearances to the contrary, is not the little *infans* animal but the little speaking human. The history of desire, Lacan says (1986, 61 ff.), drawing on selected fragments from Freud,[24] starts with the *cry*. With the cry, Freud explains, the little human being separates himself from the immediate experience of need (of dissatisfaction): he names the experience (and thus annuls it by making it an object that he is not),[25] and he names it for the attention of another human (*Nebenmensch*), who on the one hand is close to him (that is, identical, since the *Nebenmensch* "understands" him and gives him—or, better yet, *is*—the object he needs) and on the other hand, as a "Thing" (*Ding*), remains absolutely and inexplicably foreign, *Fremd*, to him (1986, 64–65).[26] Lacan expresses this double alienation by saying that the cry is a demand addressed to the Other.

The cry (the *human* cry, since from this point on it is obvious that we are not talking about an animal mewling) could be paraphrased in this way: "I demand *x* from you." The thing that differentiates the human from the animal cry (but by what mysterious necessity?) is that the human cry is already language, in the peculiar sense that Lacan gives the term: not a name or the "signal of an object," but a demand (that is to say, speech) addressed to another. "Originally, the signifier expresses a demand,"[27] and the human cry "is already a cry calling for a response . . . a cry uttered for someone to acknowledge" (SIV, 27 February 1956). In other words, the human cry is from the start a demand for recognition. It does not demand a "direct object";[28] it is an intransitive demand to be a subject. And, far from signifying a merely biological dependence on the person who satisfies needs, it manifests dependence with respect to his or her *desire*: "In the theory, we must substitute for the whole economy of gratifications this notion of a primordial dependence in relation to the desire of the other, to understand that desire is modeled by the conditions of the demand. It is a signified demand: I signify to you my demand. . . . The subject is engaged in a process of recognition: the desire of recognition and the recognition of desire."[29]

The result, in the Lacanian deduction, is a radical transmutation of the object of need: the object signified in the demand becomes the signifier of something else (of that impenetrable "Thing," *das Ding*, that Freud locates in the *Nebenmensch*). Take, for example, the nourishing breast as the particular object of need. Does the child, by its cry, demand *the breast* of the mother? Yes, but he simultaneously *demands* the breast, and that is all that matters to Lacan. The object of the child's demand is that the mother *give* the breast—in short, that she respond to his call by returning his message in an inverted form: "Demand in itself bears on something other than the satisfactions it calls for. It is demand of a presence or of an absence—which is what is manifested in the primordial relation to the mother, pregnant with that Other to be situated *behind* (en-deçà)[30] the needs that it can satisfy" (1977a, 286/690–691; translation modified). Why the "Other," and why "behind"? Because the mother is fundamentally unpredictable and all-powerful: she can respond to the demand or not, according to her whim. The true object of the demand is therefore the *love* of the mother, the sole guarantee of her presence. By demanding the breast (and, later on, presents, toys, and finally anything at all), the child is asking to be loved. More precisely, he is demanding to be the object of the mother's love, the *suckled breast* that will fulfill her. The demand, although it appears to bear on the particular and unsubstitutable object of a need, actually calls for a signifier in which the subject can identify himself in his being: "In this way, demand annuls (*aufhebt*) the particularity of everything that can be granted, by transmuting it into a proof of love" (1977a, 286/691).

Thus there is an *Aufhebung* of the object of need in the object of demand: the object is "annulled" in its particularity and "raised (*aufgehoben*) to the function of signifier" (1977a, 288/692) of the other's love. Now it is an object in which the subject loves himself (a signifier in which he signifies himself). As for the expected end of this deduction, the object of desire, are we there yet? No, for the "object" of desire is precisely *not* to be the *object* of the other's love. No matter how Lacan pretends to derive the object of desire from the object of need, transmuted into an object of demand, it is clear that he has defined it in advance (a priori) as the absence of an object. For him, desire is a desire to be desired as a subject—that is, as a non-object. By all rights, therefore, and from the beginning, it is a radical negativity, going beyond any object. But the *Aufhebung*, in strictly Hegelian doctrine, is not a pure "immediate" negation of the object. It is a "determined" negation, which maintains what it suppresses. Here, indeed, the object of need, annulled/raised to the dignity of the signifier of the mother's love, is preserved in its very negation, as a "that's not it": "What you are giving me is not what I asked for."

Indeed, the demand must truly demand some *thing* before it can annul that thing and make it the signifier of something else, of that "Thing" that is precisely not a thing—namely, the love that no object of need can demonstrate. *What* the demand demands (at the level of its statement) is always this or that particular object (the breast, a piece of candy, a kiss). But what the demand *demands* (at the level of its enunciation) is no object. The demand, as Lacan says, is "intransitive" (1977a, 254/617), "unconditional" (1977a, 265/629), and "unconditioned" (1977a, 286–287/691)[31] in that it does not depend on any object, and it calls to *be* loved, *for nothing*. With even the crudest demand a "struggle for pure prestige" starts up, a sort of sacrificial "potlatch" (SIV, 23 January 1957) whose stakes are the pure love—that is, the pure *desire*—of the other. And so the demand becomes necessarily insatiable, since no object can satisfy it. No matter how the mother gives in to the child's every demand—for food, presents, kisses—she will only manage to reduce him to the level of the "subject of the *need*" and the "*object* of love" (1977a, 287/691; my emphasis). As for the child, he will always demand something else—namely, the exact thing that she does not give (and cannot give, since it is no object): her pure love, as "the radical form of the gift of what [she] does not *have*" (1977a, 286/691; my emphasis once again).

In other words, satisfaction of the demand always leaves something to be desired—something that is nothing but is nevertheless always carried beyond the object of demand, as what this object is not: the paradoxical "object" of desire. As Lacan explains at the end of a particularly hermetic passage, this "object" emerges, through a "subtraction" of the object of need from the object of demand, as what remains of the demand once it has been satisfied:

It is necessary, then, that the particularity thus abolished should reappear *beyond* (*au-delà*) the demand [that is, as an *abolished* particularity]. It does, in fact, reappear there, but preserving the structure contained in the unconditioned [see note 28] element of the demand for love. By a reversal that is not simply a negation of the negation [and for good reason, since it is a matter of a perpetual negation], the power of pure loss emerges from the residue of an obliteration. For the unconditioned element of demand, desire substitutes the "absolute" condition [evidently an allusion to Kant: like pure reason, desire falls into the "paralogism" of making the unconditioned—a purely formal and a priori condition—into an unconditioned "thing in itself"]: this condition unties the knot of that element in the proof of love that is resistant to the satisfaction of a need. Thus desire is neither the appetite for satisfaction nor the demand for love, but the difference that results from the subtraction of the first from the second, the phenomenon of their splitting (*Spaltung*) [1977a, 286–287/691].

However obscure this passage may be, at least one thing seems clear: the object of desire is neither the object of need nor the object of the demand. And since these are the only two objects that we can get our hands on, we are once more reduced to defining this object as a non-object, or as a negated one. From this perspective, the deduction of the object of desire does not teach us anything that we did not know from the start. Since the cry of the "little man" has been defined from the beginning as a demand for recognition—that is, as a desire to be desired as a subject—it goes without saying that it cannot be satisfied by any object, since it really does not demand one. The mysterious "necessity" for this object of desire to re-emerge "beyond the demand" only translates the postulate with which we began: the "object" of man's desire is the desire of the other—*that is, a non-object.* And so it is not surprising that the "object" of desire should be so paradoxical, since there has never really been any question of there being such an object.

To recapitulate, we know now that no object of need and/or demand will ever satisfy the desire/subject. And we also believe that we know why erotic objects, for man, are so aberrant, multiple, and interchangeable. As soon as there is any question of objects of need that are metabolized ("eroticized") into signifiers of desire by virtue of the demand, it is rather obvious that any object will do as "object" of desire, since *none* will do: it will never be a question of anything but an object that manifests desire in its absence (or, if you will, a signifier that represents the subject for another signifier, which can be exchanged for him). What we still do not understand, however, is why humans decide to desire *this* object, rather than any other, as the "cause of desire" (1977a, 287/691). And what we understand even less is why the "object" of desire electively appears/disappears in(to) *one* signifier, which appears, as if by accident, to coincide with *one* sex organ. There is indeed one signifier (an object "raised to the function of signifier") that signifies the ungraspable "object" of desire better than any other. As the last part of Lacan's article on the signification of the phallus abruptly informs us, after several paragraphs meant to condemn all naturalizing reductions of the object of desire to "genitality":

The phallus is the privileged signifier of that mark in which the role of the logos is joined with the advent of desire. . . . All these propositions merely conceal the fact that it can play its role only when veiled, that is to say, as itself a sign of the latency with which any signifiable is struck, when it is raised (*aufgehoben*) to the function of signifier. The phallus is the signifier of this *Aufhebung* itself, which it inaugurates (initiates) by its disappearance. That is why the demon of Αἰδώς (*Scham*) [the "demon" of shame, as a Klossowskian note points out] arises at the very moment when, in the ancient mysteries, the phallus is unveiled [1977a, 287–288/692].

Of course, Lacan is speaking here not about the penis but about its symbol: the erected, painted, or sculpted *Phallos* (in this respect, the allusion to the ancient "mysteries" is rather clear). As in Klossowski, it is a question of the simulacrum that embodies the object of desire in its absence and thus veils it in its very unveiling (Lacan adds that the *Phallos* must be veiled as soon as it is unveiled, but this only confirms that the phallus is itself the ultimate veil of absence: the inauguration of the erected statue coincides with its disappearance, just as Diana shamelessly (un)clothes herself[32] in the phallic appearance lent to her by her "demon"). In spite of every-thing, however, this phallus of the masquerade is actually the sym-bol of *the penis*. It is the penis, sacrificed and "raised" (in every sense of that word) to the dignity of signifier. And it is this *"Aufhe-bung"* that is the locus par excellence of the mysterious *alētheia* of the "object" of desire: the symbolic (ceremonial, ritual) castra-tion of the penis, for the sake of its theatrical simulacrum (1977a, 289/694), "initiates" the subject into desire by making the subject disappear under the signifier that "marks" and masks it. Therefore, Lacan says, the phallus is the "model signifier,"[33] the "signifier of signifiers" (1966, 630), the "unparalleled signifier" (1977a, 277/642), and as such it is *the* signifier of desire—that is, in Lacan's terms, the "signifier of the signified," "for it is the signifier intended to designate as a whole the effects of the signified, in that the signifier conditions them by its presence as a signifier" (1977a, 285/690); and when it comes to symbolizing "what matters to the subject, what he desires . . . , he does so, in the final analysis, with the phallus. The signifier of the signified in general is the phallus" (SV, 12 February 1958).

We must understand that the phallus is not the signified itself (that is, the ungraspable "object" of desire metonymically signified by every object), but it is this "object's" major signifier in that it signifies it better than any other signifier does. Just as a painting or a novel can be represented within itself *as* a representation, so the phallus is what represents within itself (or is represented by) all other signifiers. It is the signifier that we seek through all other sig-nifiers, all other objects. Where does the phallus get this surprising privilege? We can easily see why Lacan felt the need to give the phallus this eminent position (to give the signifier a bit of sex and body, if only in "the form of a bloody scrap—the pound of flesh that life pays in order to turn it into the signifier of . . . signifiers"; 1977a, 264/629–630). But we still do not see how this is justified within the doctrine of the signifier. Why does the negated-annulled-lost-castrated-symbolized-raised *penis* play this role of the signifier "on pointe," if all signifiers are equal and interchangeable with re-spect to the absence that they signify? Why not the clitoris or the vagina (after all, we do not lack examples of symbolic manipulations or representations of the female sexual organ, from excision to the "mythical vulva")? Why not *any* part of the scarred, tattooed, pierced, "lost" body? Lacan insists strongly on this: the phallus is not a "part-object" like the rest (1977a, 198, 283, 285/555, 688, 690); on the contrary, it is what the rest all represent to the extent that it is missing (1977b, 103/95).[34] We might as well say right away that this phallocentrism is more obscure than it seems, and we should not be content to see it as the symptom of an androcentrism that surreptitiously confuses the signifier of desire with the masculine penis. If the penis is predestined to its promotion as the major signifier of desire, it is not, for Lacan, in its capacity as real organ. But in what capacity, then?

The Scepter and the Statue

The hint of an answer is given a bit farther on in the article on the signification of the phallus. "The desire of the mother," Lacan tells us, "*is* the phallus" (1977a, 289/693). Thus we are also better able to understand the prevalence of the phallic signifier in the libidinal economy of the two sexes. Since the desire of the "little man" (boy or girl) is directed toward the desire of the other, it is clear that he will be enormously interested in whatever signifies (manifests) this desire to him. Behind all the necessarily deceptive signs of love that the mother gives in response to the child's demands, there looms what she does not give—that is, what all her behavior testifies that she does not have: "If the desire of the mother *is* the phallus, the child wishes to be the phallus in order to satisfy that desire" (1977a, 289/693).

But this scarcely gets us anywhere, for we would like to know why the mother herself desires the phallus. Is it simply because she does not have a penis and is looking for one as an object of genital satisfaction (as a "direct object")? That is obviously not the case, for Lacan takes great care to speak of the "phallus" and the "desire" of the mother: if the phallus "*is* the desire of the mother," it is because it is *not* the penis, because it is the penis annulled/raised to the rank of signifier of the absence of the "object" of desire. Several episodes later, we learn that it is the phallus forbidden to the mother by the law of the father (1977a, 289/694): not only the penis that she does not actually have but also the phallus symbolically castrated by the law that commands the mother not to give herself the phallus by way of the child (that symbolic equivalent of the penis, as psychoanalytic theory indeed informs us: "My dear little phallus").

As for the father, he is the father only to the extent that he himself has done his mourning for the phallus and thus desires it himself: "Nothing [of paternity] will come to pass without . . . that fundamental mutilation thanks to which the phallus becomes the signifier of power . . . the scepter" (SV, 12 March 1958). If the father forbids the mother to give herself the phallus (to keep it for herself), this is certainly because she must receive it from him, because, apparently, he has it: the dialectic of interhuman exchange, Lacan recalls, with support from Lévi-Strauss's *The Elementary Structures of Kinship*, is androcentric in that men give/exchange the phallus through the mediation of women and children (I will give you one woman who will produce children, so that you will give me another) (SIV, 27 February 1957; SV, 12 March 1958). But this—which actually does seem to root phallocentrism in a fundamental androcentrism—does not at all mean, according to Lacan, that the father possesses the phallus by nature, by virtue of a potent, fertile penis. On the contrary, he "has" it only to the extent that he has given it up beforehand by incurring symbolic castration: the phallus is a *title*, which he has received so that he can bestow it in accord with symbolic pact and law. In other words, the phallus may very well express masculine power (the power that ultimately explains why women do not exchange men/phalluses), but it does so only symbolically (that is, we must understand, not sexually). The phallus is the penis annulled-castrated-raised to the function of "scepter," of inherited signifier, which is passed on according to the law of exchange and kinship: "If this exchange must be described as androcentric . . . it is, M. Lévi-Strauss tells us, because of the occurrences of political power that make themselves felt in it, power that falls to man to exercise. It is therefore because it is also the scepter that the phallus prevails—in other words, because it belongs to the symbolic order."[35]

This amounts to saying that we will never know why the "scepter" is phallic: masculine in fact, it is not so by right (the scepter, as the "signifier of power," can legitimately be held by a Cleopatra or a Semiramis). In the Lacanian system, the phallus does not really belong to anyone, for both man and woman always receive it from another, another who can bestow it only because he or she has received it as the signifier of his or her desire. Therefore, no genesis will ever tell us why it is the castrated-symbolized *penis* that functions as the major signifier of human desire, for wherever we turn we will find it always already in the form of a signifier, always already absent as a real penis. In accord with the doctrine of the signifier, the phallic *signifier* is posed a priori as a negated-superseded-transcended object, which literally forbids our understanding why it should be a question of a *phallic* signifier. The trap is impeccable. We can submit to this transcendental closure and accept the phallus, Φ, as a handy "zero symbol" that can signify anything because it signifies nothing in particular; then, like Bouvard and Pécuchet, we will see the phallus everywhere, to the precise degree that it is nowhere: "Long ago, towers, pyramids, candles, mile-posts, and even trees signified the phallus—and for Bouvard and Pécuchet everything became a phallus."[36] Or, on the contrary we can stubbornly mire ourselves in our own empirical naïveté, and in vain we can ask why it is just the phallus that serves as the universal "password" of desire.

Will we have better luck if we turn to the clinic, that domain of firm certitudes? Indeed, Lacan often refers to Freud's discovery of the phallus's role in the libidinal economy of children and neurotics: the primacy of the male genital organ for boys *as well as* girls at the moment of the so-called phallic stage; the subsequent reduction of the difference between the sexes to the opposition "phallic/castrated," which entails in the boy a fear of losing what he has (anxiety of castration by the father, causing him to abandon the mother at the time of the normal "decline" of the Oedipus complex) and in the girl a desire to possess what she does not have (penis envy, causing her to enter into the Oedipus complex by turning toward the father as the bestower of penis and children). But this "observation of the facts" (SV, 12 March 1958) cannot help us, for if we stay at the level of the facts, we can never explain why a single organ should obsess both sexes, especially if we confuse it, as Freud did, with the real penis (or clitoris): an "evident paradox" (1977a,

284/688), which, according to Lacan, leaves the door wide open to all the "feminist" (1977a, 198/555) and "culturalist" (1977a, 284/689) deviations that make phallic primacy in the girl a secondary formation, added on to her properly feminine sexuality (Karen Horney, Melanie Klein, Helene Deutsch, Ernest Jones). But this is precisely the "paradox" that Lacan means to found in theory. Since the privilege of the phallus cannot be that of the real organ, it *must*, he explains, be that of the phallic signifier—which puts us right back on the merry-go-round, since we still do not understand why this signifier is sexual.

But suddenly we remember that we have forgotten something: the imaginary, an essential part of the Lacanian system. Apart from the real penis and the symbolic phallus, mustn't there also be an imaginary phallus? In apparent opposition to this are Lacan's most explicit declarations: "In Freudian doctrine the phallus is not a phantasy, if by that we mean an imaginary effect" (1977a, 285/690). But, as we shall see, this must be understood as a *Verneinung*. If the symbolic phallus is *not* an imaginary phallus, it is in the precise sense of its being one "by not being one": "The object of castration is imaginary. It is the phallus." [37]

There actually is an "imaginary function of the phallus" (1977a, 198/555), and this is indeed how Lacan initially explained the phallus's prevalence, at a time when the category of the "symbolic" had not yet made its appearance. If we turn to the article on the family complexes, we find that the phallus is thematized there in the form of the specular double: "The primordial imago of the double, on which the ego models itself, at first seems to be dominated by fantasies of (the) form, as it appears in the fantasy common to both sexes, of the *phallic mother* or in the *phallic double* of the neurotic woman" (1984, 48). But, as Lacan explains a bit farther on in connection with the castration complex, this prevalence of the phallic double is not at all related to some "male domination" (as Freud, still "closed . . . to the notion of the autonomy of forms," had proposed; 1984, 59). The object to which the castration fantasy refers is a "narcissistic object," whose "form, born before any locating of the body proper, . . . does not depend on the subject's sex. . . . It represents the defense that the narcissistic ego, identified with his specular double, opposes to the renewal of anxiety that, at the beginning of the Oedipus complex, tends to disturb him" (1984, 60–61). In short, the phallus is an imaginary form of the body thanks to which the subject defends himself from the anxiety of that "tearing apart" due to prematurity (1984, 60).

Suddenly everything becomes clear. Now we see why the phallus is privileged—not in its capacity as male sexual organ, but in its capacity as "form," "phallic *Gestalt*" (1981, 198), *erected* and *visible*. Lacan returns to this quite explicitly in the seminar on the object relation:

> There is a whole series of things *in the signified* ["namely, the body," he clarifies a little farther on] that are there, *but which are borrowed by the signifier* . . . in order to give the signifier, if we may say so, its first weapons—namely, those extremely elusive and yet very irreducible things, of which precisely the phallic term, the pure and simple erection, the pure and simple raised stone, is an example, of which the notion of the human body as erected is another . . . a number of elements, more or less related to bodily posture and not simply to the felt experience of the body [SIV, 5 December 1956; my emphasis].

Elsewhere, Lacan also notes that there is a "world" between ape and man, "between the rapport of a certain animal species, *more or less erect in posture*, with what *hangs* between his legs and whatever it is in man that makes . . . the phallus the object of a cult . . . this something that *makes the erection as such a signifier*, and which makes us all feel that it is not for nothing that the raised stone in very ancient cultures has such power" (SV, 25 June 1958; my emphasis). The erection of the phallic statue therefore properly belongs to man, as *homo erectus*. And what predisposes the phallus to function as the "signifier of power" (as "master signifier") is first of all the fact that it is erected, raised upright, like the human body or the statue of stone. This is not surprising, since erection is power and height, the ability to stand upright, on one's own legs, that fascinates the infant, the "being grown up" that polarizes his rivalry. In a word, the phallus is the imaginary "Master," the (quite literally) colossal[38] double in which the "little man" anticipates the mastery of his own body.

This is also to say, in which he *sees himself*, "before" himself: here again, Lacan explains things very clearly, reprising in his own way what Freud had said about the link between upright posture and the predominance of the visual functions in human sexuality.[39] If there is only one symbolization of sex, it is because symbolization occurs only for what is visible: "Besides, it isn't the penis, but the phallus, that is to say, something whose symbolic usage is possible because it can be seen, because it is erected. There can be no possible symbolic use for what is not seen, for what is hidden" (1988b, 272/315). And this is supposed to explain the profound misogyny of the symbol:

Strictly speaking, there is no symbolization of the woman's sexual organ as such. . . . And this is because the *imaginary* provides nothing but an absence, whereas elsewhere there is a very prevalent symbol [to be understood, for otherwise this passage becomes incomprehensible, as a *form*, a symbolizable *image*]. . . . The feminine sexual organ has the character of an absence, a void, a hole, which causes it to be less desirable than the masculine sexual organ in terms of provocativeness [1981, 198–199; my emphasis].

In other words, only what is exhibited in the exteriority of the visible is capable of becoming the *object* of a symbolization that annuls, absents, and hides it. No matter how much "felt experience" of her uterus and vagina the little girl has (and Lacan does not deny this at all, since he says that ignorance of the vaginal cavity at the time of the phallic phase is "suspiciously like *méconnaissance*"; 1977a, 282/687), the fact remains that she cannot see it and is reduced to imagining it (that is, to imagining *herself*, like Klossowski's Diana), with the help of the boy's erect phallus. If the phallus is raised in the center of the city (if society is always a society of men), it is because man's is the only sexual organ capable of being publicly exhibited and therefore communicated and symbolized. More simply, let us say that it is the only *theorizable* sexual organ. The primacy of the phallus is not merely an "infantile theory," not even a masculine theory: it is theory, period—the theory of the primacy of theory.

We see, then, in spite of all Lacan's negations, that the prevalence of the phallic symbol rests on a "prevalence of the imaginary form of the phallus" (1981, 198), which itself refers us to that "predominance of the visual functions" mentioned already in the article on the family complexes—that is, to the whole onto-photo-logy of the imaginary:

The tendency by which the subject restores his lost unity has its place from the start in the center of consciousness. It is the energetic source of his mental progress, a progress whose structure is determined by the predominance of the visual functions. If the search for his affective unity promotes within the subject *the forms by which he represents his identity to himself,* its most intuitive form is provided, at this stage, by the specular image [1984, 44; my emphasis].

This is another way of saying that the phallus is privileged, in Lacanian theory, not in its capacity as masculine sexual organ, but in its capacity as visible form or figure of the ego. Phallocentrism, before being an androcentrism or (to use Derrida's term) a "phallogocentrism,"[40] is a phallo-ego-*eido*-centrism. What is sought in the phallus is not a sexual object or organ, but rather that very peculiar "object": the specular or ideal ego, that is, the ob-ject in which the subject can see himself "before" himself and thus "represent his identity to himself." Thus it is not surprising that the phallus, actually penile and masculine, is simultaneously so asexual in Lacan. It is nothing but the ob-ject in which the subject, before any sexual characterization, represents him*self* to himself, in his fixed, permanent, substantial identity. The phallus, erected and majestic, is the statue of the ego—or, if you will, it is the identificatory model par excellence, the *Vor-bild* or *Gestalt* typical of humanity in general.

Oedipus Revisited

It remains for us to understand what predestines the phallus to its promotion to major *signifier* of human desire. In truth, we can ask why it is the erected form of the phallus that furnishes the signifier with "its first weapons," as Lacan enigmatically asserts, just as we may ask what authorizes Lacan to conflate so nimbly the predominance of the phallic image with that of a symbol. Who, after all—apart from Lacan—says that "the first signifier is the notch" (1977b, 141/129), the "single stroke" (*trait unaire*) of the "1," the "vertical stick" (SIX, 6 December 1961) that resembles the phallus? Why must the signifier be a *scepter*, a "*bar*" which . . . strikes the signified" (1977a, 288/692) and which "*petrifies* the subject" (1966, 840), or a *whip* (SV, 5 February 1958)? Nothing in the theory of the signifier seems to authorize this surreptitious analogism, which, however, is habitual in Lacan. If the signifier is "arbitrary"-diacritical, there is no reason for its form to have the least "attachment," as Saussure said, to any content whatsoever, even if this content were an ideal and prevalent form of the imaginary body.

Thus we really must understand that the privilege of the imaginary phallus is an entirely negative one. In a word, the signifier in Lacan is all the more phallic in that it *must not be phallic.* If the imaginary phallus constitutes the symbolized par excellence (if it is what is "borrowed" from the signified by the signifier), it is because it is this very thing that must be annulled/raised—we could almost say extirpated, exterminated, castigated—in the symbol. In fact, the imaginary phallus is what embodies the identity of man, and therefore it is precisely what man, if he is truly human, can only desire, by negating it. The phallus is certainly what man wants *to be* (an ego of bronze, an object without lack or "hole," a beautiful totality closed on itself); but it is also, and by the same token, what man *wants* to be, in the very precise sense of his *not* being it, of his not being any object "in-itself," no transcendent ego. Man, as subject, cannot be the phallus except by transcending it and transcending himself in it. And this, in the Lacanian system, is why he *must* not be the phallus. The law of castration, which enjoins every human to lose the phallus by annulling/raising it to the function of signifier, only expresses that ontological prescription inherited from Kojève and Sartre: the human being is not what he is and he is what he is not, and therefore he cannot conform to what he is except through nonconformity. In short, he cannot (and must not) identify with himself except through non-identification.

This can be translated as follows: the human being (man or woman) must identify with the phallus, but as a signifier—that is, as that with which he or she cannot and must not identify. "Identify without identifying"; "Be the phallus without being it." The law of symbolic castration enjoins us to substitute for the imaginary phallus the symbolic phallus—namely, the imaginary phallus negated: "In fact, what must be recognized is the function of the phallus, not as object, but as signifier of desire. . . . The solution to the problem of castration does not arise from the dilemma to have or not to have it; the subject must first recognize that he *is* not it."[41]

Let us see, then, how this ontological prescription/prohibition is tested in empirical description—that is, in the description of the Oedipus; and to do this, let us return to the point where we left the infant not long ago, when he wanted "to be the phallus" of the mother. Why "to be"? Because human desire, as we know, is fundamentally a desire to be a subject, not a desire to have an object. As a result, the mother, contrary to the official version of the Freudian Oedipus, is not desired in her capacity as object of love (as object chosen according to the "anaclitic" type) but in her capacity as desiring subject. The child demands to be loved—that is, he demands, beyond all the gratifications that reduce him to the status of "object of love," to be desired as a subject: "The child's desire asserts itself . . . in that it is the desire of the desire of the mother" (SV, 22 January 1958). Even more simply, he *desires* to be.

But the desire of the mother—such is the a priori of the Lacanian Oedipus—"*is* the phallus." Why? Because the mother bathes in the symbolic, and because that "third"—the father—forbids her to desire herself in her child by making it her little phallic "double." "*Thou shalt not reintegrate thy product*" (SV, 29 January 1958): the father enjoins the mother to desire "something other than" the child—namely, the imaginary phallus that she herself had to give up, in order to receive it in the form of its symbolic equivalent, the child-phallus. Therefore, the child is the phallus of the mother only insofar as he is *not* it: he is her symbolic phallus—that is, the signifier of her desire, the substitute for the x that she desires (in which she desires herself) "beyond" him.

But from all of this (which, as we shall see, is the operation of the "paternal metaphor"), "the child catches only the result" (SV, 22 January 1958)—namely, the "signified." The x that the mother's whole conduct signifies to him (since she obviously desires "something") is what he will wish to be, in order to be what the mother desires. In short, he will fall into the inevitable and disastrous error of confusing the signifier with the signified, the symbolic phallus with the imaginary phallus. Confronted with the alternative to be or not to be the "object" of the desire of the other, he will imagine himself to be just that object (that ego, that phallic double) of the mother that he is not (since he is only its signifier). This is the first stage of the Lacanian Oedipus, its strictly *identificatory* stage:

What the child seeks is . . . "to be or not to be" [English in the original] the object of the desire of the mother . . . the point that corresponds with what is ego and what, here, is his other ego, that with which he identifies, the "something other" that he will seek to be. . . . As if in a mirror, the subject identifies with the object of desire of the mother. . . . To please the mother . . . it is necessary and sufficient to be the phallus [SV, 22 January 1958].

The child's first identificatory model, then, is not, as Freud thought, the father of "the early history of the Oedipus complex"[42] or even the breast of the oral phase. It is the imaginary phallus, in which the ego freezes himself into an object (and, by the same token, "fixes" himself to the all-powerful mother, of whom he becomes, so to speak, the "first weapon").

   According to Lacan, it is only in a second phase that the Oedipus takes on the form we know in Freud: that of a rivalrous identification with the father. Realizing that the mother does not have the phallus (and that he himself, by the same token, is not it), the child begins by interpreting that castration, which by rights is a symbolic and legal castration, as a real privation: the father is the one who *has* the phallus, since he violently deprives the mother (and hence also the child) of it. There follows a no less violent rivalry with the depriving father, which Lacan presents as a rivalry for an object ("to have or not to have the phallus"), but which is obviously a purely identificatory rivalry, since it is once more a question of "to be or not to be" the phallus of the mother. As in Freud, Oedipal hostility toward the father is conflated with identification with the father, except that the stakes in this rivalry are not the maternal object that the child would like to have, but rather the phallic "object" that he would like to be, in his capacity as ego. Here, the Oedipal conflict is very clearly (much more clearly than in Freud, anyway) a "struggle for pure prestige."

   The result is that the problem of the Oedipus in Lacan (even more than in Freud) becomes that of the "decline" of the identificatory rivalry for the phallus, especially in the boy. The girl, in reality, does not have the phallus (she "is *without having it*," says Lacan[43]), and she is thus much more naturally inclined to leave it to the father who has it, in order to receive it from him as a woman (in coitus) and/or as a mother (in the form of a child): "For her, it is much simpler: *she does not have to make this identification* [with the legal father, as we shall see], nor does she need to keep it as a title to virility: she knows where it is, . . . where she must go to get it; it is on the father's side, [she must go] toward him who has it" (SV, 22 January 1958; my emphasis). In other words, the fact of not having a real penis makes her access to symbolic castration, which enjoins her not to be the imaginary phallus, almost natural. (This solution may actually be found to be a little too "simple," even from Lacan's own point of view, for isn't this a surreptitious resurgence of the reference to the *reality* of the difference between the sexes, to the reality of the "hole" that the girl hastens to fill through an imaginary identification with the phallus?)

The boy, on the contrary, must actually identify with the father who has the phallus, in order to come to a virile position; and this, as Lacan remarks, is the cause of the weakness, with respect to perversion, of the male sex (1977a, 320/823): the boy must simultaneously identify with the father (so as to have the phallus and to become masculine) and not identify with him (so as not to be his rival, so as not to be the phallus of the mother). As Lacan says once again, he "*is not* without having" the phallus,[44] so that it will be very difficult for him not to confuse the symbolic phallus that he must have without being it, and the imaginary phallus that he is by the fact of having it. Hence it is only too easy for him to remain "fixed" in rivalrous identification with the phallus of the mother, violently refusing its privation by the father: a transvestite identifying with the phallus hidden beneath the clothing of the mother, a homosexual identifying with the mother who has the masculine phallus "at hand," a fetishist who identifies with the mother insofar as she gives herself the phallus in the form of equivalents (boots, corsets, and so on) (SV, 22 and 29 January 1958).

How, then, can the boy get out of the double bind that simultaneously enjoins him to be and not to be the phallus, to identify and not to identify with the phallic father? We recognize here the problem that Lacan had already stumbled on in his article on the family complexes:[45] if the Oedipal father simultaneously says, "Be like me" (a man) and "Do not be like me" (in regard to the mother), how is it possible henceforth to prevent the normative ("secondary") identification with the father from being confused with the rivalrous ("primary") identification with this same father? There-fore, we are not surprised to see Lacan returning to a solution analogous to the one he advocated in that article, in 1938. Just as he proposed then to distinguish between rivalrous identification with the "superegoic" father and normalizing identification with the *function* of the "ego-ideal," here he proposes to distinguish be-tween identification with the imaginary phallus and identification with the symbolic phallus—that is, *with the same imaginary phallus, insofar as one must not identify oneself with it.*

Indeed, this is the third phase of the Oedipus, according to Lacan. The child (or, more precisely, the boy) must realize that the father *has* the phallus, not inasmuch as he *is* the phallus of the mother (that is, a "rival object") but inasmuch as he possesses it legitimately, and that the mother, by the same token, cannot have it in any case: "Inasmuch as he [the father] intervenes as the one who has the phallus, and not as the one who is the phallus, something can happen to reinstate the agency of the phallus as the object *de-sired* by the mother" (SV, 22 January 1958; my emphasis). This will happen only if the mother, instead of making the child her little phallic double, returns him to the father as to the one who legally possesses the phallus. In short, it is necessary that she play the game of the symbolic pact/exchange, by referring to the word and the law of the father as to her own law, as to a "given word" that she intends to respect (when this is not the case, we get the whole gamut of neuroses, psychoses, and perversions). The pivotal moment of the Oedipus is not, as in Freud, the threat of castration by the rival-father; it is the castration of the mother insofar as she recognizes it symbolically: "I do not have (the right to have) the phallus, and therefore you cannot be it, unless you yourself become a father, by receiving/giving in your turn the symbolic phallus that you are not."

What happens then, according to Lacan, is that the child (more precisely, the *boy*), instead of identifying with the father who is the imaginary phallus of the mother, identifies with the father who has the phallus symbolically (which the girl, as we have seen, does not need to do): "The identification with the father occurs at this third phase, the phase in which he intervenes as him who 'has' it. This identification is called the *ego-ideal*" (SV, 22 January 1958). Lacan expresses this once again by saying that the boy "metaphorically" identifies with the father, by identifying with his symbolic phallus (as a "title of virility") *instead* of identifying with the imaginary phallus of the mother: he becomes "his *own* metaphor" (SV, 22 January 1958). The Oedipus is resolved, Lacan assures us, through a "paternal metaphor" that substitutes the signifier of the "Name of the Father" for the signifier of the "Desire of the Mother." Hence the following formula (1977a, 200/557):

$$\frac{\text{Name-of-the-Father}}{\text{Desire of the Mother}} \cdot \frac{\text{Desire of the Mother}}{\text{Signified to the subject}}$$

$$\rightarrow \text{Name-of-the-Father} \left(\frac{\text{O}}{\text{Phallus}} \right).$$

It is read in this way: the metaphorical function of the Name-of-the-Father is to put an Other in the place of the phallus.

It can be reformulated, perhaps slightly less "algorithmically," by saying that the child (the boy) becomes a virile man (at least potentially) by identifying with the phallus with which he must not identify. Lacan, in fact, is speaking of the substitution of one signifier for another, but in reality it is a question (from the point of view of the child himself) of a sort of transmutation of the identification, which mysteriously passes from positive to negative. From this perspective, we are irresistibly drawn back to the mechanism of the *Umwendung* of identification already cited by Freud to explain the "exit" from the Oedipus complex.[46] The child (the boy) really does continue to be the phallus insofar as he identifies with the one who has it. The only difference is that now he is it "by not being it," insofar as he identifies not with the *object* but with the *signifier* of the desire of the mother—namely, with the object negated by the paternal "no" (SV, 29 January 1958). In short, he is a "no"-object; in other words, a subject: he desires himself beyond himself, such as he is *not*. At present, the phallus is the signifier of his desire—that is, of the non-object that he is (or, what amounts to the same thing, of the object that he is not) for the desire of the other. Or, again, the phallus is the signifier of the subject, insofar as the subject identifies himself in it ("represents his identity" in it) under erasure, in the mode of a forbidden, barred, repressed identification: the subject is the phallus insofar as he is not it, insofar as he "metaphorizes" himself in it and defers his own identity in it.

If we now ask how this symbolic identification is a non-identification, how this phallus-signifier is so *different* from the imaginary phallus that it metaphorizes (for, after all, according to Lacan's own admission, the boy must *identify himself with it* in order "not to be it"), the only answer we get is Zazie's: [47] because "zatzeewayitiz" (*cékomça*), because the symbolic phallus must not be the imaginary phallus that it nevertheless really is, and such is the fundamental Law of the Oedipus, enjoining Man (*homo*, but especially *vir*) "*not*-to-identify with," "*not*-to-be," the phallus. Lacan, unlike Freud, never questions the origin or the genesis of that universal prohibition of identification, for he knows only too well that it would then be necessary for him to seek the "solution" on the side of that same identification (the identification with the father and/or phallus with whom one must not identify, and so on). The result is that the difference between these two types of identification is purely and simply postulated as "the Law," without our even being allowed to ask why the phallus of symbolic identification is *not* the phallus of imaginary identification, or why that symbolic identification is *not* an identification. That question is literally forbidden, for what would become of us if we doubted the Law and the Word of the Father? Psychosis, neurosis, and perversion would await us at every turn. Thus the whole Lacanian system encloses and barricades itself in the a priori of the "no," interpreted as the universal Law of humanity: "Do not identify"; "Do not be what you are"; "Desire yourself beyond every object"; "Be nothing."

Obviously, Lacan's whole complex reformulation of the Oedipus complex ultimately rests on the rigid "dualist ontology" of Kojève: man is what he is (a desiring subject, an ek-static transcendence) only by not being what he is (a transcendent object, a given identity). If the phallus, in Lacan, is posed as the universal "object" of desire, this is because it eminently embodies the identical-and-objective-being of the imaginary ego—that is, what the human subject, if he wishes to live up to his vocation, must perpetually negate, overcome, transcend, and desire. In it, the subject desires himself as the object he is not, as the non-object he *has to be*. As for the recourse to the Lévi-Straussian theory of the "elementary structures of kinship," in sum, it only dresses up that profound ontological appeal by furnishing it with a sort of "scientific" guarantee. If the symbolic father enjoins the mother "not to reintegrate her product" (much more than he forbids the child to possess the mother, as in Freud), this is first of all because it is necessary for the child not to identify with the object-phallus that he is, so as to desire himself beyond himself. In this sense, the Law is an ontological law (or a "mis-ontological" one, since it is a matter of negative ontology): it does not forbid one's *having* an object of pleasure or enjoyment (*jouissance*), it forbids one's *being* that object. In short, it forbids identification in all its forms, by prescribing that the subject conform to nothing: "Act in conformity with your desire" (1986, 362).

It is not a question here of a description of the Oedipus, but rather of a prescription that constitutes the stakes of what Lacan calls the "ethics of psychoanalysis": "Desire!" "Do not give in to your desire!" (1986, 368). As far as the reality of the modern Oedipus (the Freudian Oedipus) is concerned, Lacan was the first to know that it hardly conforms to that sort of symbolic initiation to desire. On the contrary, the crisis of the symbolic is spread all over: the "deficiency" of the paternal function, the "foreclosure" of the Name-of-the-Father, the perpetual calling into question of the "Law" and the symbolic "pact," the confusion of lineages and the generalized competition of the generations, the battle of the sexes, the loss of familial landmarks. In other words, the crisis of symbolic identification is everywhere, and it becomes impossible to separate it, as Lacan would have liked to do, from so-called imaginary identification. Thus, the call to a "symbolic Law," so obviously obsolete, must be understood in Lacan as a sort of analytic myth intended to serve as a prop for an onto-ethics of human desire. The Lacanian Oedipus is not the Oedipus as it is; it is the Oedipus as it *must* be. It is the anti-mimetic Oedipus, the identificatory anti-model to which the analyst, through his silence, enjoins the analysand to conform: "Identify with my desire"; "(Do not) be like me"; "Imitate the inimitable." Besides, this is why Lacan's "model" was not *Oedipus Rex*, the neurotic Oedipus who "submit[s] to the interdiction" (1986, 354) while simultaneously rivalizing with it, but rather *Oedipus at Colonus*, the Oedipus who "incur[s] castration" (1986, 854), who voluntarily tears out his eyes and rails, unreconciled, against the curse of existence: "The last speech of Oedipus, as you know, was . . . μὴ φῦναι. . . . μὴ φῦναι means—*rather, not to be*. This is the preference on which a human life must end . . . the triumph of being-toward-death, formulated in the μὴ φῦναι of Oedipus, in which we find the μὴ, the negation identical to the entry of the subject, in the support of the signifier" (1986, 353, 361–362).[48]

As for the analysis (or the "pass") that leads the subject to that absolute "disbeing" (1968, 26), "nuptials with destruction, considered as the culmination of his vow" (1986, 357), Lacan may very well assert, while implicitly criticizing Freud, that analysis "is not the rite of the Oedipus" (1977a, 316/818). But this is because he had made it the rite of symbolic castration: the harsh initiation of the "harsh desire of . . . desiring" (1986, 357), the tragic schooling of the tearing away from self and total disidentification, the infinitely painful access to that "place from which a voice is heard clamoring 'the universe is a defect in the purity of Non-Being'" (1977a, 317, 819).

The Crystal Stopper

A few more words on the theory of the "*objet a*"[49]—indeed, the exposition of Lacanian doctrine would be incomplete if we did not mention, at least briefly, that ultimate avatar of the "object" of desire. Not that the theory of the *objet a* actually modifies the doctrine of castration; as we shall see, it really only furnishes that doctrine with a clothing, in the sense in which Lacan says, for example, "It is only the clothing of the self-image that comes to envelop the object cause of desire, which most often supports . . . the objectal relation. The affinity of *a* with its envelope is one of the major articulations to have been advanced by psychoanalysis" (1975c, 85). But the fact that Lacan felt the need thus to "clothe" the hole of castration is not in itself a matter for indifference. In reality, this imaginary clothing corresponds, in Lacan, to a question that is difficult to avoid, one that the doctrine of castration left entirely open—gaping, we could even say: the question, once again, of the "*object*" of desire.

The phallus, as we have already confirmed, is precisely no object, no self-image, since it is, properly speaking, the negation of object and self-image under the condition of "the Law." But the problem is that desire nevertheless must have an object; otherwise, it would desire nothing at all. As Alain Juranville quite justly notes, "There must, all the same, be some *object*. Not the object of desire, since its failing is radical. But an object that is tied to desire, let us say, an object 'for desire.'"[50] Human desire, being a finite desire (1977b, 31/32)—a finite transcendence—necessarily embodies itself, appears to itself in an ob-ject, if only to negate it immediately. This, again, is Actaeon's problem: Actaeon would not desire the Goddess if she did not take on body in his gaze, if she did not throw him the infinitely deceptive simulacrum of her buttocks and her breasts, in which she herself sees and desires herself. In other words, the phantasy (the simulacrum, the image) is necessary to the perpetuation of desire, even from Lacan's point of view (we could say, from the point of *view*, period). Indeed, the subject must identify in some way with the object of the desire of the Other in order to desire himself in it, failing which he would be nothing but a pure desire of the pure desire of the Other—that is, nothing: an absolute void in "the purity of Non-Being."

In a certain way, it was this very difficulty that the doctrine of castration was initially supposed to resolve, since the phallus was precisely that object of the desire of the Other with which the subject must simultaneously identify and not identify. But it is also this same doctrine that Lacan, in the early 1960's, felt the need to complete with his theory of the *objet a*, as if he were not totally satisfied with it. Why? Essentially, it seems, because the phallus had been so well defined as a signifier that it no longer allowed the slightest identification on the subject's part: a much too "iconoclastic" theory, as Klossowski would have said, and which must therefore necessarily find its limit, or even its punishment. In fact, as Lacan often explains, the phallus, Φ, "signifier of signifier," is never anything but the "signifier of a lack in the Other" (1977a, 316/818), in the sense of its being the signifier of the lack of every signifier that could signify to me what the Other desires and, by the same token, *what I am* for him. To the question "What does he want?"—which is, identically, a "What does he want from me?" (1977a, 312/815), understood as a "How does he want me?" (SX, 14 November 1962)—there is no response from the Other except perhaps a signifier that represents me in my absence for another signifier, and so forth. Nothing, in other words, permits me to identify myself in the

signifiers furnished by the Other, and that is what the phallus signifies. It is the S(Ø), the signifier of the barred Other that, in return,
signifies to me my own ek-sistence as barred subject, divided and
separated from myself: $\mathcal{S}$(O), vanished subject, in *aphanisis*, perpetually "fading" (1977b, 207–208/189) in the signifiers that manifest me as what I am not.

It is easy to see how Lacan, under these conditions, would have
felt the need to lend a bit of "stuff" (1977a, 314, 315/816, 818) to
that ungraspable subject of the signifier and, by the same token, a
bit of body and objectivity to his desire. In the end, do human beings copulate with signifiers? Do they seek only *symbols* of their
desire (and that of the other) in their partners? As Lacan ends up
conceding, rather brusquely, desire, "in the final analysis, always remains the desire of the body, desire of the body of the other and
nothing but desire of his body" (SX, 8 May 1963). Besides, how can
we explain the singular fixity of the phantasy, which securely fas-
tens the subject's desire onto this particular object, this particular
imaginary scenario in which he plays, for example, the part of an
object that is beaten, sucked, defecated, gazed at by the other? Isn't
this a sort of ultimate identification of the subject, irreducible to the
perpetual vicariance of signifiers? "This subject . . . is no more than
such an object. Ask the writer about the anxiety that he experiences
when faced by the blank sheet of paper, and he will tell you who *is*
the turd of his phantasy" (1977a, 315/818).

Moreover, Lacan asserts this quite clearly in his seminar on
anxiety: the *objet a* "is what resists that assimilation to the function
of signifier, . . . what, in the sphere of the signifier, . . . always
presents itself as lost. . . . Now, it is just this scrap (*déchet*), this off-
cut (*chute*), this thing that resists 'significantization,' that comes to
find itself constituting, as such, the foundation of the desiring subject" (SX, 13 March 1963). In short, the *objet a* is the object of
phantasy—namely, that stopgap object (*objet bouche-trou*; 1977b,
269–270/242) that the subject "substitutes for the Ø" (1977a,
320/823) by identifying with what the Other lacks (with the "lost
object," as Freud said—to which Lacan adds, "[The] *a*, the object
of identification . . . is what one no longer *has*" [*ce qu'on n'a plus*];
SX, 23 January 1963). In this fascinating and opaque object, the
subject becomes the turd, the breast, or the "phallus (imaginary ob-

ject)" (1977a, 315/817) lost by the other by virtue of the signifier—
that is, the "object that cannot be swallowed . . . which remains
stuck in the gullet of the signifier" (1977b, 270/243) because no signifier can (or should, in the case of the phallus) signify it definitively: "indices of an absolute signification," Lacan writes (1977a,
314/816). In phantasy, in other words, the subject imagines himself
as the object that could fulfill the desire of the Other, as that infinitely precious and absolutely unique object that would finally respond to the enigma of desire: "*Ché vuoi?*" "What do you want
from me?" "Who am I for you?"

And yet we must be very exacting here, for to read the fore-
going may give the impression that the *objet a* is really a new re-
hashing of the imaginary object—namely, the very one that the
"object" (or, what amounts to the same thing, the subject) of desire
cannot be in any case. And indeed, in the evolution of Lacan's
thought, the symbol *a* actually does refer to the imaginary "small
other" ("*petit autre*") regularly denounced by Lacan as the cause of
the *méconnaissance* of desire (cf. the "schema L" of the 1950's).
Therefore, it is all the more urgent to emphasize that the *objet a*,
although actually remaining imaginary in Lacan, is not altogether
imaginary. More precisely, let us say that it is only *partially* imaginary, in its capacity as "part-object," unintegrable into the total image of the body; and, as such, it "cannot be grasped in the mirror"
(1977a, 315–316/817–818). Far from being merely the imaginary
object that "fills the gap constituted by the inaugural division of the
subject" (1977b, 270/243), the *objet a* is just as much what manifests that gap at the very moment when it seals it. It is, Lacan says,
the "presence of a hollow" (1977b, 180/164); and this does not
mean that, as signifier, it represents the absent subject to another
signifier, but rather that it *embodies* and ultimately *images* the division of the subject, the break in the image, the cut of castration:
Oedipus's bloody eyes rolling on the ground, the severed breasts of
Saint Agatha of Zurbarán, phallic *vanitas* floating before Holbein's
Ambassadors.

The *objet a*, by Lacan's habitual definition, is a "morsel of
the body" (SX, 30 January 1963), a detachable/detached "pound
of flesh": "The *objet a* is something from which the subject, in
order to constitute itself, has separated itself off as organ" (1977a,

103/95). Let us understand this first in the most literal sense: the living being, as Lacan recalls, never stops separating himself from "parts" of himself (placenta, feces, urine, sperm, and so on). But he also separates himself from the breast "superimposed" on the body of the mother that he himself is (1977b, 195/178), from the erectile organ at the moment of detumescence following orgasm (SX, 15 May 1963), from the eye (which sees without seeing itself; SX, 15 May 1963), and even from the voice (which can hear itself only on condition of being externally emitted; SX, 22 May 1963). As we can see, these "separations" are extremely diverse, but they have in common that they are separations from oneself, "internal" separations (SX, 15 May 1963). In them, the body sacrifices parts of itself, so to speak, by "cutting" itself along "a margin or border—lips, 'the enclosure of the teeth,' the rim of the anus, the tip of the penis, the vagina, the slit formed by the eyelids, even the horn-shaped aperture of the ear" (1977a, 314–315/817). Hence the ambiguity of the "parts" thus separated from the body, since in relation to it they are both the same and other, both similar and dissimilar.

Now, it is quite obviously this ambiguity, this drifting between imaginary continuity and real separation, that primarily interests Lacan. On the one hand, in fact, these "parts" or "organs" are eminently suitable for representing the subject himself, insofar as they arise from an autopartition. Hence Lacan makes them objectivizations of the subject, "small other" objects in which the subject images, embodies, and identifies himself. On the other hand, these objects are *really* lost (the *objet a*, says Lacan, is "what represents the S[ubject] in his irreducible reality"; SX, 6 March 1963); their loss is not only irrecuperable but also constitutive of the subject as such (here, Lacan cites the maternal breast, or the placenta, which "certainly represents that part of himself that the individual loses at birth"; 1977b, 198/180). The subject is therefore not at liberty to identify with it, since he can engender himself (*se parere*) as an individual totality only on condition of separating himself from it (*separare*): "It is from his partition that the subject proceeds to his parturition" (1966, 843)—with the result that the *objet a*, a part without a whole, does not enter into the specular image (1977a, 316/818), since, on the contrary, it is from its "cut" that the total image of the body is engendered. The subject can see "himself" in it only as a heterogeneous, odd part or, again, as a *hole of which he himself is the rim* (a structure that, as we know, Lacan illustrated with a great many paradoxical topological figures, such as the Moebius strip and the Klein bottle). Hence "the phallus, that is, the image of the penis, is negativated (*négativé*) in its place in the specular image . . . as a part lacking in the desired image" (1977a, 319–320/822; translation modified): ($-\varphi$), a pathetic, obsolete, dog-tired organ. Or, again, it is my own image in the mirror, gazing at me with strange anxiety-producing *unheimlich* eyes, which do not belong to me (SX, 9 January 1963): some sort of brilliant marbles, fully ready to leap from their sockets.

The *objet a* thus has the remarkable property of furnishing an image of the subject, *insofar as he is lacking in that image*: a marvelous broken mirror, muddy and opaque, in which the subject can see himself as he is not and with which he can identify himself in his absence of identity: a marvelous Medusa head, marvelous *alētheia* of the subject. Thus we can understand the tremendous interest that this paradoxical "mirror" would have had for Lacan: in it, he could finally hold the possibility of imaging the subject (the subject and not the ego), by giving body to his desire (a body that, this time, would no longer be an image of the body). In it, more precisely, Lacan could hold a sort of *non-specular imaginary*,[51] one particularly suitable for portraying the unportrayable symbolic castration. Indeed, the loss of *objets a*, Lacan tells us, is *analogous* to the loss (the disappearance) of himself that the subject submits to by virtue of the signifier, and that is why it holds such importance in the strictly libidinal economy of the drives. The lost organ, a part of the real body, non-sexual in itself, comes to portray that "hole in the real," the subject of the signifier, the subject of desire:

I have been able to articulate the unconscious for you as being situated in the gaps that the distribution of the signifying investments sets up in the subject, and which figure in the algorithm in the form of a lozenge [$\lozenge$], which I place at the center of any relation of the unconscious between reality and the subject. Well! It is insofar as something in the apparatus of the body *is structured in the same way*, it is because of the topological unity of the gaps in play, that the drive assumes its role in the functioning of the unconscious [1977b, 181/165; my emphasis].

In other words, the corporeal gaps "mirror" the unimaginable cut of castration, and it is from these "erogenous zones" that the drive goes out to "drive round" (1977b, 168, 177–179/153, 162–163)[52] the lost *objet a*—that is, the hole: a rim conjunct with another rim, a disjunctive conjunction that is therefore "figured" in the Lacanian algorithm by the lozenge of fantasy that a-joins $, the

castrated subject of the symbolic, and *a*, the real lost object (1977b, 209/190). Let us imagine this lozenge as a kiss embracing absence, like a mouth-to-mouth conjoining of two wounds: a rapport of non-rapport, a sexual (non-)rapport ([*non-*] rapport sexuel). As Lacan says, "Two lacks overlap here" (1977b, 204/186): in the lost organ, the subject will represent his very own loss, the "fundamentally lost object" that he is for the desire of the Other. More precisely, in the lost organ he will make himself what he is *not*, by identifying himself with *what* the Other lacks and desiring himself in it as what the Other *lacks*. Fantasy, insofar as the subject identifies himself in it with the lost object of the Other (breast, feces, phallus, gaze, voice), puts the disappearance of the subject, his eclipse of/from the scene, on stage (SX, 8 May 1963). The subject, always *in* the scene of the fantasy, is at the same time always excluded, elided, divided (beaten, sectioned, defecated, and so on) "in his relation to the object, which usually does not show its true face" (1977b, 185/168). Therefore, according to Lacan, fantasy functions less as an image or painting of the subject than as a *frame* (SX, 12 June 1963): a window, a bull's-eye surrounding the *objet a*, a slit cutting the rim of his enigmatic appearance/disappearance, a keyhole serving as a prop to the fading of the subject in the scene where he sees himself. In a word, the *objet a* of the fantasy causes to appear/disappear in(to) the imaginary the subject's unimaginable appearance/disappearance into the signifier, the fading of the object that he is *not* for the desire of the Other: "The *objet a* . . . serves as a

symbol of the lack, that is to say, of the phallus (1977b, 103/95)—
that is to say, of the subject. The *objet a* of phantasy portrays the
subject *on the verge* (*au bord*; literally, "on the rim") of disappearing, suspended (and thus "propping up"his desire) *on the verge* of
castration: "the enclosure of the teeth" nibbling the nipple, lips en-
circling the glans, the anal sphincter severing the fecal or penile col-
umn, the eye glued to the keyhole, an anorexic mouth closed on
nothing. Let us imagine this (1977b, 178/163):

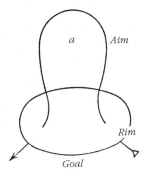

Lacan illustrates this structure of drive and fantasy in many
(often obscure) ways, but the example to which he most often returns is that of the scopic *objet a*: the gaze, by which the subject
wishes to be seen. This is obviously no accident. The phantasy
(Lacan, at least, does not doubt this) is indeed essentially spatial
and visual (SX, 12 June 1963), and vision is in turn the true domain
of the imaginary. In space, as Lacan emphasizes, nothing is ever
separated, and this is why the body always appears in it as total, as
a "good form," one and identical (SX, 22 May 1963). Under these
conditions, we can see that the scopic phantasy is the phantasy par
excellence, under the aspect of the "stopgap" (*bouche-trou*), of the
filling in of loss and castration: "The scopic drive . . . most completely eludes . . . castration" (1977b, 78/74). How, then, does the
subject *appear* there *in his disappearance*, as the lost object of the
desire of the Other?

As a gaze—a gaze, not an eye. Lacan strongly insists on this
point, taking up a distinction already made by Sartre:[53] the gaze, as
the gaze of the Other (of "*autrui*," as Sartre prefers to say),[54] cannot

be seen as the eye, the organ of vision. More precisely, it cannot "see itself"[55]: "What one looks at [the gaze of the Other, who "gazes at you"] cannot be seen [cannot see itself]" (1977b, 182/166). There is a "split" between eye and gaze (1977b, 73/70). Indeed, the eye is always an eye-object in that I see the eyes of another person or see my own eyes in a mirror. I cannot ever see myself from the place where I gaze (1977b, 144/132), since I could do so only on condition of seeing myself "before" myself. In this sense, the eye actually is a separated organ—namely, my own lost, objectivized gaze. And yet it is also the object in which, by virtue of the very structure of vision, I appear fully to find myself: the specular illusion of Valéry's "I saw myself seeing myself," which Lacan rigorously equates with the illusion of the *cogito* (understood as self-consciousness; 1977b, 80–81/76–77) and, more generally, with the primacy of vision in the philosophic tradition (1977a, 71/68).[56] The eye is the imaginary object par excellence, the *objet "petit autre"* in which I separate myself from myself the better to recognize myself.

In the gaze, on the contrary, I do not recognize myself. Why not? Because that eye, as Lacan says, returning to Sartre's expression, "gazes at me" (*me regarde*[57]; 1977b, 95–96/89), in both senses of that expression.[58] Indeed, that eye is no longer the visible object at which I gaze, it is the eye of another *subject* who gazes at (who concerns) *me*. This is a reversal of the perspective in which Sartre, as we know, situates the upsetting encounter with the other (as another "for-itself") and in which Lacan sees instead the singular (and anxiety-producing) manifestation of the desire of the Other. If the gaze "gazes at me," it is also in the sense in which it "concerns me" as a subject. In it, as Sartre insists, I certainly become the *object* of the gaze of the other, as soon as he poses me as the "in-itself" that he himself is not: under the nihilating gaze of the other, Sartre asserts, I suddenly become a transcendent ego, I freeze myself in the identity of "voyeur" that I henceforth *am* for him, in the most total shame.[59] But, Lacan adds, this is only the better to become the non-object, the "lost" and annihilated object of the desire of the Other. Indeed, the Other gazes at (concerns) me *beyond* the visible eye (the object) that I am for him, as (according to Lacan) the very example of the "voyeur surprised" chosen by Sartre demonstrates: "Is it not clear that . . . it is not the nihilating subject, correlative of the world of objectivity, who feels himself surprised, but the subject sustaining himself in a function of desire?" (1977b, 84–85/80; translation modified); "the other surprises him, the subject, as entirely hidden gaze" (1977b, 182/166). What the other looks for in my voyeur's eye, glued to the keyhole, is in fact my gaze—that is, precisely that "object" in which he cannot see himself: the enigma of what he himself is for my desire, which is the reason for his. In short, he seeks "himself" in it, as a non-object—that is (let us in turn object to Lacan), as a "nihilating subject."

The result is that I can no more see (identify, recognize) myself in the gaze of the Other than he can see himself in mine: "You never gaze at me from the place from which I see you" (1977b, 103/95). The gaze is an opaque mirror (an "underside of consciousness"; 1977b, 83/79) in which I can identify myself only as the closed, definitively enigmatic, lost "object" of the desire of the Other, and which nevertheless *is seen*, causing the disappearance that I "am" (as the subject of desire) to *appear*. Lacan clearly objects on these grounds to Sartre, who asserts, "The Other's gaze is the disappearance of the Other's *eyes* as objects which manifest the gaze."[60] Lacan replies, "Is this a correct phenomenological analysis? No. . . . The gaze is seen" (1977b, 84/79; translation modified), that "underside of consciousness" is phenomenalized. How? As an incongruous *stain* (1977b, 74/71) in the painting-mirror of the visible—not, therefore, as an eye in which I see myself see or see myself seen, but as an eye that gazes at (concerns) me all the more in that it does not see me, in that it stains the mirror: the pupils of a blind man, or a beauty mark that comes to disturb the perceptual "good form" (SX, 22 May 1963); the eye of an octopus, or the ocelli of animals (1977b, 73–74/70); brush strokes as they stain the canvas (1977b, 114–115/104–105).

Witness, deploying itself before Holbein's *Ambassadors*, "this strange, suspended oblique [phallic] object" that bars the painting (1977b, 88/82). You see it, and yet you see nothing. You see nothing, and yet it gazes at (concerns) you in proportion to your not seeing a thing: "What do you want from me?" You are there, yourself, "in the picture" (in the phantasy), "out of place in the picture" (*faisant "tache dans le tableau"*; 1977b, 96/89): the pure enigma that you are for the desire (of the painter? of the ambassadors?) that gazes at (concerns) you by *giving* you this painting to see (1977b, 101/93). Then you "begin by walking out of the room in which no doubt it [the painting] has long captivated you. It is then that, turning round as you leave—as the author of the *Anamorphoses* [Jürgen Baltru-šaitis] describes it—you apprehend in this form . . . what? A skull" (1977b, 88/83; translation modified). It was an *anamorphosis*, a refined variation of *trompe l'oeil*. Seeing the painting before you, you could not see what you were in it. But now, no longer seeing it, seeing it from the side, you can finally see in it what you are—nothing, a hollow in the visible, an empty *vanitas*: "Holbein makes visible for us here something that is simply the subject as nihilated—nihilated in the form that is, strictly speaking, the *imaged embodiment* of the *minus-phi* $[(-\varphi)]$ of castration. . . . It *reflects our own nothingness*, in the figure of the death's head" (1977b, 88–89, 92/83, 86; my emphasis; translation modified).

Thus we see, in this more than exemplary example, what the *objet a* of phantasy represents for Lacan: an "embodiment" of the non-objective object of desire, an "image" of the unimaginable castrated phallus, a "reflection" of the non-existent vacuity of the subject—in short, an impossible image, a sort of ultimate limit of identification, a self-portrait in which the subject will see himself as he cannot see himself, a vision of horror in which his own nullity appears to him. What am I for you? Shit; refuse. Who are you for me? That in which I mutilate you (1977b, 268/241)—which is to say that, in the imaginary, the *objet a* plays a role exactly analogous to the one played by the phallic signifier in the domain of the symbolic: that of embodying the absence of the subject. In reality, the same logic is at work in both realms, with just a slight difference of register. Just as the symbolic phallus was the object of the desire of the Other with which the subject must "*not* identify," so at present the *objet a* of phantasy is the lost object of the Other with which the subject identifies, without being able to identify himself in it. Just as the phallus was the *signifier* of the enigma of what I am (*not*) for the desire of the Other, so at present the *objet a* is its *image*.

Does this mean that Lacan, late in life, finally reworked the rigid opposition between the symbolic and the imaginary, recognizing in the latter the capacity to "reveal" the truth of the subject in its abyssal non-being? In a sense, yes, since Lacan reached the point of making the *objet a* the ultimate identification of the subject, beyond which there is simply nothing: a pure identification with the unidentifiable, a pure Being-*there* of an enigmatic void. And yet this profound reworking did not challenge the aim that had been supporting the distinction between the symbolic and the imaginary: the ever more stubbornly renewed aim of a total disidentification of the subject, tending toward the apocalyptic revelation of his nothingness. From this point of view, the objective of analysis did not change, for it was always a question, as far as Lacan was concerned, of bringing the subject to this point of disappearance, where it is revealed to him that he is nothing—nothing of what is, nothing but the pure desire of the pure desire of the Other. But how to reach this infinitely vanished point, if not by dropping the final screen: the *objet a*?

Thus was Lacan's incessantly separative project pursued, this time operating on the *objet a* itself. The analyst, Lacan finally acknowledged, cannot be content with being a pure symbolic Other, a silent answering machine perpetually returning to the patient the question of his desire: "It is not enough that the analyst should support the function of Tiresias. He must also, as Apollinaire tells us, have breasts" (1977b, 270/243)—which should be understood as meaning that he must, in the transference, embody the *objet a* of the phantasy. But this is only so that he can break this last identification, in which the subject fascinates himself—hypnotizes himself, Lacan says significantly (1977b, 273/245)—in and as the object that fulfills the desire of the Other. How does the analyst go about this? By separating the *objet a* from the identification, by literally making it jump, fall, drop from the self-image. So the subject has hypnotized himself in that mysterious "crystal-stopper," the analyst's gaze? Well, then, the analyst will throw away (lose) that stopper, to finally reveal the void that the mouth of the bottle had so lovingly embraced:

As everyone knows, it was by distinguishing itself from hypnosis that analysis became established. For the fundamental mainspring of the analytic operation is the maintenance of the distance between the I [the "idealizing capital I of identification"] and the *a*. . . . [The analyst] isolates the *a*, places it at the greatest possible distance from the I that he, the analyst, is called upon by the subject to embody. It is from this idealization that the analyst has to fall in order to be the support of the separating *a* [1977b, 273/245].

We thought we understood that the *objet a* was the ultimate identificatory object, what we identify with *on the verge* (*au bord*) of no longer being anything, in order to sustain ourselves awhile longer in our desire. But we were wrong. We still had to learn not to be that object, to tear ourselves away from it, to lose it definitively. We were nothing but a hole in the image; and now, our eyes gouged out, we must plunge into that hole.

Better never to have been born, for how can we ever separate from ourselves to the point of becoming, not even the lost *object* of the Other but, his *lost* object—not even his blank, impenetrable eyes, but the empty, bleeding sockets of his desire to see where there is no longer anything to see? How, we ask, can we survive this experience, which even Oedipus himself could not bear? "How can a subject who has traversed the radical phantasy *live* the drive?" (1977b, 273/246; my emphasis; translation modified). Let us listen one last time to Lacan's response, oracular words, words of truth: "This crossing of the plane of identification is possible. Anyone who has lived through the analytic experience with me to the end of the training analysis knows that what I am saying is true" (1977b, 273/246).

Actaeon, chasing the Goddess, found her at last. His dogs devoured him eagerly. "Some say that his specter long haunted the countryside; he would stone those who ventured out into the night, and who knows what other devilries he caused; since it was impossible to find his remains, the oracles decreed that a statue be erected to him on the hillside, its gaze fixed afar; thus he lies in wait for *her* still, as if fixed in that vision forever; he who refused the simulacrum had his love of truth immortalized in a simulacrum."[61]

Notes

Notes

In Place of an Introduction

1. The epigraph for this chapter is from Raymond Queneau, *Le dimanche de la vie* (Paris: Gallimard, 1973), 160.

2. It was at Lacan's home that Caillois and Bataille met (R. Caillois, interview with G. Lapouge, *La Quinzaine littéraire*, 16–30 June 1970), and there is no doubt that Lacan followed closely the activities of the Collège de Sociologie, in which several of his other friends (Leiris, Klossowski, Kojève) collaborated. Michel Surya, in the biography *Georges Bataille, la mort à l'oeuvre* (Paris: Séguier, 1987), states (pp. 242, 256–57, 347) that Lacan was even a member of the small circle that operated around the secret society Acéphale.

3. Lacan, 1977a, 74/286; Lacan, 1988b, 55/73; Valéry, "La Pythie," from *Oeuvres* I (Paris: Gallimard, Pléiade, 1957), 136: "Qui se connaît quand elle sonne / N'être plus la voix de personne / Tant que des ondes et des bois" [my translation—Trans.].

4. E. Roudinesco, *La bataille de cent ans: Histoire de la psychanalyse en France* II (Paris: Editions du Seuil, 1986), 116. This point is also noted by F. Roustang, *Lacan, de l'équivoque à l'impasse* (Paris: Minuit, 1986), 14: "Lacan succeeded in the impressive feat of never appearing in public or private except as the analyst. . . . Whereas Freud exposed himself through his dreams, his correspondence, and his case histories, Lacan did everything in his power to avoid leaving any trace of his subjectivity."

5. A cave in southern France—Trans.

6. The original French is "*Moi, la vérité, je parle.*"—Trans.

7. Queneau wrote on this subject in "Premières confrontations avec Hegel," *Critique* 195–96, 1963. The list of those attending Kojève's course on Hegel speaks for itself: Jacques Lacan, Georges Bataille, Raymond Queneau, Pierre Klossowski, Alexandre Koyré, Eric Weil, Maurice Merleau-Ponty, Raymond Aron, R. P. Fessard, Jean Desanti, Patrick Waldberg, Aron

Gurwitsch, Henry Corbin, André Breton, and, less frequently, Jean-Paul Sartre and Emmanuel Lévinas. For the person last named, see S. Petrosino and J. Rolland, *La vérité nomade* (Paris: La Découverte, 1984), 177. On the importance of Kojève's teaching for postwar French philosophy, see the excellent analyses of Vincent Descombes, *Modern French Philosophy*, trans. L. Scott-Fox and J. M. Harding (Cambridge: Cambridge University Press, 1980), to which I have often made reference while writing this book. See also J.-M. Besnier, *La politique de l'impossible* (Paris: La Découverte, 1988); M. S. Roth, *Knowing and History: Appropriations of Hegel in Twentieth-Century France* (Ithaca: Cornell University Press, 1988); and J. P. Butler, *Subjects of Desire: Hegelian Reflection in Twentieth-Century France* (New York: Columbia University Press, 1987). On the relation between Lacan and Kojève, see P. Van Haute, "Lacan en Kojève: het imaginaire en de dialectiek van de meester en de slaaf," *Tijdschrift voor Philosophie* 48 (1986), 391–415; E. S. Casey and J. H. Woody, "Hegel, Heidegger, Lacan: The Dialectic of Desire," *Psychiatry and the Humanities* (New Haven: Yale University Press), 75–111; E. Roudinesco, 149–56.

8. A play on the words *publication* (publishing) and *poubelle* (garbage can)—Trans.

9. Alexandre Kojève, *Introduction to the Reading of Hegel* (New York, London: Basic Books, 1969), 76/272; partial translation by James H. Nichols, Jr., from the French *Introduction à la lecture de Hegel* (Paris: Gallimard, 1947). The first page number refers to the English translation, the second to the original French; hereafter, "Kojève" is followed by the two numbers, or by xx/ and a page number where no English translation exists —Trans.

10. Kojève, 76/272.

11. G. W. F. Hegel, *Phenomenology of Spirit*, trans. A. V. Miller (Oxford: Clarendon Press, 1977), 51. I have changed the translation of *Begriff* from "Notion" to "Concept"—Trans.

12. Kojève, 159/435 (quoted by Descombes, 27). An important self-critical note added to the second edition nevertheless modifies this idyllic thesis. Instructed, he says, by a trip to Japan, Kojève recognized that Man does not disappear at the end of history. He simply becomes a snob, like those posthistorical humans the Japanese: "Now, since no animal can be a snob, every 'Japanized' posthistorical period would be specifically human" (Kojève, 162/437).

13. M. Blanchot, *L'entretien infini* (Paris: Gallimard, 1969), 304, 307 (partially quoted by Descombes, 114). Kojève himself described that ungraspable "experience" of posthistorical man in two articles dedicated to Queneau and Sagan: "Les romans de la sagesse," *Critique* 60 (1952), and

"Le dernier monde nouveau: Françoise Sagan," *Critique* 111–12 (1956).

14. This word means "idleness" but also, literally, "unworking."—Trans.

15. After having established, in an explicit reference to the Kojèvian problematic of the God-Man, that "Hegel has nothing to do with the 'apotheosis' of a madwoman . . . ," Bataille "concludes" his strange story in this way: "The story, shall I continue? / I've finished./ From the sleep that left us, for a short time, in the depths of the taxi, I awoke first, sick. . . . The rest is irony, a long wait for death. . . ." G. Bataille, *Oeuvres complètes* III (Paris: Gallimard, 1971), 31.

16. C. Baudelaire, "L'essence du rire," *Variétés critiques* III (Paris: Grès, 1924), 95.

17. Bataille V, 130.

18. See Roudinesco, 155.

19. Kojève, 9/16.

20. Here, the citation comes from the J. B. Baillie translation, *The Phenomenology of Mind* (New York: Harper Colophon Books, 1967; original Macmillan edition 1910), 237, because the Miller translation mysteriously omits any mention of "death, the absolute Master"—Trans.

21. Kojève, xx/539.   22. Kojève, xx/556.

23. Kojève, xx/551.   24. Kojève, 5–6/13.

25. Hegel, *Hegel's Science of Logic*, trans. A. V. Miller (London: Allen and Unwin, 1969), 50.

26. Hegel, *Phenomenology* (return to the Miller translation), 10.

27. Hegel, *Phenomenology*, 19.

28. "The death of Jesus participates in comedy insofar as it is impossible, without arbitrariness, to introduce the forgetfulness of his eternal divinity—which belongs to him—into the consciousness of an infinite and infinitely powerful God. The Christian myth anticipates, precisely, Hegel's 'absolute knowledge' by grasping the fact that nothing divine (in the pre-Christian sense of *sacred*) is possible unless it be *finite*" (Bataille XII, 330).

29. On this subject, see J. Derrida, "The Ends of Man," *Margins of Philosophy*, trans. Alan Bass (Chicago: University of Chicago Press, 1982), 121.

30. Hegel, *Phenomenology*, 14.

31. Kojève, xx/550.

32. Hegel, *Phenomenology*, 10.

33. Kojève, 9/16.

34. Kojève, xx/572–73.

35. Kojève, xx/293.

36. For the following discussion of Heidegger's ideas, I have adopted

the convention of translating *Sein* (*être* in French) as "Being," and *Seiendes* (*étant* in French) as "being."—Trans.

37. Kojève, xx/548.

38. Heidegger, *Being and Time*, trans. Macquarrie and Robinson (New York: Harper & Row, 1962), 72, 75 (and generally all of sec. 10).

39. Kojève, xx/550; my emphasis.

40. Derrida, *Margins*, 115.

41. Denis Hollier, ed., *The College of Sociology*, trans. Betsy Wing (Minneapolis: University of Minnesota Press, 1988), 398–99.

42. Kojève, 3–4/11.

43. Hegel, *Phenomenology*, 105.

44. Kojève, 3/11.

45. Kojève, 5/12.

46. Kojève, 5/13.

47. Kojève, 212–15/485–87. On Kojève's "dualistic ontology," see M. Henry's useful and solid statement in *The Essence of Manifestation*, trans. Girard Etzkorn (The Hague: Martinus Nijhoff, 1973), 698: "There are not two regions of Being, one of which would be a structure incompatible with the dialectical essence. Pure and simple Being so little escapes the jurisdiction of this essence that it is rather in it that it finds its foundation. Identity *is* difference. It does not leave negativity outside itself as if negativity had to deal with another sector of Being. . . . The sphere of transcendent Being constitutes the sole ontological region known by Hegelianism, and negativity is so little alien to this region that it rather constitutes the essence and the foundation thereof. Negativity, let us repeat, has no Being of its own."

48. Kojève, 187/463.

49. Kojève, xx/548–49.

50. Kojève, 215/487: "Since Kant, Heidegger seems to be the first to have posed the problem of a dual ontology." See also Kojève's article on A. Delp, *Tragische Existenz: Zur Philosophie Martin Heideggers*, in *Recherches Philosophiques* 5 (1935–36), and the commentary by Roth, *Knowing and History*, 89–90.

51. Kojève, 5/12.   52. Kojève, 5/12.

53. Kojève, 6/13.   54. Kojève, 6/13.

55. Kojève, 9/16.

56. Queneau, *Le dimanche de la vie*, 210.

Chapter 1

1. G. Politzer, *Critique des fondements de la psychologie* (Paris: Rieder, 1928). Was it academic prudence or deliberate silence? The fact is

that Politzer's name is conspicuous by its absence in the index of Lacan's thesis. Later, Lacan (1966, 661) corrected this "lapse of memory" by invoking "Politzer's great spirit." On the "Politzerism" of the young Lacan, see M. Mannoni, *La théorie comme fiction* (Paris: Seuil, 1979), 131.

2. P. Nizan, *L'Humanité* (10 Feb. 1933): "We should point out a book that—counter to the currents of official science, and despite the precautions that must be taken by the author of an academic thesis—translates a sure and conscious influence of dialectical materialism." J. Bernier, "Compte-rendu de lecture," *La critique sociale*, reprinted by Editions de la Différence (1983), 139: "It is not without great satisfaction that we see a young representative of our extremely bourgeois psychiatry illustrate the Marxist conception of the human personality" (both cited in Roudinesco, 130).

3. Freud, "Psycho-Analytic Notes on an Autobiographical Account of a Case of Paranoia (Dementia Paranoides)," *Standard Edition* [hereafter *SE*, followed by volume number] *of the Complete Psychological Works of Sigmund Freud* XII, ed. James Strachey (London: Hogarth Press, 1958), 63–65.

4. Freud, "On Narcissism: An Introduction," *SE* XIV, 90.

5. Freud, "Some Character-Types Met with in Psychoanalytic Work," *SE* XIV, 332 ff.

6. Hegel, *Phenomenology*, 117 (translation modified).

7. Philippe Julien, *Le retour à Freud de Jacques Lacan* (Paris: Erès, 1986), 27 (see also 40, 53).

8. Hegel, *Phenomenology*, 10.

9. In French, *l'Oedipe* and *le complexe d'Oedipe* are normally synonymous and are usually both translated as "the Oedipus complex." In what follows, however, the distinction between the two is important, and so I will translate the first as "the Oedipus" and the second as "the Oedipus complex."—Trans.

10. Freud, letter to W. Fliess, 31 May 1897, *The Origins of Psycho-Analysis*, trans. Eric Mosbacher and James Strachey (New York: Basic Books, 1954), 206: "Another presentiment tells me . . . that I am about to discover the source of morality."

11. Freud, *Totem and Taboo*, *SE* XIII, 142–143: "The violent primal father had doubtless been the feared and envied model of each one of the company of brothers: and in the act of devouring him they accomplished their identification with him, and each one of them acquired a portion of his strength. . . . They hated their father, who presented such a formidable obstacle to their craving for power and their sexual desires; but they loved and admired him too. After they had got rid of him, had satisfied their hatred and had put into effect their wish to identify themselves with him, the

affection which had all this time been pushed under was bound to make itself felt."

12. Freud, *Group Psychology and Analysis of the Ego, SE* XVIII, 121.

13. Freud, *The Ego and the Id, SE* XIX, 34.

14. Freud, "Some Neurotic Mechanisms in Jealousy, Paranoia and Homosexuality," *SE* XVIII, 231–32.

15. "This tarrying with the negative," says the preface to the *Phenomenology of Spirit*, "is the magical power that converts it into being" (Hegel, *Phenomenology*, 19).

Chapter 2

1. The title of this chapter is borrowed from M. Balmary's *L'Homme aux statues* (Paris: B. Grasset, 1979), trans. Ned Lukacher, *Psychoanalyzing Psychoanalysis* (Baltimore: Johns Hopkins University Press, 1982). The epigraph—"Je sens sous les rayons, frissonner ma statue"—comes from Paul Valéry, *La jeune Parque* (Paris: Gallimard, NRF, 1927), 18.

2. Freud, "The 'Uncanny,'" *SE* XVII, 248.

3. Freud, "'Uncanny,'" 248.

4. Freud, "'Uncanny,'" 235.   5. Freud, "'Uncanny,'" 240.

6. Freud, "'Uncanny,'" 234–35. The reference to Rank is to "Der Doppelgänger," *Imago* 3, 356, 358, trans. Harry Tucker. *The Double: A Psychoanalytic Study* (Chapel Hill: University of North Carolina Press, 1971).

7. H. Wallon, "Conscience et individualisation du corps propre," *Journal de Psychologie* (Nov.–Dec. 1931), reprinted in *Les origines du caractère chez l'enfant* (Paris: Boivin, 1933); hereafter, references are to the second edition (Paris: Presses Universitaires de France, 1949). On Wallon, whom Lacan knew well (since it was Wallon who asked Lacan to write the section on the family in the *Encyclopédie française*) and with whom he shared a certain Hegelianism (rather Marxist in Wallon), cf. E. Jalley, *Wallon, lecteur de Freud et de Piaget* (Paris: Editions sociales, 1981), and Roudinesco, 157. Wallon's and Lacan's theses on the specular image are analyzed in detail by M. Merleau-Ponty in his course at the Sorbonne, *Les relations avec autrui chez l'enfant* (Paris: Centre de Documentation Universitaire, 1951; 2nd ed., 1975); here, Merleau-Ponty justly notes that Lacan's research "extends that found in Wallon while at the same time being different" (2nd ed., 58). In this respect, one cannot help being struck by Lacan's stubborn silence concerning this important debt. The article on the family complexes, which already claims "to supplement" the Freudian doctrine of "affective identification" with "a theory of that identification whose developmental moment we designate with the term *mirror stage*" (1984, 41),

makes no mention of Wallon. Likewise, "in the text entitled 'The Mirror Stage,' Lacan says not a word about Wallon . . . and he attributes to Baldwin an approximate periodization that in fact belongs to Darwin. Wallon extensively quotes Darwin; Lacan does not. Via the false reference to Baldwin, he skips over Wallon," according to B. Ogilvie, *Lacan: La formation du concept de sujet* (Paris: Presses Universitaires de France, 1987), 113.

8. Wallon, *Les origines*, 172–73.

9. Wallon, *Les origines*, 172.

10. Wallon, *Les origines*, 172–73.

11. E. Roudinesco writes, "Lacan separates himself from the Wallonian outlook by describing the process from the angle of the unconscious rather than from that of the conscious" (157). But this is to retroactively project onto the theory of the mirror stage a distinction that Lacan, *at the time*, explicitly refused—cf. this text of 1946 (1966, 183): "Let it suffice to say that the consideration [of the "elementary phenomena" of paranoid psychosis] led me to complete the catalogue of structures—symbolism, condensation, and others that Freud explicitly mentions as those, I shall say, of the *imaginary mode*; for I hope that people will soon abandon the use of the word 'unconscious' to designate what manifests itself in consciousness." Likewise, recalling the arguments of Wallon, P. Julien (45) writes: "The child has an image of itself similar to its image of other bodies outside itself in the world: one body among others. Now Lacan subverts this accepted interpretation. There is no formation of the ego by *its* exteriorization, by a movement from the interior to the exterior, by a projection, but rather the opposite: the ego is exteroceptive from the very beginning, or it is nothing at all." But this is precisely what Wallon had said. J.-A. Miller is much closer to the truth when he says, "Lacan reorganized the Freudian discovery from a point of view that was foreign to [Freud], the mirror-stage . . . which comes from Henri Wallon for its empirical basis and from Hegel revised by Kojève for its theory" ("Une histoire de la psychanalyse," interview with F. Ewald, *Magazine littéraire* 271, Nov. 1989, 22).

12. Freud, "On Narcissism: An Introduction," *SE* XIV, 76–77: "We are bound to suppose that a unity comparable to the ego cannot exist in the individual from the start; the ego has to be developed. The auto-erotic instincts, however, are there from the very first; so there must be something added to auto-erotism—a new psychical action—in order to bring about narcissism."

13. L. Bolk, *Das Problem der Menschenwerdung* (Jena: 1926), French trans. in *Arguments* (4th year, 18, 1960), 4: "From the bodily point of view, man is the fetus of a primate come to sexual maturity." Lacan makes reference to Bolk's work in "Some Reflections on the Ego" (1951) 15, and in *Ecrits* (1966) 186.

14. Hegel, *Phenomenology*, 10.

15. Hegel, *Hegel's Logic*, ed. J. N. Findlay, trans. William Wallace (Oxford: Oxford University Press, 1975), sec. 82.

16. Hegel, *Phenomenology*, 11–12. On the question of reflection and speculative thought, see J. Hyppolite, *Logique et existence* (Paris: Presses Universitaires de France, 1952), especially the chapter "La réflexion et les réflexions"; see also R. Gasché, *The Tain of the Mirror* (Cambridge, Mass.: Harvard University Press, 1986), 23–54.

17. Hyppolite, 106.

18. Hegel, *The Spirit of Christianity and Its Fate in Early Theological Writings*, trans. T. M. Knox (Chicago: University of Chicago Press, 1948), 258, cited by Michel Henry, *Essence*, 692. Henry makes the following comment: "In other words, reflection does not designate a particular mode of the life of consciousness; it rather constitutes its essence . . . because the splitting and the division (the term 'reflection' designates here nothing else) are thought of as the conditions of possibility of presence, as the very essence of the phenomenon interpreted beginning with the idea of light (φῶς)."

19. M. Heidegger, *Nietzsche IV*, ed. David Krell (New York: Harper & Row, 1982), 167. See also "Science and Reflection," trans. William Lovitt, in *The Question Concerning Technology and Other Essays* (New York: Harper & Row, 1977), 163.

20. The current French translation of Heidegger's *entdecken* (itself a translation of the Greek *alētheuein*) is *dévoiler*. I have consistently translated this as "to unveil"; Heidegger's English translators variously translate *entdecken* as "to unconceal," "to uncover," "to discover," and "to disclose."—Trans.

21. Heidegger, *Nietzsche IV*, 173.

22. The Bollingen edition of *Plato: Collected Dialogues*. I give Heidegger's more literal translation in brackets.—Trans.

23. Heidegger, *Nietzsche IV*, 173.

24. Heidegger, *The Question of Being*, trans. William Kluback and Jean Wilde (New York: Twayne, 1958), 57, regarding Junger's *Der Arbeiter* and concerning "the meta-physical of metaphysics, transcendence, changes, when, within the confines of the differentiation, the *Gestalt* of the essence of man appears as the source of the giving of meaning. Transcendence, understood in the manifold sense, turns back into the corresponding re-scendence and disappears in it. A retreat of this kind through *Gestalt* takes place in such a way that its state of being present is represented and is present again in the imprint of its stamping."

25. Heidegger, *Nietzsche IV*, 105.

26. Heidegger, *Nietzsche IV*, 106.

27. See, for example, J.-L. Nancy, *Ego sum* (Paris: Aubier-Flammarion, 1979), 27 ff., and especially the masterful analysis of the cogito by M. Henry, *Généalogie de la psychanalyse* (Paris: Presses Universitaires de France, 1985), Chapters 1–3. This analysis has been recently confirmed and extended by J.-L. Marion, "Générosité et phénoménologie: Remarques sur l'interprétation du cogito cartésien par Michel Henry," *Les études Philosophiques* (Jan.–Mar. 1988).

28. René Descartes, *The Philosophical Writings of Descartes* II, trans. John Cottingham, Robert Stoothoff, and Dugald Murdoch (Cambridge: Cambridge University Press, 1984), 19 (translation modified).

29. Sartre's essay "La transcendence de l'Ego," which appeared in 1936 in *Recherches philosophiques*—trans. Forrest Williams and Robert Kirkpatrick, *The Transcendence of the Ego* (New York: Farrar Straus Giroux, 1957—is probably the immediate "source" of Lacan's reading of the *cogito*. In addition, Lacan makes explicit reference to Sartre, in the second session of the seminar on desire and its interpretation, with respect to the imaginary character of the experience of the *cogito*: "In this experience to which philosophy confines us, one recollects the confrontation of the subject with an object and, consequently, with an imaginary object among which it is not surprising that the 'I' turns out to be one object among the others." Indeed, as Sartre wrote, "The psychic is the transcendent object of reflective consciousness. It is also the object of the science called 'psychology.' The ego appears to reflection as a transcendent object"; or again, "The *me* (*Moi*) being an object, it is evident that I shall never be able to say: *my* consciousness, that is, the consciousness of my *me*. . . . The ego is not the owner of consciousness" (*Transcendence of the Ego*, 71, 96–97); see also, in *L'être et le néant*—trans. Hazel Barnes, *Being and Nothingness* (New York: Philosophical Library, 1956)—the section entitled "The Self (*Moi*) and the Circuit of Selfness." Lacan, who later accused Sartre of taking only the imaginary register into account (1977a, 6/99; 1977b, 84/79–80), could not have missed originally finding material in Sartre to fortify his own description of the ego—and, later, even his conception of the subject; see Chapter 6 of the present volume, the section entitled "What Is Called a Subject?"

30. Heidegger, *An Introduction to Metaphysics*, trans. R. Manheim (New Haven: Yale University Press, 1959), 59–60: "This erect standing-there, coming up ⟨*zum Stande kommen*, coming to stand⟩ and enduring ⟨*im Stand bleiben*, remaining in standing⟩ is what the Greeks understood by being"; "'Being' meant for the Greeks: permanence [*Ständigkeit*]. . . . Essent is that which is permanent [*ständig*] and represents itself as such, that which appears and manifests itself primarily to vision"(64–66). On this question of Being as "stance," "statue," "standing-erect," or *stèle*, see the commen-

tary of Philippe Lacoue-Labarthe, "Typographie," in *Mimesis, des articula-tions*, a collaborative publication (Paris: Aubier-Flammarion, 1975), 190 ff., which uncovers in Heidegger an "onto-steleo-logy" (169) that very much resembles the Lacanian "mirror stage" (which is mentioned in passing by Lacoue-Labarthe, 257).

31. Heidegger, "The Question Concerning Technology," in *Basic Writings* (New York: Harper & Row, 1977), 308.

32. Cf. Heidegger, *Question of Being*, 57 (see preceding note).

33. The French word *formation* is normally translated as "education" or "training," but I have included the original in parentheses to help retain the relation with "form" and "in-form."—Trans.

34. Heidegger, "Platons Lehre von der Wahrheit" *Wegmarken* (Frankfurt am Main: Vittorio Klostermann, 1976), 230–31 [my translation.—Trans.].

35. Heidegger, "Platons Lehre," 217.

36. Freud, *The Ego and the Id*, SE XIX, 31.

37. On this point, see the developments of P. Lacoue-Labarthe on the specularization of *mimesis* in Plato ("Typographie," 210–24).

38. Freud, *Group Psychology*, SE XVIII, 106.

39. Freud, *Group Psychology*, 107.

40. Freud, *Group Psychology*, 106.

41. On precisely this point, Freud was much more hesitant. In two different places in Chapter 7 of *Group Psychology*, he lets it be understood that *Einfühlung* constitutes the original (and most obscure) basis of the "emotional tie" of identification: "Another suspicion may tell us that we are far from having exhausted the problem of identification, and that we are faced by the process which psychology [T. Lipps] calls 'empathy' (*Einfühlung*) and which plays the largest part in our understanding of what is inherently foreign to our ego in other people"; "A path leads from identification by way of imitation to empathy, that is, to the comprehension of the mechanism by means of which we are enabled to take up any attitude at all toward another mental life" (*Group Psychology*, 108, 110). On this question, see J.-L. Nancy and P. Lacoue-Labarthe, "La panique politique," *Confrontation* 2, 45 ff.

42. Freud, "Findings, Ideas, and Problems," *SE* XXIII, 299.

Chapter 3

1. The epigraph for this chapter is from Georges Bataille, "Madame Edwarda," *Oeuvres complètes* III, 22.

2. The author translates the German *Agieren* as *agir* (to act)—and not, as is usual in both French and English, as "acting out." It is possible to

translate *agir/Agieren* as "enactment," but the author prefers "acting," for the sake of preserving a certain theatrical connotation—Trans.

3. Freud, "Remembering, Repeating, and Working Through," *SE* XII; "Beyond the Pleasure Principle," *SE* XVIII, Chapter 3.

4. Hegel, *Phenomenology*, 42–43.

5. Freud, "Remembering"; "Beyond the Pleasure Principle," ch. 3.

6. Freud, "An Autobiographical Study," *SE* XX, 42.

7. The French expression *se dire*—literally, "to speak oneself"—is approximately the same as "to express oneself." Nevertheless, because of the importance of speech in Lacan's discourse, and because of Lacan's explicit denunciation of "expression" in favor of "revelation" (see Chapter 4 of the present volume), we have decided to retain the more literal translation—Trans.

8. The French word *répéter* also means "to rehearse" (a play, for example).—Trans.

9. Freud, "The Question of Lay Analysis," *SE* XX, 226–27.

10. Aristotle, *Poetics* 1452a, 29–33: "Recognition (*anagnōrisis*) is, as the very word implies, a change from ignorance to knowledge. . . . The finest form of recognition is one attended by reversal (*peripeteia*), like that which goes with the recognition in Oedipus." *The Complete Works of Aristotle*, ed. Jonathan Barnes (Princeton: Princeton University Press, 1984), translation modified.

11. Freud, *The Interpretation of Dreams*, *SE* IV, 261–62: "The action of the play [*Oedipus*] consists in nothing other than the process of revealing, with cunning delays and ever mounting excitement—a process that can be likened to the work of a psycho-analysis—that Oedipus himself is the murderer of Laïus, but further that he is the son of the murdered man and of Jocasta."

12. Passage quoted and discussed by P. Lacoue-Labarthe, "Oedipe comme figure," *L'imitation des Modernes* (Paris: Galilée, 1986), 217.

13. Again, a play on the words *voir* (to see) and *savoir* (to know): "*sa passion de (sa)voir*."—Trans.

14. Claude Lévi-Strauss, *Introduction to the Work of Marcel Mauss*, trans. Felicity Baker (London: Routledge and Kegan Paul, 1987), 18.

15. This course was assembled and published by Queneau in 1947. At the same time, the problematic of the "desire of the other" made its appearance in Lacan, finally becoming central around 1953. It seems, therefore, that Lacan, who had nevertheless been one of Kojève's "assiduous auditors" (it is under this heading that he figures in the student list of the *Ecole Pratique des Hautes Etudes*; cf. M. Roth, *Knowing and History*, 225–26), awaited the publication of the *Introduction to the Reading of Hegel* to truly profit from the Kojèvian teaching.

16. See the present volume, "In Place of an Introduction."

17. Hegel, *Phenomenology*, 104.

18. Hegel, *Phenomenology*, 109.

19. Hegel, *Phenomenology*, 110. On the Hegelian concept of "recognition," see M. Henry's commentary (*Essence*, 709–10), in which he carefully emphasizes the link between the necessity of recognition in Hegel and the ontological primacy accorded to transcendence, understood as the only possible form of manifestation.

20. Kojève, 5–6/13 (see also 40/169, 135/368, 225/497, 244/514, etc.).

21. Kojève, 6/13: "Human reality is a social reality, society is human only as a set of Desires mutually desiring one another as Desires."

22. See the theory of "triangular" or "mimetic" desire set forth by René Girard in *Deceit, Desire, and the Novel*, trans. Yvonne Freccero (Baltimore: Johns Hopkins University Press, 1965) and *Violence and the Sacred*, trans. Patrick Gregory (Baltimore: Johns Hopkins University Press, 1977). The numerous and troubling cross-references between the Girardian and Lacanian descriptions are in all likelihood explained by their common roots in Kojève's problematic. In this respect, one should read Girard's not altogether convincing declaration of anti-Hegelianism in *Deceit* (110–12), which, in reality, is only justified by the accentuation—extremely brilliant, to be sure—of the specifically *Kojèvian* theme of the "desire of the desire of the other."

23. Hegel, *Phenomenology*, 110.

24. Georges Bataille, "Hegel, l'homme et l'histoire" (1956), *Oeuvres complètes* XII (Paris: Gallimard, 1988), 363; see also the following passage (362–63), which marks well the signification of Kojève's teaching for his listeners: "Kojève's close adherence to the negating passion of Action marked him with the sign of finitude and death; in listening to him one feels that death itself spoke such a cutting, joyful language, animated with an implacable movement; his speech has the impotence and, at the same moment, the omnipotence of death. What would remain of a devastating movement in which nothing that humanity thinks does not turn to dust and disintegrate: Kojève has emphasized the hidden dissatisfaction of Hegel and he has fortunately brought to light once again that what the Wise Man calls satisfaction is a frustration, admittedly *voluntary*, but absolute, definitive."

25. Kojève, 5/12.

26. Kojève, 5/12.

27. Kojève, 7/14.

28. Hegel, *Phenomenology* (Baillie trans.), 237.

29. Indeed, this is how Kojève translated the Hegelian concept of

Genuss—cf., for example, his annotated transcription of the passage, from Chapter 4 of the *Phenomenology*, on the opposition of the working slave, who "represses" desire, and the *jouisseur* master: "For the Master, on the other hand, the *immediate* relation [to the thing] comes into being, through that mediation [i.e., through the work of the Slave who transforms the natural thing, the "raw material," with a view to its consumption (by the Master)], as pure negation of the object, that is, as *Enjoyment (Jouissance)*. . . . What Desire . . . did not achieve, the Master . . . does achieve. The Master can finish off the thing completely and satisfy himself in Enjoyment" (Kojève, 17–18/23–24). See also the footnote on p. 8 of the present volume.

30. Bataille, "Hegel, la mort et le sacrifice," *Oeuvres complètes* XII, 336–37.

31. See also the account by J.-B. Pontalis (approved by Lacan) of the seminar of 1958–59. It concerns a dream analyzed by Freud, in which the dreamer sees his father dead but *not knowing himself to be dead*: "The subject understood his father's pain, but what he does not know is that he is now inheriting it as pain itself, hence the *absurd sound* of the dream. . . . The subject can see that his father did not know of the subject's wish for death to end the father's suffering; he can see, or not (it all depends on the point of the analysis), that he has always wished that his father, as rival, die. But what he does not see is that by inheriting the pain of his father he now aims to maintain an ignorance that is necessary to him: at the end of existence nothing remains but the pain of existing. The subject rejects his own ignorance onto the other. Here the desire of death is the desire of not awakening to the message: through the death of his father he is henceforth faced with his own death, from which, till then, the father's presence protected him. . . . The subject consents to suffer in place of the other; but behind that suffering, a lure is maintained: the murder of the father as imaginary fixation. . . . The content of [*he was dead*] *according to his wish*—for example, the aggressive desire—thus appears as a protection" ("Desire and Its Interpretation" [title here rendered in English—Trans.], account by J.-B. Pontalis, *Bulletin de psychologie* XIII, 1959–60, 270). We see here how Lacan extends the critique of the Freudian Oedipus broached in the article on the family complexes: the identificatory rivalry with the Oedipal father is inevitably and fundamentally neurotic, not only because it has no (decidable) exit but even more because the parricidal desire serves as a screen for the desire of death pure and simple. "In a word, the whole scheme of the Oedipus needs to be criticized" (Lacan, 1978a, 305).

32. Freud, "Thoughts for the Times on War and Death," *SE* XIV, 289.

33. Freud, "Thoughts," 291. See also "Psychopathic Characters on the Stage," *SE* VII, 305–6: "Being present as an interested spectator at a

spectacle or play (*Shau-Spiel*) does for adults what play (*Spiel*) does for children, whose hesitant hopes of being able to do what grown-up people do are in that way gratified. The spectator . . . [longs] to be a hero. And the playwright and actor enable him to do this by allowing him *to identify himself* with a hero. They spare him something too. For the spectator knows quite well that actual heroic conduct such as this would be impossible for him without pains and sufferings and acute fears, which would almost cancel out the enjoyment. He knows, moreover, that he has only *one* life and that he might perhaps perish even in a *single* such struggle against adversity. Accordingly, his enjoyment is based on an illusion; that is to say, his suffering is mitigated by the certainty that, firstly, it is someone other than himself who is acting and suffering on the stage, and, secondly, that after all it is only a game." These passages are cited and commented upon by P. Lacoue-Labarthe, who then deduces an irreducibility of *mimesis*, itself interpreted, as in Lacan, in terms of *representation* (of death). The necessity of identification and the "closure of representation" (Derrida) would thus be one and the same thing, according to Lacoue-Labarthe: "There is an unavoidable *necessity* of re-presentation (of theatrical production, of *Darstellung*) of death, and consequently of identification, of mimesis"; from "La scène est primitive," *Le sujet de la philosophie* (Paris: Aubier-Flammarion, 1979), 206.

34. Bataille also makes this point with respect to the sacrificial spectacle: "In the sacrifice, the sacrificiant identifies with the animal struck with death. Thus he dies while seeing himself die, and even, in a certain way, by his own will—the heart with the arm of sacrifice" ("Hegel, la mort et le sacrifice," *Oeuvres* XII, 336). It is true that Bataille adds immediately, "But it is a comedy!"—apparently reintroducing the motif of spectacular representation. Nevertheless, in Bataille, the projection of identification onto the plane of representation is much smoother than in Lacan, for in Bataille the motif of "comedy" opens onto that of laughter, that of laughter onto a sovereign "communication" with the other (with the one who dies), which can no longer be understood solely in terms of representation and the economy of death (see, for example, Bataille's remarks, in the same article [338] on the "anguished gaiety" and/or the "gay anguish" of the "man of the sacrifice," who, "lacking a discursive knowledge of what he does, has only a 'sense-certainty,' that is, obscure, reduced to unintelligible emotion. . . . The agitation of which I speak is known: it is definable; it is *sacred* horror: simultaneously the most agonizing and the richest experience, which does not limit itself to tearing apart, which, on the contrary, opens itself *like a theater curtain* [my emphasis] onto a beyond of this world."

35. See the present author's *The Freudian Subject*, trans. Catherine

Porter (Stanford: Stanford University Press, 1988), the chapter entitled "Dreams Are Completely Egoistic."

Chapter 4

1. Edgar Allan Poe, "The Facts in the Case of M. Valdemar," *The Science Fiction of Edgar Allan Poe*, ed. Harold Beaver (Harmondsworth: Penguin Books, 1976), 201.

2. The current French translation of Freud's *Wunsch* is *désir*. Thus Lacan was able to amalgamate the Freudian *désir* (= *Wunsch*) and the Kojèvian-Hegelian *désir* (= *Begierde*). In English, it is impossible to play on the same ambiguity; therefore, it has been necessary to choose one or the other, according to the context—Trans.

3. Freud, *The Interpretation of Dreams*, SE IV, 160.

4. Freud, *Psychopathology of Everyday Life*, SE VI, 13: "In the Signorelli case, so long as the painter's name remained inaccessible, the visual memory that I had of the series of frescoes and of the self-portrait which is introduced into the corner of one of the pictures was *ultra-clear*—at any rate much more intense than visual memory-traces normally appear to me."

5. Freud, *Psychopathology*, 5.

6. The only trace that Freud consents to leave us is found in a note to the second chapter: "If the repressed thoughts on the topic of death and sexual life are carefully followed up, one will be brought face to face with an idea that is by no means remote from the topic of the frescoes at Orvieto" (*Psychopathology*, 13). Strachey mentions that there may be a connection with the visit to an Etruscan tomb near Orvieto, mentioned in *The Interpretation of Dreams*, SE V, 454. Here, during the analysis of a dream, Freud emphasizes the fact that he had found himself in a tomb *while alive*, which he then compares with his megalomaniacal wish for immortality: would he achieve immortality through his work (*The Interpretation of Dreams*), through that repugnant and infernal "self-analysis" represented in his dream by "a dissection of the lower part of my own body, my pelvis and legs, which I saw before me as though in the dissecting-room. . . . The pelvis had been eviscerated, and it was visible now in its superior, now in its inferior, aspect, the two being mixed together. Thick flesh-coloured protuberances (which, in the dream itself, made me think of haemorrhoids) could be seen" (452). Dissecting oneself the better to resuscitate oneself: self-analysis as apotropaic apocalypse? *Flectere si nequeo Superos, Acheronta movebo . . .*

7. Freud, "The Unconscious," SE XIV, 177. On this question, see the useful clarification by M. Tort, "A propos du concept freudien de 'représentant' (*Repräsentanz*)," *Cahiers pour l'analyse* 5 (Paris: Seuil, 1966), as well

as the decisive commentary by M. Henry, *La généalogie de la psychanalyse* (Paris: Presses Universitaires de France, 1985), 362 ff.

8. Freud, *Psychopathology*, 5.

9. *Parole* will normally be translated as "speech" except in the expression *parole donnée*. Cf. note 21 to chapter 5.—Trans.

10. While waiting to return in more detail to this question, let us simply quote several passages taken almost at random from Kojève's *Introduction*: "If this Discourse reveals Being . . . it reveals not only the Identity but also the Negativity of Being" (201/475); "The man who errs [i.e., who says what is *not*] is a Nothingness that nihilates in Being" (187/463); "Negativity is therefore nothing other than the *finitude* of Being . . . and Action is essentially *finite*. . . . But if Man is Action, and if Action is Negativity 'appearing' as Death, Man, in his human *or speaking* [my emphasis] existence, is only a death: more or less deferred, and self-conscious" (xx/548). As Bataille said, to hear Kojève was to hear Death speak. In the end, this question has its origin in the debate initiated by Heidegger in "What is Metaphysics?": "Is the nothing given only because the 'not,' i.e., negation, is given? Or is it the other way around? . . . We assert that the nothing is more original than the 'not' and negation." The preceding passages are from *Basic Writings*, ed. David Krell (New York: Harper & Row, 1977), 99.

11. Freud, "Negation," *SE* XIX. The text we are reading by Lacan is precisely an "introduction" to J. Hyppolite's commentary on this article (reproduced in Appendix I of 1988a, 289–97).

12. Freud, *Beyond the Pleasure Principle*, *SE* XVIII, Chapter 2. Lacan's commentary: "Through the word—already a presence made of absence—absence itself gives itself a name in that moment of origin whose perpetual recreation Freud's genius detected in the play of the child" (Lacan, 1977a, 65/276); "Thus the symbol manifests itself first of all as the murder of the thing, and this death constitutes in the subject the eternalization of his desire" (Lacan, 1977a, 104/319).

13. See, for example, "Delusions and Dreams in Jensen's *Gradiva*," *SE* IX, 35: "In such cases the old Latin saying holds true . . . *Naturam expellas furca, tamen usque recurret*. But it does not tell us everything. It only informs us of the fact of the return of the piece of nature that has been repressed; it does not describe the highly remarkable manner of that return, which is accomplished by what seems like a piece of malicious treachery. It is precisely what was chosen as the instrument of repression—like the *furca* of the Latin saying—that becomes the vehicle for the return: in and behind the repressing force, what is repressed proves itself victor in the end."

14. And why should this surprise us, since Heidegger was already the ventriloquist for the strange "Hegel" imagined by Kojève? We must add

that Lacan's "Heidegger," despite his more careful reading of the latter, continued to be that of Kojève. As Derrida has noted, Lacan "resituates *Dasein* in the subject"—see "Le Facteur de la Vérité," *The Post Card*, trans. Alan Bass (Chicago: University of Chicago Press: 1987), 470—and, in the end, this is really nothing "surprising"—this was already Kojève's fundamental gesture, abruptly identifying the ek-static transcendence of Being-there with the negativity of the "Subject," of "Desire," and of "*human* reality." In this sense, Lacan's frequent declarations of non-Heideggerianism (1977a, 175/528; 1981, 334) are not simply "bad faith," and this is also why the comparison between Lacan and Heidegger, legitimate as it may be, cannot be taken beyond a certain point; this comparison is to be found in the last chapter of J.-L. Nancy and P. Lacoue-Labarthe, *Le titre de la lettre* (Paris: Galilée, 1973), and in W. J. Richardson. "Psychoanalysis and the Being-Question," *Psychiatry and the Humanities*, vol. 6 (New Haven: Yale University Press, 1983). On the very comical personal relationship between the psychoanalyst of the Left Bank and the thinker of Todtnauberg, one might refer to the bits of gossip piously collected by E. Roudinesco, *La bataille de cent ans* II.

15. Note that Lacan had proposed a translation of it according to his own lights in *La psychanalyse* 1 (1956).

16. Heidegger, *Being and Time*, 55–58.

17. "Logos (Heraclitus, Fragment B 50)," *Early Greek Thinking*, trans. David Farrell Krell and Frank A. Capuzzi (New York: Harper & Row, 1975, 1984), 70–71; translation modified. Cf. also the following paraphrase of this passage given by Lacan in the first seminar during a discussion of the identity between repression and the return of the repressed: "Every successful symbolic integration involves a sort of normal forgetting. . . . In every entry of being into its habitation in words, there's a margin of forgetting, a λήθη complementary to every ἀλήθεια" (1988a, 192/216).

18. Heidegger, "On the Essence of Truth," *Basic Writings*, 137.

19. Cf. Kojève, 187–88/463–64: "Since *error* means *disagreement* with the real; since what is *other* than what is, is *false*, one can . . . say that the man who errs is a Nothingness that nihilates in Being. . . . Truth is more than a reality: it is a *revealed* reality; it is the reality *plus* the revelation of the reality through discourse. Therefore, in the heart of the truth, there is a *difference* between the real and the discourse which reveals it. But a difference is *actualized* in the form of an *opposition*, and a discourse *opposed* to the real is, precisely, an error. . . . Therefore, there is really a *truth* only where there *has been* an error. But error exists really only in the form of human discourse." And a bit farther on, there is this Lacanian (before

the fact) note: "Error, and hence truth, exist only where there is language (*Logos*)."

20. On this distinction, see "enunciation" in the translator's note to the English version of Lacan's *Ecrits* (1977a, ix). Briefly, the "I" who is making the statement is the subject of the enunciation (*sujet de l'énonciation*), and the "I" who is the grammatical subject of the statement itself is the subject of the statement (*sujet de l'énoncé*).—Trans.

21. Pierre Klossowski, *Le Bain de Diane* (Paris: Pauvert, 1956). This admirable fable of truth, which may be read in part as an erotico-theological reformulation of Heidegger's *alētheia*, appeared the same year as "The Freudian Thing," and it would not be hard to show that Lacan's "prosopopoeia" consciously takes up its writing strategy (Klossowski's strategy of the "simulacrum").

22. "*Thea* is Goddess. It is as a goddess that *Alētheia* . . . appears to the early thinker Parmenides"—Heidegger, "Science and Reflection," trans. William Lovitt, *The Question Concerning Technology* (New York: Harper & Row, 1977), 164.

23. Heidegger, "The Thing," trans. Albert Hofstadter, *Poetry, Language, Thought* (New York: Harper & Row, 1971).

24. Heidegger, "The Thing," 168, 170.

25. Klossowski, *Le Bain de Diane*, 26.

26. Freud, *Jokes and Their Relation to the Unconscious*, *SE* VIII, 115.

27. Cf. Heidegger, "Logos": "Expression and signification have long been accepted as manifestations which indubitably betray some characteristics of language. But they do not genuinely reach into the realm of the primordial, essential determination of language" (64); "So long as we only listen to the sound of a word, as the expression of a speaker, we are not yet even listening at all" (66). As for the term "revelation," it evidently comes from Kojève: "For the truth is more than a reality: it is *revealed* reality . . . the revelation of the reality through discourse" (Kojève, 187–88/463); "[Being] contains in it a discourse that reveals it; it is not only given Being, but revealed Being or Truth, Idea, Spirit" (189/464); "Desire taken as Desire . . . is but a revealed nothingness. . . . the revelation of an emptiness" (5/12), etc.

28. On this point, Lacan (1988a, 225/250; 1988b, 29–30/41–42) refers to Lévi-Strauss, but it would be easy to show that the Structuralist reference is really based on Kojève's "dualist ontology." The Lévi-Straussian rereading of the dialectic of master and slave changes nothing, for the bracketing of the question of origin was already inscribed in Kojève's dualism of Nature and History (or, if you will of the Real and Discourse). Kojève would undoubtedly have been content with Lévi-Strauss's thesis, in

which "language [and the symbolic in general] can only have arisen all at once" (Lévi-Strauss, *Marcel Mauss*, 59).

Chapter 5

1. Maurice Merleau-Ponty, "Indirect Language and the Voices of Silence," *Signs*, trans. Richard McCleary (Evanston, Ill.: Northwestern University Press, 1964), 44; translation modified.

2. On the complex moves that led to the break, in 1953, between the SPP (Société Psychanalytique de Paris) and Lagache's and Lacan's new SFP (Société Française de Psychanalyse), see E. Roudinesco, *Bataille de cent ans* II, Chapter 2, "Le grand partage," 2.

3. An allusion to a famous statement of Sartre's: although he no longer believes in Communism and/or Marxism, he does not want to let on to that fact, for fear of driving the poor workers at Billancourt to desperation.—Trans.

4. Freud, "The Ego and the Id," *SE* XIX, 18. We know that Anna Freud's *The Ego and the Mechanisms of Defense* (1936), which Lacan implicitly targets here, had been approved by her father.

5. Freud, *Beyond the Pleasure Principle*, *SE* XVIII, Chapter 3 and *passim*.

6. Freud, "Inhibitions, Symptoms and Anxiety," *SE* XX, 18: "It must be that after the ego's resistance has been removed the power of the compulsion to repeat—the attraction exerted by the unconscious prototype upon the repressed instinctual process—has still to be overcome. There is nothing to be said against describing this factor as the *resistance of the unconscious*."

7. "Agony" comes from the ecclesiastical Latin *agonia*, "anxiety" or "anguish," from the Greek *agōnia*, "struggle" or "fight" (noted by P. Lacoue-Labarthe, *Le sujet de la philosophie*, 262).

8. This aspect of Lacan's personality appears quite clearly in Roudinesco's work.

9. See also Lacan (1973a, 31): "Psychoanalytic discourse (this is my discovery) is precisely that which can found a social tie cleansed of any group necessity. . . . I measure the group effect by what it adds in imaginary obscenity to the effect of discourse." This optimism (which will be amply belied by the *destin si funeste* of the school founded by Lacan) leads one to think, *mutatis mutandis*, of the optimism of Freud, who asserted in 1910 that the diffusion of psychoanalytic theses in society would contribute by this very fact to the progressive extinction of neuroses: "You [the psychoanalysts] are not only giving your patients the most efficacious remedy for their sufferings that is available today; you are contributing your share

to the enlightenment of the community from which we expect to achieve the most radical prophylaxis against neurotic disorders along the indirect path of social authority" ("The Future Prospects of Psycho-Analytic Therapy," *SE* XI, 151).

10. Heidegger, *Being and Time*, 56; translation modified.

11. Hegel, *Phenomenology*, 42.

12. Freud, "An Autobiographical Study," *SE* XX, 65. See also "Jokes and Their Relation to the Unconscious," *SE* VIII, 179: "A dream is a completely asocial mental product; it has nothing to communicate to anyone else. . . . Not only does it not need to set any store by intelligibility, it must actually avoid being understood, for otherwise it would be destroyed," etc.

13. Freud, *The Interpretation of Dreams*, *SE* IV–V, 267, 270, 322, 440, 485, 664. See also "A Metapsychological Supplement to the Theory of Dreams," *SE* XIV, 223, 225: "Thus we know that dreams are absolutely egoistic and that the person who plays the chief part in their scenes is always to be recognized as the dreamer. This is now easily to be accounted for by the narcissism of the state of sleep. . . . The wish to sleep endeavors . . . to establish an absolute narcissism."

14. See my book *The Freudian Subject*, the chapter entitled "Dreams Are Absolutely Egoistic" (this, I swear, is the last "egoistic" note of the present volume).

15. Freud, "The Unconscious," *SE* XIV, 186.

16. In this passage from *Sein und Zeit*, there is of course no mention of the "subject," but rather of *Dasein* (of "the human reality," in the Corbin translation that Lacan would have had access to at the time). Here is the complete definition, from Macquarrie and Robinson's (non)translation: "*Death, as the end of Dasein, is Dasein's ownmost possibility—nonrelational, certain and as such indefinite, not to be outstripped*" (Heidegger, *Being and Time*, 303); and, a bit earlier: "Death is the possibility of the absolute impossibility of Dasein" (294).

17. The French reads as follows: *en ce qu'ils sont inter-essés*; that is, "in which their being (their *essence*) is an 'inter-esse'nce."—Trans.

18. *Ne rien dire*—literally, "not to say anything" or "to say nothing"—is a very common French expression meaning "not to mean anything." In what follows, I have kept to the more literal translation.—Trans.

19. In this respect, the description of empty speech brings to mind Heidegger's "idle talk" (*Gerede*), a fallen (because purely transmissive and repetitive) form of the authentic "communication" (or "sharing," *Mitteilung*) that defines "discourse" (*Rede*) (cf. *Being and Time*, sec. 35).

20. William Shakespeare, *Hamlet*.

21. "Parole *donnée*" = "given word," as in "I give you my word."

The interplay between *la parole* = "speech" and *parole donnée* = "given word" should be kept in mind in what follows.—Trans.

22. Vincent Descombes quite aptly notes this in *Grammaire d'objets en tous genres* (Paris: Minuit, 1983), 235: "Here speech does not have the same meaning as in Saussure. The remarks that Lacan makes on the evolution of criminal law in Europe make it clear that the word must be given a much stronger and, in a certain sense, more archaic, more feudal meaning."

23. Emile Benveniste, *Problems in General Linguistics*, trans. Mary Meek (Coral Gables, Fla.: University of Miami Press, 1971), 224. The article that this quotation is taken from ("Subjectivity in Language") was written in 1958, but it only restates a thesis that Benveniste had already posited in 1946, in "Relationships of Person in the Verb": "'I' designates the one who speaks" (*Problems*, 197). Lacan makes explicit reference to these analyses of Benveniste in the long development he devotes to the "You are" in his seminar of 1955 on the psychoses (Lacan, 1981, 310 ff., particularly 314).

24. Benveniste, *Problems*, 218.

25. Benveniste, *Problems*, 229. It is true that this thesis was advanced by Benveniste in 1958—therefore, after Lacan's developments on full speech and/or the given word (*la parole pleine/donnée*). It is quite possible, however, that Lacan knew of it much earlier, through private conversations with Benveniste. In fact, Lacan followed Benveniste's work very closely, to the point of alluding in 1954 (Lacan, 1988a, 248/272–73) to developments that Benveniste would not make public until 1962 ("The Levels of Linguistic Analysis," *Problems*, 101–11).

26. Benveniste, *Problems*, 224.

27. Benveniste, *Problems*, 230. *Dialectic* "intersubjectivity," of course: "And so the old antinomies of 'I' and 'the other,' of the individual and society, fall. . . . It is in a dialectic reality that will incorporate the two terms [the *I* and the *you*] and define them by mutual relationship that the linguistic basis of subjectivity is discovered" (Benveniste, *Problems*, 225). Here, it is once more confirmed that Structuralism, contrary to appearances, accommodates itself quite well to Hegelianism.

28. Lacan "Actes du congrès du Rome," quoted by Descombes, *Grammaire d'objets en tous genres*, 237.

29. J. L. Austin, *How to Do Things with Words* (Cambridge, Mass.: Harvard University Press, 1962). The proximity of Lacan's theses to those of Austin has been emphasized by Shoshana Felman, *Jacques Lacan and the Adventure of Insight* (Cambridge, Mass.: Harvard University Press, 1987), 114 ff., and by D. Bougnoux, *L'inconscient communicationnel* (forthcoming). (P. Van Haute has indicated to me that A. Vergote has also noted this in his unpublished courses.)

30. Austin, 12–13.　　　　　31. Austin, 10.

32. Austin, 139.　　　　　　33. Austin, 3.

34. Austin, 61.

35. Austin, 60. I will not go into the question here of whether Austin meant to indicate by this the *presence* of the subject at the enunciation and/ or the statement (oral or graphic) of the *I*, as J. Derrida reproaches him for doing in "Signature Event Context," *Margins*, 327 ff. It is certainly true that Austin (322) mobilizes the notion of "intention"—and therefore of "the conscious presence . . . of the speaking subject for the totality of his locutionary act"—in reference to "abuses," a sort of performative that is merely "professed," since it is pronounced without the intention of keeping one's promise. But Austin (16) does this without much conviction ("Let me hasten to add that these distinctions are not hard and fast, and more especially that such words as 'purported' and 'professed' will not bear very much stressing"), and his indications on the absence of any "interiority" prior to the utterance of the performative tend rather in the opposite direction: that of a purely linguistic—that is, "*itérable*" (Derrida)—constitution/institution of the incriminated *I*, which tends to bring him rather closer to the thesis variously defended by Benveniste, Lacan, and Derrida. Whatever may be the case with this question, to which Austin's fluctuating, aporetic thought truly precludes any answer, it is certain that the Austinian performative is related to that critical zone that Benveniste called "subjectivity in language."

36. Austin, 116.　　　　　　37. Austin, 36.

38. Austin, 103.　　　　　　39. Austin, 26.

40. Lévi-Strauss, *Marcel Mauss*, 37: "In fact, it is not a matter of translating an extrinsic given into symbols, but of reducing to their nature as a symbolic system things which never fall outside that system except to fall straight into incommunicability. Like language, the social *is* an autonomous reality (the same one, moreover); symbols are more real than what they symbolize, the signifier precedes and determines the signified."

41. On this point, see the useful clarification by O. Ducrot, "De Saussure à la philosophie du langage," in the French edition of John R. Searle, *Speech Acts*, trans. Pauchard, *Les actes du langage* (Paris: Hermann, 1972), 20–24.

42. Let us recall that Austin's major work, based on lectures given between 1952 and 1955, did not appear until 1962, and that even Benveniste, who nevertheless was already working "independently" on the same problems (cf. *Problems*, 234), did not know of it until that date. As for Lacan, he very often incriminates the "logical positivism" of the Oxford school (1977a, 61/271, 150/498; 1966, 353), which seems to indicate that he was not aware of the "pragmatic" turn initiated by Austin. Thus it would seem

that we must look to the "independent" research of Benveniste to find the source of Lacan's developments on full speech and/or the given word. The parallelism between Lacan's theory and Austin's, however, is no less astonishing and remarkable. Nevertheless, it should be noted that if Lacan did not know of Austin's work, he did know of Bateson's; witness his remarks on the Batesonian theory of the double bind (SV, 8 Jan. 1958). He could thus have been initiated into this "pragmatic" (Morris) approach to language, to which Benveniste also alluded with respect to his own theory of "instances of discourse" *I/you* (cf. *Problems*, 218). "It appears that in America there are people who are concerned with the same thing that I am explaining to you here. . . . M. Bateson, anthropologist and ethnographer, . . . has indicated something that forces us to look a bit beyond the end of our noses concerning therapeutic action" (SV, 8 Jan. 1958).

43. Cf. this much later declaration by Lacan, which attests to his attachment to the idea of creation *ex nihilo*: "Genesis . . . tells us of nothing other than the creation—indeed, of nothing—of what?—of nothing other than signifiers. As soon as that creation bursts forth, it articulates itself in the naming of what is. Is this not the essence of creation? . . . In the idea of creationism, is it not a matter of creation from nothing, and thus of the signifier?" (Lacan, 1986, 41; see also 1986, 144–47).

44. Benveniste, "Analytical Philosophy and Language," *Problems*, 231–38. On the evolution of Austin's thought, see the very clear presentation by F. Récanati, *La transparence et l'énonciation* (Paris: Seuil, 1979), Chapter 6.

45. Austin, 138. Retracing Austin's path in reverse, certain pragmaticians are now claiming that every performative utterance also has a constative/referential potential; cf. A. Berrendonner, *Eléments de pragmatique linguistique* (Paris: Editions de Minuit, 1981); D. Bougnoux, *Vices et vertus des cercles* (Paris: La Découverte, 1989).

46. Such a sentiment, said Kojève, can only be animal: "If animal Desire is the necessary condition of Self-Consciousness, it is not the sufficient condition. By itself, this desire constitutes only the Sentiment of self" (Kojève, 4/11).

47. Again, Kojève: "Human Desire must be directed toward another Desire. . . . That is why the human reality can only be social" (Kojève, 5–6/13).

48. A portmanteau word made up of *parler*, "to speak," and *être*, "to be"; hence "speaking-being."—Trans.

49. Lévi-Strauss, *Marcel Mauss*, 37.

50. Lévi-Strauss, *Marcel Mauss*, 35. See also *Structural Anthropology*, trans. Claire Jacobson and Brooke Schoepf (New York: Basic Books,

1963), 203: "[The unconscious] is reducible to a function—the symbolic function, which no doubt is specifically human, and which is carried out according to the same laws among all men, and actually corresponds to the aggregate of these laws."

51. As Descombes notes in a very incisive article, "The [Lévi-Straussian and Lacanian] theory of the symbolic . . . is a doctrine of the social contract" ("L'équivoque du symbolique," *Confrontation* 3, Spring 1980, 78 and *passim*; see also J.-L. Nancy and P. Lacoue-Labarthe, *Le titre de la lettre*, 35, 129). Moreover, Lévi-Strauss makes no mystery of it: "I believe that Rousseau, in the *Social Contract*, . . . formulated the most profound and most generalizable—that is, verifiable over a large number of societies—idea of what political organization can be, and even the theoretical conditions of any possible political organization"; cited in G. Charbonnier, *Entretiens avec Claude Lévi-Strauss* (Paris: UGE, 1963), 43. In the end, all this returns to the Saussurian definition of language: "It is the social side of speech, outside the individual who can never create nor modify it by himself; it exists only by virtue of a sort of contract signed by the members of a community"; Ferdinand de Saussure, *Course in General Linguistics*, trans. Wade Baskin (New York: McGraw-Hill, 1959, 1966), 14.

52. Lévi-Strauss, *Marcel Mauss*, 17.

53. Lévi-Strauss, *Marcel Mauss*, 18.

54. Lévi-Strauss, *Marcel Mauss*, 13. On the notion of the "individual myth," see *Structural Anthropology*, 199–203.

55. Lévi-Strauss, *Marcel Mauss*, 14.

56. Lévi-Strauss, *Marcel Mauss*, 18 (the sentence preceding this one favorably mentions Dr. Lacan).

57. From this point of view, Lacan has manifestly *hypostatized* the Lévi-Straussian "symbolic." As Descombes notes, "In the Lacanian formulations, the fiction of a univocal symbolic is reinforced. Lévi-Strauss still spoke of 'symbolic systems,' in the plural; he surrounded himself with a million precautions at the moment of advancing the concept of an 'order of orders' [cf. Lévi-Strauss, *Structural Anthropology*, 312–14, 332–34]. In Lacan, there is no longer any question of anything but 'the symbolic' and 'the Law,' with the capital letter of reverence" ("L'équivoque du symbolique," 89).

58. See, among many other passages, Freud's "An Autobiographical Study," *SE* XX, 34; "The Question of Lay Analysis," *SE* XX, 187; "Analysis of a Phobia in a Five-Year-Old Boy," *SE* X, 102–05; "From the History of an Infantile Neurosis," *SE* XVII, 52. See also S. Fish, "Withholding the Missing Portion: Power, Meaning and Persuasion in Freud's 'The Wolf-Man,'" *Times Literary Supplement*, 29 Aug. 1986.

59. On this point, see D. Spence, *Narrative Truth and Historical Truth* (New York: Norton, 1982); Roy Shafer, *The Analytic Attitude* (New York: Basic Books, 1983); A. Oppenheimer, "La solution narrativiste," *Revue française de psychanalyse* 52 (1988).

60. D. Bougnoux, "Doser l'hypnose," *Quinzaine Littéraire* (July 1989).

61. This is what L. Chertok and I. Stengers emphasize with respect to Spence's narrativist theory, and we can very easily extend their remarks to Lacan: "Thus it is that a 'radical' narrativist (Spence) has come to define the 'becoming-true' of the narration that must be produced during the cure in a purely pragmatic register: 'Once a given construction has acquired narrative truth, it becomes just as real as any other kind of truth; this new reality becomes a significant part of the psychoanalytic cure' [Spence, *Narrative Truth*, 31]. From this point of view, the 'becoming-true' is an *event* that no longer authorizes the distinction between 'truth' and 'suggestion.'" L. Chertok and I. Stengers, *Le coeur et la raison: L'hypnose en question, de Lavoisier à Lacan* (Paris: Payot, 1989), 162.

62. It is on this count that Lacan was able both to confirm and to criticize the troubling assertion of Thomas Szasz, according to which the analyst, in the transferential situation, would be the only judge of the truth of his interpretations (cf. Szasz, "The Concept of Transference," *International Journal of Psychoanalysis* 44, 1963). This did not in any way hinder Lacan, since truth, as he points out, has a "structure of fiction": "Truth is based only on the fact that speech, even when it consists of lies, appeals to it and gives rise to it. This dimension is always absent from the logical positivism that happens to dominate Szasz's analysis of the concept of transference" (Lacan, 1977b, 133/121).

63. *Truc* is roughly equivalent to "thing" or "thingamajig," used to specify "this thing over here," which has no name or whose name we do not know; but *truc* also signifies the "trick" or "knack" that someone uses to perform a seemingly magical operation.—Trans.

64. Lacan, "Conclusions" of the *Congrès de l'Ecole Freudienne sur la Transmission*, in *Lettres de l'Ecole*, 1979, quoted and discussed by François Roustang, *Lacan, de l'équivoque à l'impasse*, 21; L. Chertok, in L. Chertok, M. Borch-Jacobsen et al., *Hypnose et psychanalyse* (Paris: Dunod, 1987), 11; L. Chertok and I. Stengers, *Le coeur et la raison*, 193–94.

65. Catherine Clément, *The Lives and Legends of Jacques Lacan*, trans. Arthur Goldhammer (New York: Columbia University Press, 1983), 48–51, 108, 199. (Clément, who describes Lacan's "shamanism" in impressionistic terms, never goes so far as to suspect a deliberate and con-

scious theatrical production on the part of Lacan, in consideration of which she nevertheless reinforces the *belief* in the shaman.)

66. In addition to *Introduction to the Work of Marcel Mauss*, which is as much a (non-Maussian) theory of magic and religion as it is a manifesto of structural anthropology, the reader should note "The Sorcerer and His Magic" (1949) and "The Effectiveness of Symbols" (1949), both of which are reprinted in *Structural Anthropology*.

67. Lévi-Strauss, *Structural Anthropology*, 198.

68. Lévi-Strauss, *Structural Anthropology*, 179 ff.

69. Lévi-Strauss, *Structural Anthropology*, 201 ff.

70. Lévi-Strauss, *Marcel Mauss*, 64.

71. Lévi-Strauss, *Marcel Mauss*, 55.

72. Lévi-Strauss, *Marcel Mauss*, 55–56, 63–64.

73. See Georges Bataille, "The Sorcerer's Apprentice," in Denis Hollier, *The College of Sociology*, 12–23. As Hollier observes in his prefatory note, this title refers to the reservations of Kojève, who reproached Caillois and Bataille with wanting to play at being sorcerer's apprentices. In this respect, it is not without interest (or spice) to reproduce here Caillois's passage, quoted by Hollier: Bataille "little hid his intention of recreating a Sacred, virulent and destructive, that, in its epidemic contagion, would end by reaching and inflaming the one who first planted its seed. . . . [Kojève] replied that such a miracle worker, for his part, could no more be carried away by a sacred knowingly activated by himself than could a conjurer be persuaded of the existence of magic while marveling at his own sleight of hand"; Caillois, *Approches de l'imaginaire* (Paris: Gallimard, 1974), 58.

74. Lévi-Strauss, *Structural Anthropology*, 204; and a bit earlier (202): "The comparison with psychoanalysis has allowed us to shed light on some aspects of shamanistic curing. Conversely, it is not improbable that the study of shamanism may one day serve to elucidate obscure points of Freudian study. We are thinking specifically of the concepts of myth and the unconscious."

75. On the utilization of mathematical models (game theory, "theory of ensembles, theory of groups, topology, etc.") in the domain of "human sciences," see Lévi-Strauss's report on "Les mathématiques de l'homme," first published by Unesco in the *Bulletin International des Sciences sociales* VI, no. 4, and reprinted in *Esprit* 10, 24th year (Oct. 1956).

76. Passage quoted and discussed by F. Roustang, *Lacan, de l'équivoque à l'impasse*, 42–43.

77. He proposed to understand this in somewhat the same sense as Wittgenstein's assertion with respect to mathematics: "The situation . . . is comparable to the situation supposed in the Social Contract theory. We

know that there was no actual contract, but it is as if such a contract had been made. Similarly for 2 + 2 = 4: it is as if a convention had been made"; Ludwig Wittgenstein, *Wittgenstein's Lectures, Cambridge, 1932–1935,* ed. A. Ambrose (Oxford: Blackwell, 1979), 157.

78. This was the misadventure encountered by the two L's (Jean Laplanche and Serge Leclaire). Having tried to mathematically "develop" the formulas from "The Agency of the Letter" in their report to the colloquium at Bonneval on the unconscious, they attracted the fierce ridicule of Lacan; cf. Lacan, 1977b, 247–50/224–25; Lacan, preface to A. Lemaire, *Jacques Lacan* (Brussels: Pierre Mardaga, 1977), 12–13.

79. Thus the + sign in the formula for the metaphor set forth in "The Agency of the Letter" (Lacan, 1977a, 164/515),

$$f\left(\frac{S'}{S}\right)S \cong S(+)s,$$

does not authorize any addition, since it is merely meant to graphically demonstrate the "crossing of the bar" in the "algorithm"

$$\frac{S}{s}$$

(J.-L. Nancy and P. Lacoue-Labarthe speak in this respect of the "*Witz* of logico-mathematical notation"; cf. *Le titre de la lettre,* 100). Elsewhere (Lacan, 1966, 805) the vector $\Delta \overset{\rightarrow}{\rule{0pt}{1ex}} S$ of the "graph of desire" is compared to a mattress maker's hook (because of the famous *point de capiton,* itself arising from a prankish reading of Saussure's schema of the "floating realms"; Lacan, 1977a, 154/502–3; Lacan, 1981, 296–304). [See note 28 to Chapter 6.—Trans.] The frankly farcical character of this "graph" breaks through when we learn what it introduces, "like the picture of a question mark planted in the circle of the capital O of the Other, symbolizing, in a disconcerting homography, the question that it signifies. Of what bottle is this the corkscrew? Of what response the signifier, the universal key?" (Lacan, 1966, 815)

80. The formula "scientific myth" comes from Freud himself; cf. *Group Psychology and the Analysis of the Ego,* SE XVIII, 135.

81. Freud, "Notes upon a Case of Obsessional Neurosis," SE X, 225: "Another time he told me about his principal magic word [*Glejisamen*], which was an apotropaic against every evil. . . . The word was in fact an anagram upon the name of his lady [*Gisela*]. Her name contained an 's,' and this he had put last, that is, immediately before the 'amen' at the end. We may say, therefore, that by this process he had brought his '*Samen*' [semen] into contact with the woman he loved."

82. Serge Leclaire, *Psychanalyser* (Paris: Seuil, 1968), Chapter 5.

83. Freud, *Group Psychology*, 142. On the profoundly religious character of psychoanalytic societies (Freudian or Lacanian), see the analyses of F. Roustang in *Un destin si funeste* (Paris: Minuit, 1976), particularly Chapter 2.

84. Quoted by F. Roustang (*Lacan, de l'équivoque à l'impasse*, 17), who adds this excellent comment: "Any society of psychoanalysts would undoubtedly recognize that one of its functions is the education of analysts, but this function would always remain subordinated to the therapeutic aim, which is the end of the analysis. Lacan subverted this hierarchy of ends. For him, in the same text, 'pure psychoanalysis is not in itself a therapeutic technique,' it is didactic analysis, that is, sworn to the production of analysts. That is why an analyst becomes a didactician in his School— meaning an analyst with full membership—not after having received a label from the organization, but after having made an analysand into an analyst."

85. Lacan, SXXIII (11 Jan. 1977), reproduced in *Ornicar?* 14. It should be remarked that, for Lacan, this assertion does not at all contradict the scientific character of psychoanalysis, since science is in turn said to be akin to psychosis (Lacan, 1966, 874–75).

Chapter 6

1. Kojève, xx/545; Jean-Paul Sartre, *The Emotions: Outline of a Theory*, trans. Bernard Frechtman (New York: Philosophical Library, 1948), 44; translation modified.

2. *Appeler un chat un chat* is approximately equivalent to the English expression "to call a spade a spade."—Trans.

3. M. Blanchot, "La littérature et le droit à la mort," *De Kafka à Kafka* (Paris: Gallimard, 1981), 38; originally published as "Le règne animal de l'esprit," *Critique* 18, (1947); reprinted in *La part du feu* (Paris: Gallimard, 1949). *Le droit à la mort* (the right to death) is an implicit quotation of Kojève in relation to Terror and the "political right to death" (cf. Kojève, xx/558). More generally, the argument developed by Blanchot in this article/manifesto is entirely based on Kojève's commentary on Hegel.

4. Blanchot, 36, 38.

5. Blanchot, 40: "Thus is born the image that does not directly designate the thing, but rather what the thing is not, that speaks of a dog instead of a cat" (a metaphorical process that is not at all the sole property of writers; as Lacan used to say, the child likes to say that the dog says "meow" and the cat "bow-wow").

6. Blanchot, 23.

7. Blanchot, 29.

8. Blanchot, 41; my emphasis. Obviously, this is an allusion to Hegel's formula, "the life that contains death and maintains itself therein," and the Kojèvian paraphrase, "the death that lives a human life" (Kojève, xx/550).

9. See note 14 to the Introduction.

10. Blanchot, 36.

11. This change of hats is noticed by P. Julien, 83.

12. Undoubtedly an effect of fashion: at the time, everyone was interested in Saussure, starting with Lacan's friends Lévi-Strauss and Merleau-Ponty. See especially Merleau-Ponty's "Indirect Language and the Voices of Silence," "On the Phenomenology of Language," and "From Mauss to Lévi-Strauss," in *Signs*, as well as his course at the Sorbonne on "La conscience et l'acquisition du langage," *Bulletin de psychologie* XVIII, 236 (1964), 3–6.

13. Ferdinand de Saussure, *Course in General Linguistics*, ed. Charles Bally and Albert Sechehaye, trans. Wade Baskin (New York: McGraw-Hill, 1966), 15: "Although dead languages are no longer spoken, we can easily assimilate their linguistic organisms."

14. Saussure, 77; translation modified (quoted and discussed by Vincent Descombes, *Grammaire d'objets en tous genres*, 186 ff.). In this text, I have translated *parole* as "speech," *langage* as "language," and I have left *langue* in French. For Saussure's distinction's among the three terms, see Saussure, 7–17, where Wade Baskin has translated *parole* as "speaking," *langage* as "human speech," and *langue* as "language."—Trans.

15. A neologism that echoes those of Lacan: *parlêtre, lalangue*, etc.—Trans.

16. Saussure, 66.

17. Saussure, 69; my emphasis.

18. Saussure, 68.

19. R. Godel, *Les sources manuscrites du cours de linguistique générale de F. de Saussure* (Geneva-Paris: Droz et Minard, 1957), 237.

20. Saussure, 120.

21. "The arbitrariness of the sign amounts to positing that it cannot be thought of as other than it is, since there is no reason that it should be as it is. The arbitrariness neatly covers up a question that will not be asked— What is the sign when it is not the sign? What is language before it is language?—that is, the question usually expressed in terms of the origin. . . . Here again, confusion is frequent: the thesis of arbitrariness has the function of eliminating any question about the origin, and thus it has only a superficial resemblance to conventionalism"; J.-C. Milner, *L'amour de la langue* (Paris: Seuil, 1978), 59. It should be noted that Lacan was much

more severe with Saussure on this point than was his commentator, Milner; see Lacan, 1977a, 149–50; Lacan, 1975c, 23, 32; Lacan, 1970, 63.

22. Saussure, 113.

23. Benveniste, "The Nature of the Linguistic Sign," *Problems*, 45.

24. Roman Jakobson, "Results of the Conference of Anthropologists and Linguists," *International Journal of American Linguists* 19.2 supplement (1953), 20. Jakobson's contribution is Chapter 2; the other authors are Claude Lévi-Strauss (Chapter 1) and C. F. Voegelin and Thomas A. Sebeok (Chapter 3).

25. Benveniste, "The Levels of Linguistic Analysis," *Problems* 302, note 2; my emphasis.

26. J.-C. Milner, "Réflexions sur l'arbitraire du signe," *Ornicar?* 5, 83, note 4.

27. Let us cite once more this passage from *Introduction to the Work of Marcel Mauss*, p. 37: "Like language, the social *is* an autonomous reality (the same one, moreover); symbols are more real than what they symbolize, the signifier precedes and determines the signified."

28. And for good reason: as Derrida has noted, this "materiality" of the signifier/letter "*in fact corresponds to an idealization. . . .* 'Cut a letter in small pieces, and it remains the letter it is' [a quote from the seminar on "The Purloined Letter," in which Lacan states that this "materiality" of the signifier "is *odd* (*singulière*) in many ways, the first of which is not to admit partition"; 1966, 14]; since this cannot be said of empirical materiality, it must imply an ideality (the intangibility of a self-identity displacing itself without alteration). . . . If this ideality is not the content of meaning, it must be either a certain ideality of the signifier (what is identifiable in its form to the extent that it can be distinguished from its empirical events and re-editions), or the *point de capiton* ["*Capitonner* means to quilt; *point de capiton* is Lacan's term for the 'quilted stitch' that links signifer to signified." Note by Alan Bass.—Trans.] which staples the signifier to the signified. . . . One can understand that Lacan finds this 'materiality' 'odd' [*singulière*]: he retains only its ideality"; Jacques Derrida, *The Post Card: From Socrates to Freud and Beyond*, trans. Alan Bass (Chicago: University of Chicago Press, 1987), 464. Derrida is right: what Lacan calls the "materiality" of the signifier is nothing other than its "incorporeal" ideality, according to Saussure ("The sign is by nature incorporeal"; quoted in R. Godel, *Les sources manuscrites*, 67). But Lacan is in no way ignorant of this, and that is exactly why he always underscores its *nullibiété* and its "unquantifiable" character (Lacan, 1966, 23–24), or again, its "subtlety" (Lacan, 1977a, 87). In reality, Lacan insists on the "materiality" of the signifier only in order to reverse (with a gesture that one may, of course, find too rapid) the relation classically established between ideality and meaning: the ideality of

the signifier/letter has no other "meaning" but the strictly in-sensible *différance* of meaning (that is to say, as we will see a bit later, the negativity of the subject). As for the relation Derrida establishes between the "letter" and the *phonē* (the ideal indivisibility of the phoneme), it nevertheless seems to me to be the opposite of what he suggests in this article. Not only does Lacan make it clear later on (in 1972) that "the signifier cannot in any way be limited to its phonetic prop" (Lacan, 1975c, 22), but in "The Agency of the Letter in the Unconscious" (from 1957) he already *subordinates* the alleged phonemeticity of the signifier to the differential-spaced structure of the "letter": "These [ultimate differential] elements . . . are *phonemes* . . . the synchronic system of differential couplings necessary for the discernment of sounds in a given language. Through this, one sees that an essential element of the spoken word itself was predestined to flow into the mobile characters which, in a jumble of lower-case Didots or Garamonds [Names of different typefaces.—Trans.] render validly present what we call the 'letter,' namely, the essentially localized structure of the signifier" (Lacan, 1977a, 153). The seminar on identification returns at length to the literal character of the signifier (mark, trait), to deny that writing has in itself a function of ideographic representation *or of notation of the phoneme*. Hence, with respect to the proper name, "what the advent of writing signifies is the following: the something that is already writing—if we consider the characteristic and the isolation of the signifying trait—once named becomes capable of supporting that famous sound on which M. Gardiner puts all the stress concerning proper names. . . . The characteristic of the proper name is always more or less linked with this trait of its liaison, not with sound, but with writing" (Lacan, SIX, 20 Dec. 1961).

29. Benveniste, "The Nature of the Linguistic Sign," *Problems*, 45.

30. On the rewriting of the Saussurian schema, it would be impossible to do better than refer the reader to the detailed and indispensable reading by J.-L. Nancy and P. Lacoue-Labarthe, *Le titre de la lettre*, 37 ff. The figures on pages 177 and 180 are reproduced from Saussure, *Course in General Linguistics*, by courtesy of the Philosophical Library.

31. On these two points, see M. Arrivé, *Linguistique et psychanalyse* (Paris: Klincksieck, 1987), 127 ff., and Jean-François Lyotard, *Discours, figure* (Paris: Klincksieck, 1971), 257.

32. Benveniste, "Remarks on the Function of Language in Freudian Theory," *Problems*, 71 (and, in general, 68–72). See also J.-C. Milner, "Sens opposés et noms indiscernables: K. (*sic*) Abel comme refoulé d'E. Benveniste," *La linguistique fantastique* (Paris: Clims-Denoël, 1984), and M. Arrivé, 112–18.

33. On the Lacanian *lalangue*, see J.-A. Miller, "Théorie de lalangue (rudiments)," *Ornicar?* 1, 1975, and J.-C. Milner, *L'amour de la langue*.

34. Benveniste, "Language in Freudian Theory," *Problems*, 75: "For it is style rather than language that we would take as term of comparison with the properties that Freud has disclosed as indicative of oneiric 'language.'"

35. On this essential distinction of *langue* and discourse (or propositions, as V. Descombes prefers to say in *Grammaire d'objets en tous genres*, Chapter 5), see Benveniste, "Levels of Linguistic Analysis," *Problems*, 108–11, as well as Lacan's anticipatory and very significant reference to it, in 1954: "One can't have a theory of language (*langue*) if one doesn't take the usages of groups into account, that is to say, expressions, and syntactical forms as well. But there is a limit, which is—that the sentence, for its part, does not have a usage. So there are two zones of signification. This remark is of the greatest importance, because these two zones of signification are perhaps something to which we are referring, since *it is a way of defining the difference between speech and language*. This discovery was made recently, by . . . Benveniste. It is unpublished, and he imparted it to me as something he is working on at the moment" (Lacan, 1988a, 248/272; my emphasis). Why, then, did Lacan hasten to forget what Benveniste had taught him and go on to describe speech in terms of the "signifier"? Lacan's transgression of the distinction between *langue* and discourse (or linguistics and rhetoric) is justly denounced as illegitimate by J.-F. Lyotard, *Discours, figure*, 254–60, and by A. Vergote, "From Freud's 'Other Scene' to Lacan's 'Other,'" *Interpreting Lacan: Psychiatry and the Humanities* 6 (New Haven, Conn.: Yale University Press), 202.

36. Lyotard, *Discours, figure*, 257–58; see also Lacan, 1970, 68–69, where Lacan partially subscribes to the analysis of "Professor" Lyotard.

37. M. Merleau-Ponty, "On the Phenomenology of Language," *Signs* 89: "The significative intention . . . is . . . no more than a *determinate gap* to be filled with words—the excess of what I intend to say over what is being said or has already been said. This means . . . the significations of speech are always ideas in the Kantian sense, the poles of a certain number of convergent acts of expression which magnetize discourse without being in the strict sense given for their own account"; translation modified.

38. Saussure, 112.

39. This point has been noted by M. Arrivé, 128–30, who in this respect recalls that, for Saussure, linearity is of a synchronic nature.

40. Merleau-Ponty, "On the Phenomenology of Language," *Signs* 88.

41. Jakobson, "Two Aspects of Language and Two Types of Aphasic Disturbances," *Fundamentals of Language* (The Hague: Mouton, 1956).

42. Lacan's expression is *faire pavé dans la mare du signifié*, which plays on the common expression *jeter un pavé dans la mare*, roughly the

same as "to put a cat among the pigeons," "to totally upset the regular order of things."—Trans.

43. Jakobson, "Two Aspects," 77–82.

44. D. M. Kay, quoted in Jakobson, "Two Aspects," 58.

45. I leave aside the question of Saussure's "psychologism," noted by G. Mounin in *Saussure* (Paris: Seghers, 1968), 24–26, and by Jacques Derrida in "The Pit and the Pyramid," *Margins*, 75–76.

46. Benveniste, "Subjectivity in Language," *Problems*, 224.

47. Lyotard, *Discours, figure*, 257.

48. The opposition of language and speech sketched out here brings irresistibly to mind Husserl's opposition between "indication," which has no *Bedeutung* ("vouloir-dire" [meaning], according to Derrida's translation), and "expression," which is animated by *Bedeutung*. Cf. Edmund Husserl, *Logical Investigations* I, trans. J. N. Findlay (London: Routledge and Kegan Paul, 1970) 269 ff.

49. Here, I am following Heidegger's interpretation of the *cogito*, not because I believe it is correct but because it gives an account of the traditional interpretation (or, if you will, the "metaphysics of subjectivity") in which Lacan inserts himself (see Chapter 2 of the present volume).

50. "This *I think*, for us, certainly cannot be detached from the fact that he [Descartes] can formulate it only by *saying* it to us, implicitly—a fact that he forgets" (Lacan, 1977b, 36/36). Since every interpretation of the *cogito* inevitably evokes a counterinterpretation, we could easily reply that Descartes does not at all "forget" that the *cogito* is a *pronuntiatum* (this is emphasized in J.-L. Nancy's analysis of the *cogito*, which on this point, it seems to me, only prolongs Lacan's analysis, just when it is proclaiming itself to be different; cf. *Ego sum*, 121–26). Conversely, we may also think this "forgetting" testifies that, for Descartes, the experience of the *cogito* has nothing to do with the certitude of an auto*representation* (this would be M. Henry's interpretation).

51. This is what P. van Haute does in a very suggestive article soon to appear, "Psychanalyse et existentialisme: A propos de la théorie lacanienne de la subjectivité." As van Haute quite justly indicates in a note to his article, the striking resemblances between Lacan and Sartre are explained by their common Kojèvian genealogy (on Sartre's "Kojèvism," see the clarification by Descombes in *Modern French Philosophy*, 48–54). In this respect, it should be noted that the insistent formula characterizing the "for-itself" in *Being and Nothingness*—"It is what it is not, and it is not what it is"—is an implicit citation of Hegel, quoted by Kojève in his course (cf. Kojève, *Introduction to the Reading of Hegel*, 200/474). As for Lacan's "critique" of the *cogito*, we have already remarked that it is rooted in

Sartre's essay *The Transcendence of the Ego* (see note 29 to Chapter 2 of the present volume). Sartre was the first to have clearly exhibited the *cogito*'s nonself-identity, and from this point of view the philosophical forgetting by which he has been overshadowed in France is quite unjust. But this is probably because it is only too obvious that, in Sartre, the so-called "critique" of the *cogito* is made for the sake of the same *cogito*, now and forever interpreted in terms of representative transcendence.

52. See J.-P. Sartre *Being and Nothingness*, 58 ff. On the "for-itself" defined as "desire" and "lack of being," see 91 ff.

53. A portmanteau word containing *dit*, past participle of *dire* ("to speak," "to say"), and *dimension.*—Trans.

54. Kojève, xx/531.

55. Kojève, 170–71/448–49.

56. Kojève, 187/463.

57. Kojève, 222–23/494.

58. Kojève, 142/374, xx/564.

59. Who for his part calls it the "in-itself" (see his eloquent description in *Being and Nothingness*, lxiii–lxvii).

60. Kojève, xx/542.

61. Kojève, 140/372–73.

62. [In the following passage from *Hegel and the Human Spirit: A Translation of the Jena Lectures on the Philosophy of the Spirit (1805–6), with Commentary*, ed. and trans. Leo Rauch (Detroit: Wayne State University Press, 1983), 89–91, 88–95, all words in brackets [ ] are the translator's, while those in braces { } are mine.—Trans.] "Language . . . gives {the thing} a name and expresses this as the being of the object. [We might ask, for example,] What *is* this? We answer, It *is* a lion, a donkey, etc.—[namely] it *is*. Thus it is not merely something yellow, having feet, etc., something on its own, [existing] independently. Rather, it is a *name*, a sound made by my voice, something entirely different from what it is in being looked at—and this [as named] is its true *being*. . . . By means of the name, however, the object has been born out of the I [and has emerged] as *being* (*seyend*). This is the primal creativity exercised by Spirit. Adam gave a name to all things. This is the sovereign right [of Spirit], its primal taking-possession of all nature—or the creation of nature out of Spirit [itself]. [Consider] *Logos*, reason, the essence of the thing and of speech, of *object* (*Sache*) and *talk* (*Sage*), the category—[in respect to all of these,] man speaks to the thing as *his* (and lives in a spiritual Nature, in this world [of Spirit]) {this parenthesis is Hegel's marginal note, added by the editor as a footnote}. And this is the *being* of the object. Spirit relates itself to itself: it says to the donkey, You are an inner [subjective] entity, and that Inner is I; your being is a

sound which I have arbitrarily invented." The *Esthetic* ("Symbolic Art," introduction) and the *Encyclopedia* (sec. 458–59) insist strongly on the negativizing "arbitrariness" of the sign, opposing it (as Saussure, 68–69, will also do) to the motivated character of the symbol: "In the sign, strictly so-called, the natural attributes of the intuition, and the connotation of which it is a sign, have nothing to do with each other. Intelligence therefore gives proof of wider choice [or "arbitrariness" as Derrida translates: *Willkür*] and ampler authority in the use of intuitions when it treats them as designatory (significative) rather than as symbolical. . . . The intuition . . . acquires, when employed as a sign, the peculiar characteristic of existing only as superseded and sublimated. Such is the negativity of intelligence." *Hegel's "Philosophy of Mind,"* trans. William Wallace (Oxford: Clarendon Press, 1971), 213. On this subject, see the commentaries by J. Hyppolite, *Logique et existence* (Paris: PUF, 1952), and by J. Derrida, "The Pit and the Pyramid," *Margins.*

63. Kojève, 140–41/372–73. This unfortunate mongrel is killed several times: xx/86–87, xx/543, xx/545–46, xx/564.

64. Blanchot, *De Kafka à Kafka,* 37.

65. Kojève 5/12; see also Kojève, 134–35/367, 255–56/524, xx/565, etc. This "presence/absence" regularly appears/disappears in Lacan (1977a, 65/276; 1988b, 313/359; 1981, 168–70, etc.), by whose intervention it became one of the commonplaces of "Structuralism."

66. Blanchot, *De Kafka à Kafka,* 37–38.

67. Blanchot, 52.

68. The same idea (and the same reference to Poe) can be found in Derrida's *Speech and Phenomena,* in which it furnishes the decisive argument against the *cogito* (here Husserlian) understood as self-presence: "When I tell myself 'I am,' this expression, like any other according to Husserl, has the status of speech only if it is intelligible in the absence of its object, in the absence of intuitive presence—here, in the absence of myself. Moreover, it is in this way that the *ergo sum* is introduced into the philosophical tradition. . . . Whether or not I have present intuition of myself, 'I' expresses something; whether or not I am alive, *I am* 'means something. . . .' The ideality of the *Bedeutung* here has by virtue of its structure the value of a testament. . . . The statement 'I am alive' is accompanied by my being dead [*être-mort*], and its possibility requires the possibility that I be dead; and conversely. This is not an extraordinary tale by Poe but the ordinary story of langauge"; Jacques Derrida, *Speech and Phenomena, and Other Essays on Husserl's Theory of Signs,* trans. David Allison (Evanston, Ill: Northwestern University Press, 1973), 95–97. Moreover, a note in Derrida's introduction to Edmund Husserl's *Origin of Geometry,* regarding

the "linguistic neutralization of existence," refers to the same group of texts by Hegel and Blanchot that we have just been examining; Derrida, *Edmund Husserl's* Origin of Geometry: *An Introduction*, trans. John Leavey (Lincoln: University of Nebraska Press, 1989), 67 n.

69. This was well recognized by Sartre in his essay *The Transcendence of the Ego*. If the *cogito* is the name of the structure of the transcendence by which the ego is related to itself, then the ego can grasp itself only as a transcendent object, and the "transcendental field" itself is "impersonal . . . *without an 'I'*" (19). Hence the idea of a "transcendental field without a subject" (*Being and Nothingness*, 235) that Derrida will take up (although believing that he is borrowing it from J. Hyppolite): "Writing creates a kind of autonomous transcendental field from which every present subject can be absent" (Derrida, introduction to *Origin of Geometry*, 88). Of course, it will have been understood that this transcendental field "without a subject" defines precisely the subject of representation (cf. Descombes, *Modern French Philosophy*, 77)—that is, what Lacan, very lucidly, simply calls "the subject."

70. Hegel, *Philosophy of the Spirit*, 91.

Chapter 7

1. The title of this chapter repeats the title of the play by Pablo Picasso (*Le Désir attrapé par la queue*); *la queue*, "tail," is common slang for "penis." The epigraph is from Lacan's fifth seminar (sv, 26 Mar. 1958).—Trans.

2. Klossowski, *Le bain de Diane*, 15.

3. Klossowski, 45.

4. Klossowski, 45.

5. Klossowski, 51.

6. Klossowski, 88.

7. Klossowski, 88.

8. Klossowski, 15.

9. Klossowski, 20; an untranslatable play on the word *croissant*, both "crescent" and the present participle of the verb *croître*, "to grow."—Trans.

10. Klossowski, 104.

11. *Diane . . . reconnaîtra les chiens*, a play on *Dieu reconnaîtra les siens* (God will recognize His own).—Trans.

12. Sartre, *Being and Nothingness*, 86–87.

13. Sartre, *Being and Nothingness*, 87–88.

14. Kojève, 5–6/12–13.

15. Sartre, 87.

16. Lacan, "The Object-Relation and Freudian Structures," summary by J.-B. Pontalis (approved by Lacan), *Bulletin de psychologie* X, 7 (1956–

57), 427. [The titles of this and the following seminars are here translated into English—Trans.] As Lacan was undoubtedly aware, it was this same example of the hydroelectric plant that Heidegger used in order to *denounce* the "pro-vocation" [or "challenging-forth," the English translation of *Heraus-forderung*—Trans.] of nature by modern technology. Cf. Heidegger, "The Question Concerning Technology," *Basic Writings*, 297–98.

17. Lacan, "The Formations of the Unconscious," summary by J.-B. Pontalis (approved by Lacan), *Bulletin de psychologie* XII, 4 (1957–58), 251.

18. Hence, according to Lacan, anxiety emerges equally at the approach of the desire of the Other (SX, 14 Nov. 1962 and 27 Feb. 1963) and at the approach of the object that would fulfill that desire (SX, 5 and 12 Dec. 1962): the subject wants at all costs to avoid being the *object* of desire of the Other (if not, he would no longer desire), but the imminence of his *desire* is equally that of death and nothing.

19. I borrow the expression "transcendental signifier" from J. Derrida, "Le facteur de la vérité," *The Post Card*, 477.

20. It is indeed rather striking that the problematic of the phallus, although present in the article on the family complexes, was almost completely eclipsed in Lacan until the seminar of 1955–56 on the psychoses (lectures of 21 Mar. 1956 and 4 June 1956), becoming completely central in the two following seminars ("The Object-Relation . . ." and "The Formations of the Unconscious"). The complex (and remarkably "encrypted") relations between Lacan and Klossowski would be worth a special study in this respect. For example, it is clear that the developments of the seventh seminar—on Sade, courtly love, and the Gnostic tradition—are directly inspired by Klossowski's *Sade, mon prochain*, never cited in that seminar, but whose "extreme perspicacity" is nevertheless hailed in passing, in "Kant with Sade" (1966, 789). The seminar on identification also makes a brief but significant allusion to Klossowski: "It would not be difficult for me to recall to you that on other paths, the works, and then the reflections upon the works, of a Pierre Klossowski converge with the path of research on fantasy that we have elaborated this year" (SIX, 27 June 1962). Inversely, it should be noted that Lacan is the "key" to the character Doctor Ygdrasil in Klossowski's *Le souffleur*; conversation with the author, recorded by A.-M. Lugan-Dardigna, *Klossowski, L'homme aux simulacres* (Paris: Navarin, 1986), 93, note 20.

21. On this artifice of presentation, see A. Juranville, *Lacan et la philosophie* (Paris: Presses Universitaires de France, 1984), 90 ff.

22. Kojève, 4–5/12.

23. Freud, *SE* XX, 154–55.

24. Freud, "Project for a Scientific Psychology," *SE* I, 317: "At early stages the human organism is incapable of achieving [a] specific action. It is brought about by extraneous help, when the attention of an experienced person has been drawn to the child's condition by a discharge taking place along the path of internal change [i.e., by the child's screaming]. This path of discharge thus acquires an extremely important secondary function— viz., of bringing about an understanding with other people; and the original helplessness of human beings is thus the primal source of all moral motives."

25. Freud, "Project," *SE* I, 366: "There are, in the first place, objects (perceptions) which make one scream because they cause pain. . . . Where otherwise, owing to the pain, one would have received no clear indications of quality from the object, the report of one's own scream serves to characterize the object. This association is thus a means of making conscious memories that cause unpleasure and of bringing attention to bear on them. . . . It is a short step from here to the discovery of speech."

26. Freud, "Project," *SE* I, 331–32: "Let us suppose that the object presented by the perception is similar to the [percipient] subject himself— that is to say, a fellow human-being (*Nebenmensch*). The theoretical interest taken in it [here Freud is examining memory and judgment] is then further explained by the fact that an object *of a similar kind* was the subject's first satisfying object (and also his first hostile object) as well as his sole assisting force. For this reason it is on his fellow-creatures that a human being first learns to cognize. The perceptual complexes arising from this fellow-creature will in part be new and non-comparable—for instance, its features (in the visual sphere); but other visual perceptions (for instance, the movements of its hands) will coincide in the subject with his own memory of quite similar visual impressions of his own body—a memory with which will be associated memories of movements experienced by himself. The same will be the case with other perceptions of the object; thus, for instance, if the object [the *Nebenmensch*] screams, a memory of the subject's own screaming will be aroused and will consequently revive his own experiences of pain. *Thus the complex of the Nebenmensch falls into two portions, one of which imposes itself by a constant structure, which remains together as a "thing" (als Ding);* while the other can be *understood* by the activity of memory—that is, can be traced back to information about the subject's own body." The italicized passage in the final sentence has been altered to conform to Lacan's French translation of Freud (Lacan, 1986, 64).

27. Lacan, "The Formations of the Unconscious," XII, 2, 3 (1957–58), 183.

28. The French *complément d'objet* adds to the English "direct object" the idea of complementarity: the object completes a lack.—Trans.

29. Lacan, "The Formations of the Unconscious," XII, 2, 3 (1957–58), 185.

30. Sheridan translates *en-deçà*, as "within," but here Lacan means to say that the maternal Other is situated "before" or "behind" the satisfaction of the need.—Trans.

31. Here, Sheridan translates *l'inconditionné* as "the unconditional element," whereas, properly speaking, it should be "the unconditioned element."—Trans.

32. *Impudiquement se dérobe: se dérober* means "to hide oneself" or "to be hidden," but, literally, also "to disrobe oneself."—Trans.

33. Lacan, "The Object-Relation . . . ," X, 12 (1956–57), 743.

34. On this question, see Derrida, "Le facteur de la vérité," *The Post Card*, 478, note 57.

35. Lacan, "The Object-Relation . . . ," X, 12 (1956–57), 743.

36. Gustave Flaubert, *Bouvard et Pécuchet*, in *Oeuvres Complètes* II (Paris: Seuil, "L'Intégrale," 1964), 237. I thank Andrew J. McKenna for having reminded me of this passage, which he judiciously quotes in his article "Flaubert's Freudian Thing: Violence and Representation in *Salammbô*," *Stanford French Review*, Fall–Winter 1988, 316.

37. Lacan, "The Object-Relation . . . ," X, 7 (1956–57), 428.

38. Cf. E. Benveniste, "Le sens du mot κολοσσός et les noms grecs de la statue," *Revue de philologie* (1932), 118–35, as well as the developments of J.-P. Vernant in "Figuration de l'invisible et catégorie psychologique du double: le *colossos*," *Mythe et pensée chez les Grecs* II (Paris: Maspéro, 1974), 65–78: "In the vocabulary of the statue . . . the term *kolossos*, of the animated genre and from prehellenic origins, is attached to a root *kol-* . . . which retains the idea of something erected, raised. . . . Fixation and immobility define, in principle, the *kolossos*. It is represented in two forms: either a statue-pillar or a statue-menhir, made from a raised stone, a slab planted in the soil. . . . The *kolossos* does not aim to reproduce the features of the deceased, to give the illusion of his physical appearance. . . . The *kolossos* is not an image; it is a 'double. . . .' Through the *kolossos*, the deceased returns to the light of day and manifests his presence to the eyes of the living. An ambiguous and extraordinary presence, which is also the sign of an absence."

39. Freud, "Civilization and its Discontents," SE XXI, 99, note 1: "The diminution of the olfactory stimuli seems itself to be a consequence of man's raising himself from the ground, of his assumption of an upright gait; this made his genitals, which were previously concealed, visible and in need

of protection, and so provoked feelings of shame in him. The fateful process of civilization would thus have set in with man's adoption of an erect posture. From that point the chain of events would have proceeded through the devaluation of olfactory stimuli and the isolation of the menstrual period to the time when visual stimuli were paramount and the genitals became visible, and thence to the continuity of sexual excitation, the founding of the family and so to the threshold of human civilization."

40. Derrida, "Le facteur de la vérité," *The Post Card*, 478–82.

41. Lacan, "The Formations of the Unconscious," XII, 4 (1957–58), 256.

42. Freud, *Group Psychology and the Analysis of the Ego*, SE XVIII, 105.

43. Lacan, "Desire and Its Interpretation," summary by J.-B. Pontalis, *Bulletin de psychologie* XIII, 6 (1959–60), 334.

44. Lacan, "Desire and Its Interpretation," XIII, 6 (1959–60), 334.

45. See "Totem or Taboo" in Chapter 1 of the present volume.

46. See "The Dialectic of Oedipus" in Chapter 1 of the present volume.

47. An allusion to R. Queneau's *Zazie dans le métro.*—Trans.

48. "Not to be born surpasses thought and speech"; *Oedipus at Colonus*, v. 1224 (trans. Robert Fitzgerald). Lacan's translation is obviously inspired by the one proposed by Heidegger in the margin of his commentary on *Antigone*: "'Never to have entered into being-there prevails over the togetherness of the essent as a whole.'" Heidegger continues: "Never to have taken being-there upon oneself, *mē phynai*, is said of man, of man who as the gatherer of *physis* is essentially gathered *with* it. Here *physis*, *phynai* are used in regard to man's being. . . . These poetic words express the intimate relation of being-there to being and its disclosure; they do so by naming what is remotest from being, namely, not-being-there. Here the strangest and most terrible possibility of being-there is revealed: the possibility of breaking the preponderant power of being by a supreme act of violence against itself," etc.; Heidegger, *An Introduction to Metaphysics*, trans. Ralph Manheim (New Haven, Conn.: Yale University Press, 1959), 177.

49. See Alan Sheridan's note in Lacan, 1977a, xi: "Lacan insists that '*objet petit a*' should remain untranslated, thus acquiring, as it were, the status of an algebraic sign." Algebra or not, it is perhaps useful to recall that *objet petit a* stands for "object small o(ther)."—Trans.

50. A. Juranville, *Lacan et la philosophie*, 169.

51. "An imaginary not tied to narcissism and the ego," P. Julien writes in *Le Retour à Freud de Jacques Lacan*, 198 (and, more generally, 187 ff.). Here, I closely follow this excellent presentation—one of the extremely rare ones, in the Lacanian field, that *problematizes* the theory of the *objet a*.

52. *Faire le tour* means both "to walk/drive around something" and "to trick"; see Lacan's explanation (1977b, 168), as well as Sheridan's note.—Trans.

53. Sartre, *Being and Nothingness*, 252 ff. (where H. Barnes translates *le regard*, our "gaze," as "the look."—Trans.).

54. Lacan says *Autre* (translated as "Other"); Sartre says *autrui* (usually translated as "Other"). *Autrui* is, at least etymologically, more specific, coming from the Latin *alter huic* (literally, "this other").—Trans.

55. *Se voir*, the pronominal form of the verb *voir*, can often be understood as a passive construction (in this instance, "to be seen") but can also have the more literal meaning "to see oneself."—Trans.

56. See "Story of the Eye" in Chapter 2 of the present volume.

57. Sartre, *Being and Nothingness*, 257.

58. *Cela me regarde* also means "it concerns me," "it is my concern."

59. *Being and Nothingness*, 259–61.

60. *Being and Nothingness*, 268; translation modified.

61. Klossowski, *Le bain de Diane*, 105.

Index of Proper Names

Thematic Index

Index of Schemas, Algorithms, and "Mathemes"

Library of Congress Cataloging-in-Publication Data

Borch-Jacobsen, Mikkel.
  Lacan: the absolute master / Mikkel Borch-Jacobsen; translated by Douglas
Brick.
    p.   cm.
  Translation of: Lacan.
  Includes bibliographical references and index.
  ISBN 0-8047-1556-4 (alk. paper):   —ISBN 0-8047-1728-1 (pbk.: alk. paper):
  1. Lacan, Jacques, 1901– . 2. Psychoanalysis and philosophy.
1. Title.
B2430.L146B67 1991
150.19'5'092—dc20   90-43813
                                              CIP